# MEASURING THE INFORMATION SOCIETY

Edited by
## Frederick Williams

**SAGE** PUBLICATIONS
The Publishers of Professional Social Science
Newbury Park   Beverly Hills   London   New Delhi

Dedicated to the memory of
Jesse H. and Mary Gibbs Jones

*For information address:*

SAGE Publications, Inc.
2111 West Hillcrest Drive
Newbury Park, California 91320

SAGE Publications Inc.
275 South Beverly Drive
Beverly Hills
California 90212

SAGE Publications Ltd.
28 Banner Street
London EC1Y 8QE
England

SAGE PUBLICATIONS India Pvt. Ltd.
M-32 Market
Greater Kailash I
New Delhi 110 048 India

Printed in the United States of America

Library of Congress Cataloging-in-Publication Data

Main entry under title:

Measuring the information society / Frederick
    Williams, editor.
        p. cm. — (Sage focus editions ; v. 97)
        Bibliography: p.
        ISBN 0-8039-3155-7    ISBN 0-8039-3156-5 (pbk.)
        1. Information technology—Economic aspects. 2. Information
technology—Social aspects. 3. Information technology—Economic
aspects—Texas. 4. Information technology—Social aspects—Texas.
I. Williams, Frederick, 1933-
HC79.I55M4    1988                              87-27701
338.4'7004—dc19

**FIRST PRINTING 1988**

# MEASURING THE INFORMATION SOCIETY

# SOME OTHER VOLUMES IN THE
# SAGE FOCUS EDITIONS

# Contents

# Preface

*Measuring the Information Society* is a collection of research reports on attempts to study facets of the emerging "information society" using Texas as a case in point. The collection has been prepared for individuals with special interest in the information society, whether they be researchers like ourselves, economic or social planners, advanced students, or just generally intelligent people who want to see beyond the superficial treatments about change in our times.

*** 

Nearly a decade ago, the present editor and researcher enjoyed a sabbatical leave in order to develop a book on what came to be called *The Communications Revolution*. The theme of that volume was that the modern media technologies of television, cable television, cassette, disk, tape, videotext, combined with the coming of both super and personal computers, integrated with the vast growth of telecommunications networks, were reconfiguring our natural environment.

I realize now in retrospect what a one-dimensional view that was—as if the new environment would simply displace the old. Clearly the lesson of the last decade has been that the new can only be realized through the traditional environment where it is transformed well before it happens (to borrow from Rilke's famous poetic line).

This is the deeper plot that unites the chapters of this volume. All the information age concepts—the applications to economic growth, to governance, to leisure, to public services—will only be so realized as they complete the passage via the existing economy, politics, public attitudes, and even the culture. Another way of stating the goal of our research is to understand better this process. In all, then, despite the regionalism of our research data, this is not really a book about Texas. It is about researching the information society, with Texas as an example.

—Frederick Williams
Austin

# *Acknowledgments*

We are indebted to many sources for support of this research, including the encouragement and budget assistance from Dean Robert C. Jeffrey of the University of Texas College of Communication. The College, through the Allan Shivers and Mary Gibbs Jones Centennial Chairs, supported research and conference activities. Contributions of further funds were made by Southwestern Bell Telephone Co. and AT&T.

Other sources of project support came from the UT University Research Institute, the Public Policy Laboratory of Texas A&M University, the Perryman Report, and Tracor, Inc.

Prominent citizens and changemakers also contributed to our ideas and specifically to our activities. These included George Christian, Neal Spelce, Bob Marbut, Lowell Lieberman, Pat Baldwin, Bud Shivers, Glenn Brown, Lee Cooke, John Hill, Joe Jerkins, Frank McBee, and Frank Phillips.

The Honorable Henry Cisneros, Mayor of San Antonio, contributed his enthusiastic and insightful visions of the future of Texas to an earlier publication of our project.

Denise Fynmore, Administrative Assistant for our Research Center, deserves much of the credit for keeping this volume on schedule, including her accomplishment of many valuable editing chores.

Finally, a major acknowledgment is due to those who contributed their time, ideas, and reports to this volume, and whose names appear in the Table of Contents.

9

# PART I

# Conceptual and
# Methodological Issues

# 1

# The Information Society as an Object of Study

## FREDERICK WILLIAMS

*The information society offers a general model for economic and social development of cities, states, or countries in the modern world. It is a topic that offers many opportunities for research, results of which should be of value to planners, other researchers, or students of the concept. This chapter describes the background and rationale for the present studies. It concludes with ten generalizations about the development and researching of the information society.*

## The Information Society as a Plan for Change

Given the attention devoted to economic growth based on the technologies of computing, telecommunications, and their combinations, it is not unusual that we have many cities, states, regions, and even entire countries attempting to plot their way into the so-called information age. The Japanese, for example, since the 1970s have had an economic plan for developing their computing and telecommunications businesses (Masuda, 1982). In the United States, the San Francisco peninsula corridor from the city down to San Jose ("Silicon Valley") or the outskirts of Boston ("Route 128") have been considered highly visible examples of growth based on the information economy. It has been expected, therefore, that in writing about the growth of information businesses, researchers like Rogers and Larsen (1984) have described the likelihood that economic planners in the United States and abroad can "transfer" the Silicon Valley phenomenon to their own countries or locales.

This volume is a report of studies of such change as it has been observed in the efforts of Texas to develop an information age economy. Texas offers an important example for such research. For several decades, because of the known depletion of oil reserves, there has been an active effort by the political and business leadership to diversify the economy. Information technologies have long been encouraged as an area of growth, as marked, for example, by the success of Texas Instruments, the development associated with NASA, and the coming of IBM and other major companies to the central Texas area. But probably most noteworthy was the selection in 1983 of Austin over 56 other cities as the site for the Microelectronics and Computer Technology Corporation (MCC), a research consortium of 18 major companies vying in the computer area. Unlike Silicon Valley or Boston's Route 128, the outright recruitment of MCC to Texas, the subsidies, the increased R&D funding for universities, and the large-scale program of education reform were all parts of a carefully orchestrated program supported by business, political, and educational leaders in the state. Texas had made a visible bid not only to join but lead in the information age. The boom was on.

But, by 1986, the unexpected triangulation of drastically lower oil prices, the decline of the Mexican economy, and the national slump in the microelectronics industry dealt a severe shock to the optimistic expectations of the Texas economy. In November 1986, *Texas Monthly* took the position that the departure of MCC's first chair (Admiral Bobby Inman) marked the symbolic end of the high-tech era of promises in Texas. Although Texas had planned for several decades to diversify its economy, events had overtaken the expectations for rapid growth in the high-tech sector. In that same month, Governor Mark White, a leader of high-tech development and educational reforms, was voted out of office in favor of an "old school" conservative Republican whom he had earlier replaced.

Yet an information economy continues to grow in Texas, but one conditioned by the forces of the traditional economy, the politics and public attitudes of Texans, and the slow recovery and reshaping of the microelectronics industry. The most recent development as of this writing has been the selection of Austin in February 1988 as the site of the national semiconductor consortium known as "Sematech." There is also the recognition, however, that "information cannot replace oil"; many different sectors of the economy must be nurtured, including considerable attention given to small business—the major employer of Texans, as it is for most Americans.

Study of the foregoing topics was the chief aim of a project that came to be named "The New Texas," and involved a voluntary group of 18 researchers. To these, an additional five researchers have added papers from other projects to round out the coverage of this volume. The papers include inquiries such as the following: What does one expect to study in terms of the realities of an evolving information society? What are methods for this research? What larger-scale generalizations are evident from such research, especially generalizations applicable to other states, regions, or countries? In short, what lessons can we learn from the Texas experience?

## Postindustrialism

### The Information Society

The *information society* is a fuzzy concept, yet it does reflect a triangulation of meanings. Most of all, it is a society where the economy reflects growth owing to technological advances. Knowledge and "know-how" are sources of value in themselves (as in R&D businesses) or sources of value added in the revitalization of traditional businesses and services. Just as machines are the tools of the industrial economy, computing and telecommunications technologies are the tools of a new "information" economy. Industries directly specializing in information, including the production of information technologies and services, constitute the primary sector of this economy. The revitalization of traditional agrarian, extractive, manufacturing, transportation, and service industries through information technologies is a secondary sector. Another component of the secondary sector is the use of information technologies to increase productivity of services in the public area—education, health care, and governance, to name a few.

### Postindustrial Bases for the Information Society

Much of the concept of the information society draws from the theory of postindustrialism advanced by Daniel Bell in *The Coming of*

*Post-Industrial Society* (1976). Bell sees modern industrial countries in the transition into the last of a three-stage sequence of economic evolution. First there is *preindustrialism*, an economy based mainly on extractions from nature such as mining, fishing, lumbering, or agriculture. There are many countries whose economies are totally preindustrial; in fact, most are. The United States still engages in these types of activities, but they are not the major area of growth. A next stage is *industrialism*, which is based on fabrication of nature, the production of goods; it is a manufacturing economy. Finally, the third stage, *postindustrialism*, is an economy based on the growth and applications of new knowledge, including applications in the delivery of services. This is the economy of the "knowledge worker." Whereas the preindustrial economy is a game with nature, or the industrial a game with the fabrication of nature, the postindustrial economy is a game among people where intellectual technology replaces machine technology. Bell's concept of postindustrial society has five dimensions:

(1) There is a shift from a goods-producing economy to a service-producing one. Although this includes personal services such as retail stores and beauty salons, the main growth is in transportation, communications, health, education, research, and government. The majority of American workers are now in service occupations.

(2) There is an increase in size and influence of a class of professional and technical workers. In the United States, scientists and engineers form the key group in this new class. In this century, growth in their numbers has been much greater than that of other occupations.

(3) The postindustrial society is organized around knowledge, particularly theoretical knowledge. Innovation, social organization, and management draw on the nation's intellectual technology. Information technologies have greatly added to our capability for managing knowledge. Research and development, or the joining of science, technology, and economics, is the key to this society. Theoretical knowledge is a strategic resource.

(4) A critical aim is the management of technological growth. New methods of forecasting and of technology assessment make possible new levels of planning and control over change. This involves studies of second- and third-order consequences—not just the main effects—of expected technological change.

(5) There is an emphasis on the development of methods of intellectual technology. These are the algorithms of complex problem

solving in games against nature, fabricated nature, or among people. The goal is the management of society or "organized complexity." Intellectual technology should become as important to human affairs in the postindustrial society as machine technology is for an industrial one.

The foregoing both serve to link and to contrast several contemporary forecasts about changes in our economy. Bell, for example, stresses "intellectual technology" as a primary tool of postindustrial society, the ability to manage complexity by application of theoretical knowledge. This is not only the basis of the economy but spills over into social attitudes. A population of knowledge workers would expect that social problems be managed through applications of intellectual technology. They would be impatient with traditional politics.

There is also the growth in the service sector of information workers, yet there is the problem of these workers being displaced by information technologies. Their jobs may be "deskilled" or omitted altogether.

### Other Views of the
### Information Economy

Others have written extensively of an economy based on knowledge and information work. Fritz Machlup, in his *The Production and Distribution of Knowledge in the United States* (1962), described "knowledge industries." Occupations in these areas include those of educators, physicians, governmental administrators, engineers, researchers, and jobs in the many areas of finance, communications, and the information sciences.

Peter Drucker wrote in his *The Age of Discontinuity* (1969) about the growth of "knowledge work" as one major shift in contemporary social change. His concept is particularly business oriented, with knowledge seen as the new "central capital, the cost center, and the critical resource of the economy."

Marc Porat's (1977) research included similar information concepts and acknowledged Bell's concept of a postindustrial society. Porat stressed the growth of numbers of information workers. These are a larger group than Bell's because Porat includes virtually any individual whose occupation touches on the manipulation of information. Porat's "information society" is not so much a stress on intellectual technologies as it is a recognition that increasing numbers of people are employed in information-related industries. His is more an economic than a social forecast.

Although these theories differ in details, they all point to the importance of the growing information economy. Bell, in his evaluation of trends in U.S. occupations, noted that in a comparison of turn-of-the-century and 1940 employment figures, the original ratio of three workers in service occupations and seven in the production of goods had nearly equalized. By 1960, six of ten workers were in knowledge or service-type occupations. Marc Porat (1977) drew similar conclusions about what he calls an "information"-based economy. He reported in that, in 1967, about one-fourth of the U.S. gross national product (GNP) reflected the production, processing, or distribution of information goods and services. An additional 21% was reflected in the purely informational demands of coordinating the remainder of the economy. Such activities engaged over 46% of the work force, whose earnings were over 53% of the income from labor in the United States. Similar to Bell's statistical arguments, Porat further points out that the work force employed in agriculture dropped from nearly 50% in the 1860s to 4% in the 1970s, and the industrial work force from nearly 40% in the early 1940s to 20% in the 1970s. By contrast, the number of persons in information-related occupations has grown from 10% at the turn of the century to 46% in the 1970s.

Not all observers agree with Bell's or Porat's figures because of differences of opinion on how to classify "information," "knowledge," or what Bell calls "service workers." But nobody raises any real issue about the reduction of the work force from occupations such as agriculture. There are disputes whether manufacturing occupations are really decreasing in relative numbers. There is definite agreement, however, that the knowledge industries are growing rapidly.

Although the forecast of an economy increasingly dependent on knowledge and technology is key to both Bell's postindustrialism and the contemporary reference to the "information society," the latter term does not appear in Bell's work. It is a broader, perhaps more inexact, term, found in such works as Marc Porat's analysis of changes in the workplace (*The Information Economy*, 1977), Joseph Pelton's examination of world telecommunications (*Global Talk*, 1981), James Martin's consideration of the social impacts of telecommunications (*The Wired Society*, 1978), Wilson Dizard's evaluation of world information orders (*The Coming Information Age*, 1982), or my own, popularly written, *The Communications Revolution* (1982).

## *Information Technologies and Economic Development*

### Growth of the Information Environment

What are the information technologies that will enable us to enhance productivity, competitiveness, or create new businesses? Mainly they represent computing, telecommunications, or the combination of the two. These systems also represent an interim stage of growth in the evolution of information technologies in organizations.

As shown in Figure 1.1, in the 1960s to 1970s, information technology investments were in individual support systems like accounting, then later in word processing, or manufacturing control. By the 1980s, we have seen the integration of these resources within organizations as they include what is referred to as "management information systems." On the one hand, many management information systems started as the integration, say, of computer terminals into a network that provided access to separate word processing, data entry and retrieval, or electronic mail applications. Later, the terminal, now as a desktop computer, offered standard methods for access to computer and telecommunications services, as well as local options such as word processing, spreadsheets, or computer-aided design.

As we look at current changes, it appears as if the 1990s will represent the expansion of management information systems into networks extending far beyond the individual organization. The new systems, via networking and personal computers, also extend access to higher-level management. This results in enhanced control over data resources, cash flow, manufacturing operations, supplier or customer transactions, market information, or sales. Many new telecommunications services are a part of this new environment, including, for example, telebanking, teleresearch, telemail, teleconferencing, telecommuting, telemarketing, and teletraining. The new networks add value as well as integrate efforts in

- product engineering
- manufacturing control
- market analysis
- sales & distribution
- service

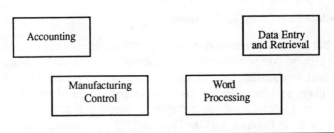

1960 s - 1970 s:  Independent Applications
To Support Systems

1970 s - 1980:  Integration of Support Systems within
Organization as Management Information System
(Internal Telecommunications)

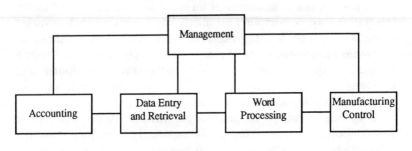

1980 s - 1990 s:  Expansion of Management Information
Support System to External Environment
(External Telecommunications)

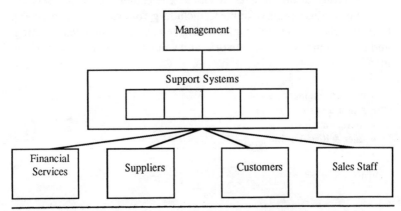

**Figure 1.1    Evolution of Information Technology Applications**

- business analysis
- decision making

Another current trend is to distinguish between the support versus the strategic role of information technology investments. Most traditional information technologies have had a mainly "support" function. Today, the most dramatic returns from investments in information technology are those that create strategic advantages over the competition. This stresses the concept of information as strategic investment. Increasingly, in the information age, the competition among businesses will be played out in the information environment. The major benefits are

- cost-effectiveness of operation
- new forms of market access and distribution channels
- competitiveness of product or service
- competitiveness of company
- ability to adapt to change
- ability to introduce new products and services

For strategic implementation, the objective is to invest in information technologies wherever the value added promises to be greatest. Because of this increased functionality, we have a greater range of options for implementing technology investments in a business or organization. To aid in deciding among these options, the concept of "value-added stream" is valuable. At what critical points or processes is value added to raw materials, to components, or services? These are targets of opportunity for information technology investment. We know from experience over the last decade that the new advances in information technology generally make contributions that are greater in some areas than in others. For example, accounting systems, or basic support-type systems, have already made their contribution. The newest opportunities are more in such areas as marketing, point-of-sale transactions, and investments that lead to company or product differentiation.

Economic trends favor the information economy. As the energy, materials, and labor costs for doing business have gone up in our economy, the costs of information technologies have declined dramatically. Moreover, we have witnessed the additional benefit that these technologies have a much wider range of functions than before, and are much more accessible not only to the individual worker or manager but the small business owner (discussed next). In the broad view, it is illuminating to see the opportunities created by these cost crossovers. Our goal in technology implementations is to transfer our operations as much as possible from the high costs of materials and labor to the decreasing costs of technologies.

### Opportunities for Small or Rural Businesses

Although popular examples of primary and secondary sector applications often involve large businesses, the number and range of innovations are greater in the small business areas. If, indeed, as many are saying, the encouragement of small businesses is an important component of economic development, then the primary and secondary sector applications of information technologies on this level are an especially important consideration. The information economy is not just huge companies and high technology; it is also "modest-tech" contributions or even what one might call "low-tech" businesses. The applications are limited only by the innovativeness of the small business entrepreneur. Often information technologies will make a small business better, or be the basis for creating new small businesses.

### Promoting the Rural Economy

These opportunities also extend to rural businesses, an important consideration for the American economy. Among the applications to rural business are

- resource conservation (e.g., irrigation systems)
- grower-processor market transaction systems
- expert systems for seed selection, fertilizers, and crop estimation
- market research
- weather forecasting and analysis
- remote management of decentralized or remote facilities
- electronic funds management and transfer
- land value enhancement (e.g., installation of information, entertainment, and security systems for retirement communities)

### Benefits in the Public Sector

Information technologies can contribute to the efficiency of nonprofit organizations. For example, the evolving managerial information network illustrated in Figure 1.1 well fits the needs of government agencies. There should come a point where federal or state, or even city, agencies will be able to route data communications with the ease that they now use voice (telephone) communications. So, too, should the citizen-client gain access to the network, and we see this as emergency alarm systems, information filing, and a few demonstrations of on-line tax payments.

There are also unrealized opportunities relative to the applications of information technologies in public education. Dissemination and interaction are key components of the educational process, so why do we not have more use of information technologies in our schools? Why not multiply and disseminate the talents of the most effective teachers through telecommunications networks? Why not invest in interactive computer instruction that can be highly adept at individualizing learning? Why do we not have "Computer-Aided-Teaching" like "Computer-Aided-Manufacturing?"

It is well known that the current use of computers in public schools is gravitating away from attempts to make instruction more innovative and productive to treating computing as an academic topic in itself. In the late 1970s and early 1980s, the most ambitious scenarios for microcomputer implementations held that computers could make instruction in the three-Rs much more efficient by the development of new instruction strategies, by self-instruction, and personal adaptation of materials. In pondering the educational challenge of the information age, one is reminded of the words of scientist and business leader Dr. Simon Ramo (the "R" in TRW), who has emphasized that to be competitive not only with the Soviets but with our Western allies in the closing years of this century, Americans need education "by, for, and about technology."

Other important public sectors for information technologies include health care delivery, law enforcement, and recreation.

## A Mandate for States

Another important factor in examining current trends is to recognize that the Reagan years encouraged individual states to take increased responsibility for their own development and not depend as heavily as in the past on federal incentives and subsidies. This has meant that states have been increasingly on notice to plot the course of their own development, to seek their own "competitive edges" in the U.S. and world economies. The 1980s has been a growth era for the establishment of state policies for economic growth as well as ancillary policies for educational reform, science and technology, and new economic opportunities in general.

## New Social Considerations

### The "Sociologizing" Mode

There is also a social dimension to the concept of postindustrialism. Daniel Bell, for example, proposes a substantial value component in that he expects a shift in advanced societies from an exclusive emphasis on productivity to more concern with social consequences and objectives. He contrasts these two ends as the *economizing* and *sociologizing* modes, which he feels can be made more meaningful than the traditional distinctions between capitalism and socialism.

The economizing mode refers to functional efficiency in management. The sociologizing mode seeks to achieve desirable social functions that may require some loss in economic efficiency. In particular, the sociologizing mode introduces noneconomic values into this system. The economizing mode reflects the traditional values of industrial society, where goals are associated with costs/benefits, maximization, or optimization. Less attention is paid to the social consequences of growth and productivity. Gains are measured in goods rather than quality of life. The sociologizing mode, on the other hand, represents an attempt to incorporate social factors in the implementation of technology. Here there is a formal attempt to assess social needs, to anticipate social costs of innovations. Social ends become objectives of change.

To summarize the evolving picture of postindustrialism, the result is a society in which social goals are thoroughly researched and processes are implemented to achieve them. Technologically driven change would be guided by research-based policy in which all the social consequences would be considered. A new knowledge class would demand that intellectual technology be as much applied to quality of life as to any other ends in the society. The political process itself might be revised to be less haphazard relative to public decisions over complex technological problems. Bargaining and negotiation might well replace political debate. Decisions would be made against the context of well-researched alternatives rather than in the heat of political rhetoric. Postindustrialism is eventually more than an economic order—it is a new social order.

## Life-Style Changes

A further important part of this theory of change is that as the basis for an economy evolves, so will characteristics of the society within which it is maintained. For better or worse, skills and values related to information technology use may move from the workplace to the home. The value of information may prompt individuals to do more information seeking in their personal lives as they have had to do in their professional ones. Further, in the information age, there is the expectation that many information technologies will be increasingly available in the home, and this has profound social consequences.

Information technologies already pervade our social institutions and personal lives. Our national and regional politics are carried out largely via the medium of television, and this is increasingly now the case with local campaigns. Most of our leisure time is also spent with television, now on the average of about six hours daily in American homes. Cable television connections and videocassette ownership have recently exceeded the 40% mark, and home computing 20%. These figures grow annually.

## Employment

Information technologies offer a mix of negative and positive consequences for the job market. For one, there is the question of the effects of information technologies on the rapid expansion of jobs in the service sector. Service jobs—not necessarily high-paying ones—are the fastest-growing type of occupation. This includes retail clerks, secretaries, nurses, repair and service technicians, janitors, and restaurant personnel, among others. Many of these are a form of labor not entirely replaceable by technologies. But for some, technologies may negatively impose a form of "deskilling" where the pay related to the job is reduced. Moreover, many of these positions do not lead to opportunities for advancement (data entry clerks seldom become programmers or computer engineers).

There is also the observation that displaced workers may have options only involving lower-paying service jobs (e.g., the factory worker who now serves hamburgers). An example of deskilling is the use of price scanners in supermarkets, coupled with increasing self-service departments, both of which lessen the qualifications and the pay required for staff. Who will take these positions? Will the compensation be enough to maintain a reasonable standard of living or to be competitive with welfare?

On the positive side are service occupations directly related to information businesses, as in manufacture, repair, or sales. Also, if information technologies increase the success of small business revitalization, growth, or development of new small business, the net effect on employment is positive. But the key question often asked at conferences on information-age economics is whether workers displaced by technologies are always directly absorbed into new jobs created by those technologies. The increasingly frequent answer is "no," unless new industries are intentionally created. So it seems that the expansion of the job market will take more than simply the growth of the information sector.

The most opportune and more career-oriented positions in the information age are in technical fields, such as the various types of engineering careers, computer and telecommunications applications, and operations management, to name a few. These offer considerable opportunity for upward mobility if one has the training, but they are far fewer than the aforementioned service occupations. Will there be enough of these positions to guarantee the survival of the middle class?

### The Negative Side

Since the rise of the mass society brought on by the industrial revolution, there has always been a fear that technology and change are done at some cost to the individual. In modern terms, it is the feeling of a loss of individualism, that the person has become subordinate to the system in an increasingly technological and corporate-dominated society.

In the antigovernment and anticorporate demonstrations of the 1960s in America, it is no coincidence that the best-selling book on college campuses was Herbert Marcuse's *One Dimensional Man* (1964). His thesis is one of the suppression of the individual, of independence, of freedom of thought, and especially the loss of the right to critical opinions as society becomes technologically advanced. As corporate advances stress objectives and efficiency, according to Marcuse, there is a corresponding loss of intellectual and political freedom. Criticism or opposition is counterproductive to objectives. It is inefficient. How ironic, Marcuse stresses, that the rights and liberties that mark the origins of industrial society are eventually bound to become its victims. As Marcuse (1964, p. 1) put it, "the achievement cancels the premises."

French philosopher Jacques Ellul (1964) has offered an even more gloomy future for technological society. *Modernization* and *technology* have become synonymous. In the process, we have "technologized" ourselves at the expense of traditional human values; humanity has become subservient to the technological state. In Ellul's thinking, there is no way that we can adopt technology without these social consequences. They are inherent. More so than even Marcuse, Ellul sees no way out of the dilemma.

Marcuse and Ellul, of course, would consider Bell's forecast a most improbable, if not impossible, future. At least one critic has accused Bell of painting a picture of what could be conceived only as a White, middle-aged, liberal's political fantasy. Yet in the last several decades, we have clearly vacillated between economizing and sociologizing modes in our society. In the late 1960s, we were in the sociologizing mode of Lyndon Johnson's "Great Society." In the later Nixon and Ford administrations, we saw an emphasis on the economizing mode. Jimmy Carter clearly emphasized sociologizing goals. Ronald Reagan was elected mainly on the basis of a directly opposite platform.

We have seen "environmental impact reports" required but have also witnessed the squashing of the occupational safety and health efforts. The Office of Technology Assessment has been an on-again, off-again entity. Nuclear power is a meeting ground for sociologizing-economizing debates, as in the conservation of natural resources and offshore oil drilling. Even if we have many of the characteristics of postindustrialism grow about us, Bell's sociologizing bias has not been particularly as forecast. We are not clearly of one mind in where we want to go with our rapidly developing technological society.

### The Key Role of Education

In an economy where "knowledge" is a raw material, education and training—especially in science and technology—take on a critical value. The well-known *A Nation at Risk* report (National Commission on Excellence in Education, 1983) decried the lack of science in public school curricula, let alone the poor quality of training available for science teachers. The importance of upgrading educational opportunities is not a case of simple altruism as much as it is a necessity for training a work force that is competitive in information age occupations. This includes the retraining of workers displaced from obsolete jobs. Education is a tool for change. Neither in theory nor practice can a society be competitive in the information age without an educated work force. There is also an increasingly visible need in the new economy for vocational training to accommodate the many growing technical occupations for the work force. These are the repair workers, sales workers, supervisors, and the paraprofessionals.

Finally, good arguments can be made for the return on investment in funds for research activities in higher education. In an information society, "knowledge production" is a central activity, and this, along with the training of researchers, is the mission of the modern research university.

## Texas as a Focus for Research

### An Environment for Change

Although areas such as Silicon Valley and Boston's Route 128 have received the bulk of the attention given to high-technology industry in the United States, there are other areas such as San Diego; Denver; Orange County, California; North Carolina; and the central corridor of Texas that are more representative of programmatic attempts at economic development than the former examples. These are less extraordinary examples and offer ample evidence of the consequences of *planned* development.

There are important points to be made about Texas as an example of a society in transition, at least attempted transition.

* Since the late 1960s, there has been a conscious attempt to diversify the economy, especially into technology-based industries (Tracor, Inc., a *Fortune* 500 company was founded in Austin in the late 1940s; IBM and Motorola settled in Austin well before the high-tech boom).

* In the 1980s, these attempts converged in an alliance of government, business, and higher education to promote central Texas as an R&D center for microelectronics. The high point of these activities was the selection of Austin over 56 other cities as the site of the Microelectronics and Computer Technology Corporation (MCC), now a research consortium of 20 U.S. companies. MCC's chief executive officer, retired

admiral Bobby Inman, a native Texan, was the symbol of leadership of Texas in the information age.

* The Select Committee on Science and Technology was personally appointed by the governor to advise on further development of the state in the new economic era. Special research funds were legislated for university researchers; private interests funded 32 $1-million chairs in engineering and computer science at the University of Texas at Austin.

* The most major public school reforms undertaken at one time in the United States were implemented in 1985 as a key program for state development. An equally prestigious committee was appointed to reorganize Texas higher education for the new challenges.

* All the foregoing took place in a state that by the mid-1980s ranked in the top three in the United States in population, total personal income, nonagricultural employment, retail sales, value-added manufacturing, construction, contracts, bank deposits, gross farm income, and foreign trade, as well as having the second lowest unemployment rate.

Despite the economic downturn of 1985-1987, it clearly remains that Texas is on the cusp of major change. Much of this can be interpreted relative to information age concepts—not hypergrowth, "Silicon Prairies," or just seducing Frostbelt companies to relocate in the South. Also, it is more than a case of the demise of the oil economy. Indeed, there is a growing diversification of the economy. Politics in Texas increasingly reflects the growth of a two-party system. Attention has been given to educational improvement. And statistically speaking—in terms of attitudes, jobs, politics, and values—Texas is changing. The challenge to Texas in the closing years of this decade is to chart a more careful course for progress, taking care to avoid false expectations but certainty not retreating from the premise that we, the nation, and the world are in a period of socioeconomic change.

Our goal in the studies reported in this volume was to examine the attempted entry of a state into the information age—not as a grandiose vision, but through a calculated view developed relative to theory and research in this topic that have been evolving for at least a quarter of a century. That the high-tech economy has not been realized as envisioned is disappointing in many respects, but it is a basis for a most realistic assessment—one with the glitter stripped away—of the information society moved from the conceptual level to the everyday realities of the economy, politics, and public attitudes.

## *Lessons from the Research*

### Overview

As stated at the outset of this chapter, our main objective in this research was to examine selected aspects of the practical realization of the information society concept. In this section, we have attempted to cast ten major generalizations. These are meant not only for other researchers, but for city, state, or even national planners, to consider as they plot their entrance into the information age.

### Ten Generalizations

(1) The transition to an information age economy and society is as much the result of the existing economy, politics, public opinion, and the deeper cultural values of the society as it is the vision of a postindustrial era. How will the current environment affect the desired changes? Realize that current crises can take away the planning energies and recourses for desired change.

(2) Education is a strategic investment for the information age. This includes not only the training of the professional and managerial classes, and vocational education in many technically oriented occupations, but higher education as a research investment.

(3) More attention needs to be given to the processes of technology transfer, or, more generally, to the diffusion of innovations. These processes have been actively encouraged in the past (e.g., in agriculture and family planning) and can be enhanced as catalysts of change in the information age.

(4) Do not anticipate that change can be promoted faster that voters are ready to accept it. This was one of the main factors relevant to the slowdown of change in our present studies. Legislators will put reelection before advancing controversial ideas.

(5) Multidisciplinary research, including interrelated studies of the economy, public attitudes, the diffusion process, and educational planning, are especially valuable for study of the information society. This includes the necessity for combined qualitative and quantitative methods. Many of the broad themes of change in the information society—for example, education—are at the intersection of economic trends, job changes, and public attitudes.

(6) In current change processes, there is a particular challenge to governance units below the federal level. The eight years of the Reagan

administration have placed far more challenge on state policymaking than has been experienced in this century. There is heightened interest in science and technology policy, business development policy, telecommunications policy, and education policy. The new technologies also impose challenges on intercity and city-level planning.

(7) We need to give much more attention to modeling the *change* process, not only economic studies but studies of technology transfer, public attitudes, acceptance of educational reforms, and even expectations for the future.

(8) There is always a potential for key variables to accelerate in a negative direction. In Texas, if economic opportunity does not reach the large minority populations, especially those of the Rio Grande Valley, the state not only fails in its development plans but change could become increasingly difficult to promote. The need for social welfare, law enforcement, and remedial education may become so great as to take funds away from investments that lead directly to growth.

(9) We need to know much more about the detailed effects of an information-type economy on employment. What are the key jobs in the information economy? The debates continue as to the degree to which jobs replaced by information technologies are then regenerated in different sectors of the economy, either through the extension of traditional businesses or the creation of new ones.

(10) The process of promoting change may not be as potentially efficient as most people seem to assume. This may be because we are simply not adept at promoting development, or perhaps the process has become so complex that it can no longer be efficiently encouraged.

# PART II

# The Information Economy

# 2

# The Growth of the Information Sector

## HEATHER E. HUDSON
## LOUIS LEUNG

*One of the classic modern studies on the information society was undertaken by Marc Uri Porat (1977), in which he studied the growth in employment in selected information-intensive occupations. If, indeed, the information society is growing, we would expect more people to be employed in the gathering, processing, and use of information, including the manufacturing and servicing of information technology. Such was the finding of Porat, which indicated that the United States is definitely moving in the direction of highly visible growth in the information type of occupations. He also established a research model that could be followed in subsequent studies. This model has been applied to a study of Texas undertaken by Heather E. Hudson and her associate Louis Leung. The researchers, indeed, find that information occupations are growing in Texas, and in some cases were greater than in the national economy. Of particular importance, according to the authors, are the implications for education, particularly vocational education, if certain of these occupations are to be filled by Texans. Dr. Hudson is well known for her many studies of the impact of information technologies on the economy of developing countries. At the time of this writing, she was on the faculty of the University of Texas College of Communication, where Mr. Leung is a doctoral degree candidate. She is soon to join the University of San Francisco.*

## *The Information Sector*

### Introduction

We are living in an era of transition. A century ago, the United States was beginning to shift from a primarily extractive economy (based on agriculture, forestry, and mining) to an industrialized economy in which a majority of economic activity consisted of the transformation of raw materials into manufactured goods. Today we are witnessing a shift from an industrially based economy to an information-based economy. In Texas, the transition may be even more dramatic and far-reaching, as agriculture and the petroleum industry coexist with information industries, and adopt the tools of the information age to improve primary sector productivity.

Along with capital and labor, information is a vital component of the modern economy. Information is intrinsic to every phase of economic activity including research and development, planning, management, marketing, education, and training. The rapid evolution of information and communications technologies during the past decade has brought powerful new tools to create, process, and transmit information, as well as new industries that produce information equipment and services.

Using census employment data, this chapter examines the growth of the primary information sector in Texas from 1973 to 1983, comparing it with the growth of the Texas economy in general, and with the growth of the information sector in the United States as a whole. The study also reports the growth of the information sector in five major metropolitan areas, namely Austin, Dallas-Fort Worth, El Paso, Houston, and San Antonio. The data are also broken down to show comparative growth in various components such as information services, media, technology, trade, and research and development.

Finally, we discuss the implications of this analysis for employment and education requirements within the framework of population growth and demographic changes in Texas, including the continuing urbanization of the population and the increasing minority population.

### Identification of the Information Sector

In 1962, Fritz Machlup published a pioneering work titled *The Production and Distribution of Knowledge in the United States* in which he identified the production of knowledge as an economic activity. This was the increase in the ratio of knowledge-producing labor to physical labor as a characteristic of the information age.

This relationship, many believe, is strongly associated with the increase in productivity and thus to the rate of economic growth. Machlup refers to "production and distribution, acquisition and transmission, creation and communication" as the key economic activities in an information economy. In his analysis of the economy, Machlup uses an "industry approach" to the study of knowledge production, examining education, research and development, the media of communication, information machines, and information services sectors as the five knowledge-production industries. This theme was further developed by Daniel Bell in his 1976 work, *The Coming of Post-Industrial Society*, in which he identified information as the key element of the postindustrial era (see Chapter 1).

### Porat's Typology

In 1977, the Department of Commerce published a study by Marc Porat that attempted to measure the extent of information activities in the economy by listing and classifying the industries that constitute the "information sector."

Porat (1977) divided information activities in the economy into a primary and a secondary information sector. He defines "information industries" as those that "intrinsically convey information" or are "directly useful in producing, processing or distributing information." The primary information sector includes all industries that produce information goods or equipment or market information services as a commodity. It includes, for example, advertising, accounting, financial services, legal services, mass media, telecommunications, printing, computer manufacturing, and trade in information goods. The secondary information sector consists of all information services produced for internal consumption by government and noninformational firms. These services include management, research, inventory control, scheduling, accounting, marketing, and so on. Bell (1981) characterizes these as the private and public bureaucracies. Their contribution is more difficult to measure because they are functions within other sectors and because their output is not information products but other goods and services.

Using this categorization and census data on U.S. industries, it was estimated that, by 1974, information activities contributed about 54% of GNP, of which 29% was attributed to the primary information sector and 25% to the secondary information sector (Bell, 1981).

Porat classified the primary information sector into five major categories:

- markets for information—knowledge production and information distribution industries such as mass media and some educational institutions;
- information in markets—information management, advertising, risk management (insurance, finance, brokerages), and so on;
- information infrastructure—information processing including printing, data processing, telecommunications, and so on, and information goods manufacturing industries ranging from paper and ink to television sets and computers;
- wholesale and retail trade in information goods—bookstores, computer stores, theaters, and so on;
- support facilities for informational activities—buildings used by information industries; office furnishings, and so on.

## Method of the Present Study

### Categories

Our research uses Porat's definition of the primary information sector to compare growth of information industries in the United States and Texas over the past decade. We have, however, reaggregated those of Porat's subcategories and selected clusters that we think are most useful, for our analysis, in tracing the growth and change in the primary information sector. These categories are given in Table 2.1

### Source of Data

To obtain an estimate of the growth of the information sector in recent years in Texas, we used the U.S. Census Bureau's data published in annual *County Business Patterns* reports. Data for individual industries are classified by Standard Industrial Classification (SIC) Codes, which Porat also used in his study. Data for each SIC code include the total number of employees, the annual payroll, and the total number of establishments in the industry, classified by number of employees. State demographic data were obtained from the Population

TABLE 2.1
Five Subsectors of the Primary Information Sector

1. Research and Development
   (7391)  Commercial research and development laboratories
   (7397)  Commercial testing laboratories
    (892)  Nonprofit education and scientific research agencies

2. Information Services
   Private Information Services
    (628)  Services allied with the exchange of securities or commodities
     (66)  Combinations of real estate, insurance, loans, law offices
   (7392)  Business, management, administrative, and consulting services
     (81)  Legal services
    (891)  Engineering and architectural services
    (893)  Accounting, auditing, and bookkeeping services
    (899)  Services, not elsewhere classified

   Search and Nonspectulative brokerage industries
   (6052)  Foreign exchange establishments
   (6053)  Check cashing agencies and current exchanges
   (6055)  Clearing house associations
    (616)  Loan correspondents and brokers
    (623)  Security and commodity exchanges
     (64)  Insurance agents, brokers, and services
    (653)  Agents, brokers, and managers
    (654)  Title abstracts companies
   (7313)  Radio, television, and publishers' advertising representatives
    (732)  Consumer credit reporting agencies, mercantile reporting agencies, and
           adjustments and collection agencies
   (7361)  Private employment agencies
   (7362)  Temporary help supply services
   (7829)  Services allied to motion picture distribution

   Advertising Industries
   (3993)  Signs and advertising display
   (7311)  Advertising agencies
   (7312)  Outdoor advertising
   (7319)  Miscellaneous advertising
   (7331)  Direct mail advertising agencies

   Nonmarket Coordinating Institutions
    (861)  Business associations
    (862)  Professional membership organizations
    (863)  Labor union and similar labor organizations
    (865)  Political organizations

   Insurance Industries
     (63)  Life, accident, fire, and casualty
    (636)  Title insurance

(continued)

TABLE 2.1    Continued

Finance Industries (components only)
- (60)   Commercial, savings banks and related institutions
- (61)   Credits institutions

Speculative Brokers (components only)
- (62)   Security brokers, commodity contractors
- (6794) Patent owners and lessors

3. Media

Regulated Communication Media
- (4832) Radio broadcasting
- (4833) Television broadcasting

Unregulated Communication Media
- (271)  Newspapers: publishing, publishing and printing
- (272)  Periodicals: publishing, publishing and printing
- (273)  Books: publishing, publishing and printing
- (274)  Miscellaneous publishing
- (735)  News syndicates
- (7813) Motion picture production, except for television
- (7814) Motion picture and tape production for television
- (7823) Motion picture film exchange
- (7824) Film or tape distribution for television
- (7819) Motion picture service industries
- (7922) Theatrical producers (except motion picture) and miscellaneous theatrical services

4. Information Technology

Electronic Consumption or Intermediate Goods
- (3652) Phonograph records
- (3671) Radio and television receiving type electron tubes, except cathode ray tubes
- (3672) Cathode ray picture tubes
- (3673) Transmitting: industrial and special purpose electron tubes
- (3674) Semiconductors and related devices
- (3679) Electronic components and accessories, not elsewhere classified
- (5065) Electronic parts and equipment

Electronic Investment Goods
- (3573) Electronic computing equipment
- (3825) Electric measuring instruments and test equipment
- (3651) Radio and television receiving sets, except communication types
- (3661) Telephone and telegraph apparatus
- (3662) Radio and television transmitting, signaling, and detection equipment and apparatus
- (3693) Radiographic x-ray, fluoroscopic x-ray, therapeutic x-ray, and other x-ray apparatus and tubes
- (381)  Engineering, laboratory, and scientific and research instruments and associated equipment

TABLE 2.1    Continued

---

5. Information Trade

Household Investment Goods
(5732)  Radio and television stores
(5946)  Camera and photographic supply stores and hand calculators

Consumption Goods
(5942)  Bookstores
(5994)  News dealers and newsstands
(7832)  Motion picture theaters, except drive-in
(7833)  Drive-in motion picture theaters

---

NOTE: Numbers refer to SIC codes.

Data System of the Texas Department of Health and the Texas Education Agency; U.S. demographic data are from the U.S. Census.

**Comparative Analysis:**
**United States and Texas**

The study began with a comparative analysis of the growth of the primary information sector in the United States and Texas by comparing data for industries (SIC codes) that fall within Porat's definition of the primary information sector. This study tracks the number of employees and the number of establishments by employment size within each information industry from 1973 to 1983. An alternative approach might be to track the change in annual payroll. We found this approach impossible to pursue, however, because of the large number of unreported entries in the years under examination, as industries apparently attempted to avoid detailed disclosure of operations.

**Geographical Analysis: SMSAs**

In addition, this study reports the growth of the primary information sector in five major metropolitan areas based on Standard Metropolitan Statistical Areas (SMSAs). By definition, an SMSA contains at least one city with a population of at least 50,000. It includes the county of that city and adjacent counties that are metropolitan in character and economically and socially integrated with the county of the central city. Therefore, this study aggregates data for the following SMSAs:

- Austin (Hays and Travis counties);
- Dallas-Fort Worth (Collin, Dallas, Denton, Ellis, Hood, Johnson, Kaufman, Parker, Rockwall, Tarrant, and Wise counties);

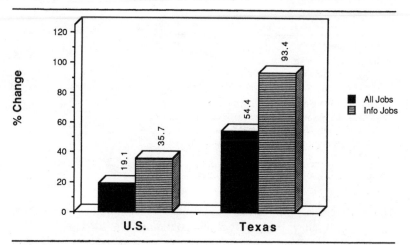

Figure 2.1    Growth of All Jobs and Information Jobs in the United States and Texas (1973-1983)

- El Paso;
- Houston (Brazoria, Fort Bend, Harris, Liberty, Montgomery, and Waller counties); and
- San Antonio (Bexar, Comal, and Guadalupe counties).

Data for the time period 1973 to 1983 were analyzed. For 1973, however, we found that there were many gaps in the employee data, making it necessary to use 1975 as the baseline year for comparative analysis of information industry growth in the SMSAs.

## Results

### Texas Compared to the United States

Figure 2.1 shows the growth in all jobs and in primary information sector jobs for the United States and Texas during the period 1973 to 1983. During this period, the population in Texas grew at three times the national rate (described later). Therefore, it is not surprising that the growth of jobs in Texas was also much greater (54.4% in Texas compared to 19.1% in the United States). The number of primary information sector jobs, however, also increased at a faster rate in Texas than in the United States. Information jobs increased a total of 93.4% in Texas during the decade compared to 35.7% in the United States as a whole.

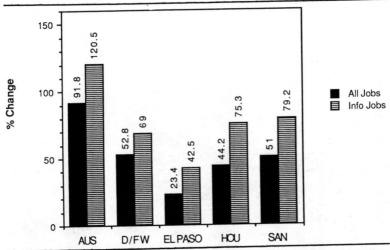

Figure 2.2    Growth of All Jobs and Information Jobs in SMSAs (1975-1983)

Figure 2.2 compares the increase in total jobs and information jobs in the five SMSAs. Here we see that, again, job creation in Texas' major cities exceeded the national average, as these cities attracted workers from outside Texas to the Sunbelt. In the cities, information jobs also increased at a faster rate than all jobs, with the highest percentage growth in Austin (120.5%). Dallas-Fort Worth, Houston, and San Antonio all had growth rates in the information sector of approximately 70% to 80%.

In order to provide an indicator for comparison across geographical areas that is not dependent on population growth, we constructed an information employment index that is the ratio of the number of primary information sector jobs to all jobs for 1983 (see Figure 2.3). Here we see that Austin has the highest percentage of primary information sector jobs at 29.2%, followed by Dallas-Fort Worth at 24.3%. Houston and San Antonio each have about 20% of jobs in the primary information sector, or about the Texas average. The growth of the high-tech industry in Austin supplements other information jobs in higher education and state government (which are not reflected in this data base). Dallas-Fort Worth has seen major growth in electronics and telecommunications, while San Antonio has a growing electronics and biomedical sector, and Houston has developed electronics, biomedical, and aerospace industries. El Paso lags with only 13.1% of jobs in this sector, and an economy dependent on manufacturing and trade with Mexico.

44    The Information Economy

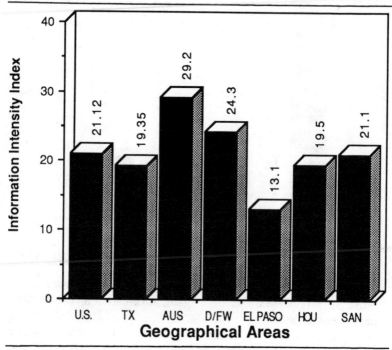

Figure 2.3    Information Employment Index (1983)

According to this index, Texas lags slightly behind the United States as a whole, which had 21.1% of all jobs in the primary information sector in 1983. This index indicates that the economy in Texas is still heavily dependent on the primary sector, which is the petroleum industry and agriculture.

**Growth of Establishments in the Information Sector**

Another way to analyze change in the economy is to examine growth in the number of businesses. Using census data on industries classified by SIC codes, we segregated establishments in the primary information sector by number of employees. Figures 2.4 and 2.5 show the growth of establishments in the primary information sector in the United States, Texas, and the five SMSAs during the period 1973 to 1983. As was true with number of jobs, Texas outdistances the United States in the number of new businesses by a factor of about 3:1 in all but the smallest establishment category. The number of medium-sized establishments with 50-99 employees increased fastest in Texas (115.6%), whereas small

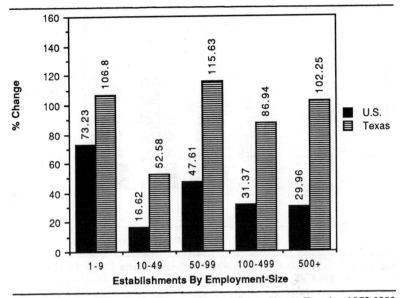

Figure 2.4    Growth in Establishments (United States Versus Texas):    1973-1983

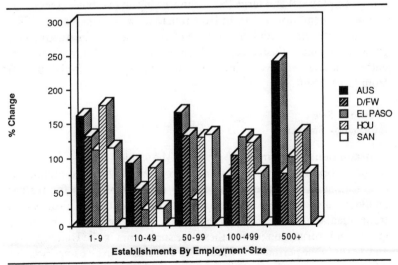

Figure 2.5    Growth of Establishments in SMSAs (1973-1983)

"mom and pop" establishments with 1-9 employees grew the fastest in the United States (73.2%). Texas also showed dramatic increase in number of firms with 100-499 and more than 500 employees, which of course represents the greatest number of new jobs. At the SMSA level,

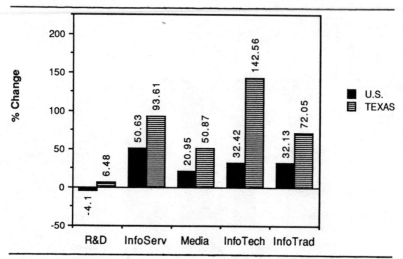

Figure 2.6    Growth in the Five Subsectors (United States Versus Texas): 1973-1983

as shown in Figure 2.5, Austin had the highest growth rate in medium (50-99 employees) and large (500 or more employees) businesses in the primary information sector. In Houston, there was an increase of 178% in small-sized firms, and an increase of 162% increase in Austin. This growth in small businesses (1-9 employees) could represent new entrepreneurial activity in information services and possibly spin-off from larger firms.

### Growth in Five Information Subsectors

In addition to examining the growth of the whole primary information sector in Texas in terms of both number of employees and number of establishments, we have identified five major subsectors for further analysis: information services, information technology, information trade, media, and research and development. Figure 2.6 compares the growth of information jobs in these five subsectors in the United States and Texas in the period of 1973 to 1983. Texas leads in all categories, but in information technology it shows the highest absolute growth (142.6%) and relative growth (4.4 times the U.S. rate). The influx of microelectronics industries in Austin, Dallas-Fort Worth, San Antonio, and Houston would certainly account for a large portion of this increase. In an industry-by-industry analysis within the information technology subsector, we found that telephone and telegraph apparatus

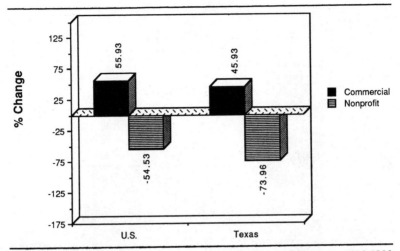

% Change

125
75
25
-25
-75
-125
-175

55.93

45.93

-54.53

-73.96

■ Commercial
▦ Nonprofit

U.S.                    Texas

Figure 2.7    Research and Development (United States Versus Texas): 1973-1983

(SIC 3661) grew 174.8% in Texas, topping the list of all the SICs in this subsector. The industry in the same subsector within the second fastest growth in employment is radio and television transmitting, signaling, and detection equipment and apparatus (SIC 3662) with an increase of 159.8%, and electronic parts and equipment (SIC 5065) with an increase of 119.6%.

The subsector with the second fastest growth in Texas is information services with an increase of 93.6%. The fastest growing industry was loan correspondents and brokers (SIC 616) with an increase of 688.9% in number of jobs from 1973 to 1983. The number of jobs in credit institutions (SIC 61) increased 65.3%, while jobs in life, accident, fire, and casualty insurance increased 28.0%. For the United States, however, this was the fastest growing subsector with a 50.6% increase in number of jobs. Again, loan correspondents and brokers showed a substantial increase in jobs of 840.9%.

In the media subsector in Texas, miscellaneous publishing (SIC 274) had the greatest increase in jobs at 225.5%. Periodical, newspaper, and book publishing experienced growth ranging from 32% to 76%. In the United States, theatrical producers (SIC 7922) and miscellaneous theatrical services grew more than 104%, and motion picture and tape production for television (SIC 7814) grew 99.5%.

In the information trade subsector, jobs in both bookstores and radio and television stores increased more than 70% in Texas and in the United States, while there was a significant drop in drive-in motion picture theaters. We might expect since 1983 a dramatic growth in small

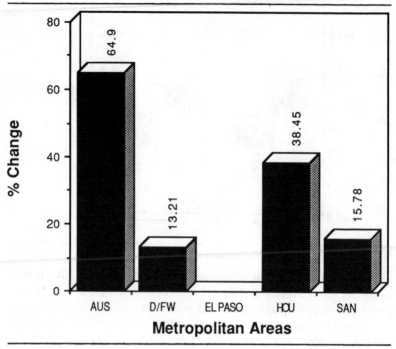

Figure 2.8    Research and Development in SMSAs (1975-1983)

businesses selling information equipment such as microcomputers, computer software, VCRs, and videocassettes.

Surprisingly, the data show only a 6.5% increase in Texas and a decline of 4.1% in the United States in jobs in research and development during the period of 1973 to 1983. The negative growth in R&D in the United States from 1973 to 1983 can be explained, however, if we further analyze the individual SICs within this subsector. Figure 2.7 shows that there was a significant drop in employment in all nonprofit education and scientific research establishments. The decline in Texas was 74.0%, while in the United States, there was a drop of 54.5%. Nevertheless, commercial research and development laboratories (SIC 7391) and commercial testing laboratories (SIC 7397) showed an increase of 45.9% and 55.9% in jobs in Texas and the United States, respectively.

**Growth in the**
**Five Subsectors in the SMSAs**

Figures 2.8 to 2.13 show the growth in employment in the five subsectors in each of the five metropolitan areas during the period 1975

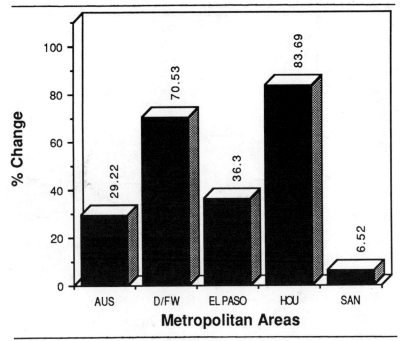

Figure 2.9    Media in SMSAs (1975-1983)

to 1983. Again, it should be noted that we excluded 1973 data from the analysis because a large number of employment figures were unreported by various industries, apparently to avoid detailed disclosure of operations. First, Figure 2.8 shows Austin with the highest growth in employment in R&D at 64.9%, followed by Houston with 38.5%. The zero percentage increase in R&D in El Paso reflects that there was no R&D activity reported in either 1975 or 1983.

In media (see Figure 2.9), Houston and Dallas-Fort Worth reported growth of 83.7% and 70.5%, respectively. Of the industries reporting the most growth in both of these metroplexes, we found a 541% increase in miscellaneous publishing, 126% increase in book publishing in Houston, and a 179% increase in motion picture services industries in Dallas-Fort Worth. Radio and television broadcasting also reported growth in number of employees of 129% in Dallas-Fort Worth and 79% in Houston.

In the area of information services (see Figure 2.10), the number of employees in all SMSAs grew more than 60%. In Austin, industries such as loan correspondents and brokers; agents, brokers, and managers; advertising agencies; title insurance; security brokers, commodity contractors; legal services; and accounting, auditing, and bookkeeping

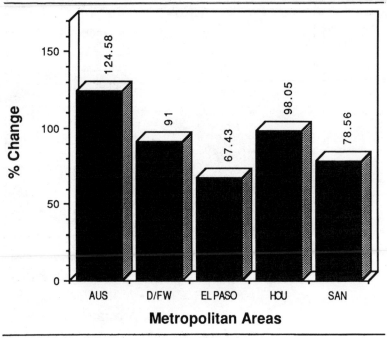

**Figure 2.10**  Information Services (1975-1983)

services all reported growth of more than 150%. In Houston, business, management, administration, and consulting services grew 337%, miscellaneous advertising went up 223%, and title insurance also reported growth of 216%.

Austin reported the biggest jump among all SMSAs in the information technology subsector (see Figure 2.11) with an increase in employees of 565.3%, including a 400% increase in semiconductors and related devices and a 272% boost in electronic parts and equipment. Although the Dallas-Fort Worth areas experienced an overall increase of only 39.5% in this subsector, electronic components and accessories (SIC 3679) rose 475%, and electronic parts and equipment (SIC 5065) grew 129% in the eight-year period. In Houston, a total growth of 32.7% in jobs in the information technology subsector was reported; however, electronic components and accessories grew 180% and electronic parts and equipment went up 94%.

Growth in the information trade subsector (see Figure 2.12) spanned all five metropolitan areas, and was particularly strong in Houston, El Paso, and Dallas-Fort Worth. Radio and television stores experienced over 100% growth in all SMSAs except El Paso and San Antonio. Bookstores came second, with increases in employees ranging from 30%

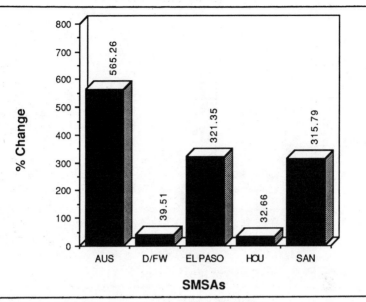

Figure 2.11    Information Technology in SMSAs (1975-1983)

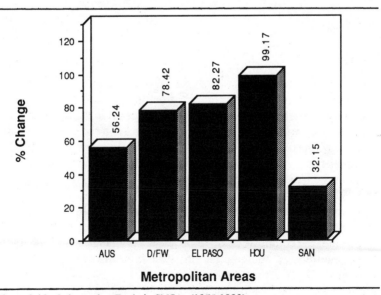

Figure 2.12    Information Trade in SMSAs (1975-1983)

to more than 100%. With the recent trend in video and consumer electronics, there has been major growth in all cities in small businesses such as video rentals and home electronics and computer stores.

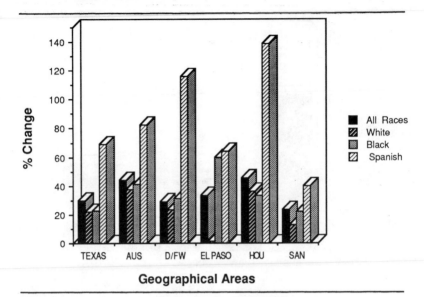

**Figure 2.13   Percentage Change in Population (1973-1983)**
SOURCE:    Texas Department of Health, *Population Data System* (1986).

## Implications

### Changing Demographics:
### Putting the Findings in Context

In order to interpret the implications of the shifts in the Texas economy, it is necessary to examine the changes in the Texas population. First, during this period, the population in Texas grew 29.9%, or nearly three times the rate for the United States population as a whole (10.5%), as northerners migrated to the Sunbelt and immigrants from Mexico and Central America joined the Texas labor force. The five SMSAs also showed major growth during this period, with Houston growing the fastest with an increase of 45.8% from 1973 to 1983, followed by Austin (44.35%) and El Paso (33.6%).

Second, the composition of Texas society is changing. In 1986, more than one-third of the population were minorities, with Hispanics making up 22.4% of the population and Blacks, 11.5%. The growth rates of the Hispanic population are dramatically higher than average growth rates for all races, due to both immigration and higher fertility rates. From 1973 to 1983, the number of Hispanics in Texas increased 68.7%, with growth rates of 138.4% in Houston, 116.7% in Dallas-Forth Worth, 82.2% in Austin, and 63.9% in El Paso. The Black population in

Texas is growing at about the same rate as the White population, but at a faster rate than Whites in some urban areas including El Paso, Dallas-Fort Worth, Austin, and San Antonio (see Figure 2.13).

Although these growth rates may be reduced in the next decade due to changes in the Texas economy and national immigration policies, they suggest that the state will need to create new jobs at a rate much higher than the national average, and that a significant percentage of its young people may not be qualified for anything but the least skilled and lowest paid jobs.

### Education

Although a detailed analysis of the status of public education is beyond the scope of this chapter, two important elements deserve attention: achievement levels and dropout rates. Texas high school graduates lag behind their counterparts in most other states in basic skills required as prerequisites for higher education and entry-level jobs with career potential. Texas ranked 45th out of 50 states on combined SAT scores in 1986. Although these scores are generally correlated with the number of students taking the test, even controlling for this variable, Texas ranks low. Of the 22 states in which 30% or more of eligible students took the SAT test, Texas ranked 17th, or in the lowest quarter. The average score in Texas was 877 (out of a total possible score of 1600), with 32% of high school graduates taking the test (for 1982, which is the latest data available for graduates from the College Board). The average score for the 22 states was 894, with an average of 50% of graduates taking the test (derived from College Board data reported in the *Dallas Times Herald*, September 23, 1986).

Although SAT scores are far from a perfect indicator of high school achievement, they do at least indicate mastery of basic skills. Texas must make major improvements to catch up with the New England states and California, which had higher SAT scores even though a higher percentage of graduates took the test than in Texas.

### *Special Challenges for Texas*

The implications of the present analysis are that education will be vital for young people who seek careers rather than simply dead-end jobs. Although careers for some may require university education, for others, the minimum requirement will be high school graduation with solid mastery of high school subjects to enable them to be trained in entry-level jobs. Those who drop out or manage to graduate without really learning in high school may be stuck in the fast growing but low paying service jobs such as janitor and fast-food worker.

Quality education can also be important in attracting new information-based employers. Among factors that influence the location choices of high-technology firms, availability of technical, skilled, and professional workers ranks highest. Thanks to advances in telecommunications and transportation, high-tech firms do not need to be near their suppliers or customers. Proximity to customers ranked 10th and proximity to raw materials and component supplies ranked 12th out of 14 factors (Robert Premus, quoted in Snyder, 1984).

**Unanswered Questions and**
**Unresolved Issues**

This research has touched on only a few aspects of the growth of the information sector. Among other important research questions are the following:

* What is the extent of the secondary information sector in Texas, that is, the information handling activities within industries such as agriculture, petroleum, or manufacturing? The secondary sector may be much larger than the primary sector, and may be a source of new jobs as well as a major market for information equipment and services.

* What types and levels of education and training are required for various information jobs? Which jobs require specialized education as a prerequisite, and which require a general liberal education as a foundation for on-the-job training? What types of retraining and continuing education are required in the information sector?

* To what extent will information work (in both primary and secondary information sectors) take place outside the cities? Will the combination of information and telecommunications technologies make it possible for more information work to be located in small towns as well as in the "exurbs" surrounding the major SMSAs?

* What are the implications of the growth of the information sector in Texas for state policy? At present, there is no entity in the state government responsible for telecommunications and information policy, yet the changes in the state's economy and education needs of its citizens are critical to its future. The state will need to assess how new information technologies and services can meet the needs of individuals, industry, agriculture, government services, and education so that policies can be formulated to help Texans excel in an information-intensive environment.

# 3

# The Economy of the New Texas

## JAMES SMITH

*Any study of the growth of the information sector of the economy must be examined relative to the patterns of the overall economy. The present chapter presents a large-scale view of the current and future economy of Texas by James Smith of the Bureau of Business Research at the University of Texas at Austin. Except for the "boom and decline" cycle in the early 1980s, the overall pattern of the growth of Texas remains quite constant and positive. In his other writing and speaking, Smith reminds planners that they must look at this larger picture rather than being preoccupied by short-term fluctuations. James Smith has spent most of his professional years as an economist in the private sector. He was the Director of the Wharton Economic Forecasting Service prior to joining the University in 1986.*

## A Time of Change

### Current Statistics

That the Texas economy in 1987 is incredibly different from the past is shown most dramatically by the strong rebound in employment from the depressing effects of the large decline in oil prices in 1986. In April 1987, the total number of people employed in Texas was reported by the Texas Employment Commission as 7,552,000 on a seasonally adjusted basis. April marked the fifth consecutive month that total employment exceeded the level of the same month one year earlier and it was the fourth month out of the last five to post an all-time record high for that

55

TABLE 3.1

Total Employment in Texas and the United States,
1970-1987

| | Texas | United States | Texas as a Percentage of the United States |
|---|---|---|---|
| 1970 | 4,399,000 | 78,678,000 | 5.6 |
| 1971 | 4,500,000 | 79,367,000 | 5.7 |
| 1972 | 4,688,000 | 82,153,000 | 5.7 |
| 1973 | 4,846,000 | 85,064,000 | 5.9 |
| 1974 | 5,016,000 | 86,794,000 | 5.8 |
| 1975 | 5,123,000 | 85,846,000 | 6.0 |
| 1976 | 5,378,000 | 88,752,000 | 6.1 |
| 1977 | 5,626,000 | 92,017,000 | 6.1 |
| 1978 | 5,920,000 | 96,048,000 | 6.2 |
| 1979 | 6,213,000 | 98,824,000 | 6.3 |
| 1980 | 6,386,000 | 99,303,000 | 6.4 |
| 1981 | 6,702,000 | 100,397,000 | 6.7 |
| 1982 | 6,867,000 | 99,526,000 | 6.9 |
| 1983 | 7,033,000 | 100,834,000 | 7.0 |
| 1984 | 7,442,000 | 105,005,000 | 7.1 |
| 1985 | 7,515,000 | 107,150,000 | 7.0 |
| 1986 | 7,433,000 | 109,597,000 | 6.8 |
| 1987[a] | 7,533,750 | 111,399,000 | 6.8 |

SOURCE:  Bureau of Labor Statistics; 1970-1986 data are annual averages.
a.  Average of first four months.

particular month. Furthermore, the data for February showed it in a tie with March 1985 (at 7,592,000) for second best all-time high and both were only 1000 jobs below the record set in June 1984. The figure for April is the fourth highest ever recorded for Texas.

The first four months of 1987 averaged 7,533,750 people employed in Texas. This represents an increase of 123,500 jobs or 1.7% over the first four months of 1986, not far below the national average of a 2.4% increase. The momentum has been building, as job growth in Texas accounted for 1 out of every 6.4 jobs created in the entire United States in the first quarter of 1987 as compared with the last quarter of 1986. Table 3.1 shows the growth in employment in Texas since 1970 compared with the United States.

Since 1970, there have been 32,721,000 jobs created in the United States; a performance unmatched by any other country in the history of

TABLE 3.2
Employment Distribution by Major Categories,
Texas and the United States: 1970 and 1985

| | 1970 | | 1985 | |
| | Texas | United States | Texas | United States |
| | (in percentages) | | (in percentages) | |
|---|---|---|---|---|
| Durable manufacturing | 11.1 | 15.8 | 8.9 | 11.8 |
| Nondurable manufacturing | 9.1 | 11.5 | 6.2 | 8.0 |
| Mining | 2.9 | 0.9 | 3.9 | 1.0 |
| Construction | 6.6 | 5.1 | 6.7 | 4.8 |
| Wholesale trade | 7.0 | 5.6 | 6.7 | 5.9 |
| Retail trade | 16.7 | 15.6 | 18.8 | 17.8 |
| Transportation, communication, and utilities | 7.0 | 6.4 | 5.7 | 5.4 |
| Finance, insurance, and real estate | 5.2 | 5.1 | 6.6 | 6.1 |
| Government | 18.3 | 17.7 | 16.4 | 16.8 |
| Other services | 16.1 | 16.3 | 20.1 | 22.5 |

SOURCE: Bureau of Labor Statistics.

the world. One out of every 9.6 of these jobs was created in Texas, which represents 3.1 million jobs or a 71.3% increase since 1970.

## Diversification

This growth has been remarkably diversified. In a recent study (Willis, 1987), it was shown that from 1970 to 1985, there were only 3 of 40 major employment categories in which growth of employment in Texas was less than that of the nation. Growth employment in Texas outpaced the national performance in every category in the services sector, which accounts for over 70% of total employment in the United States. Table 3.2 shows these changes.

This diversification in employment in the midst of rapid growth of the Texas economy is also documented in data provided by the Bureau of Economic Analysis of the United States Department of Commerce. These data show that for the 1979-1985 period, total employment in the United States grew by 1.68% a year on average, while Texas employment grew by 3.22% a year. This ranked Texas fifth in the country behind Alaska (5.54%), Florida (3.86%), Arizona (4.62%), and New Hampshire (3.86%). The fastest growing sector of the Texas economy in this period was the finance, insurance, and real estate sector, which grew by 6.79% a year, a rate of growth exceeded only by Delaware among the other 49 states. The mining sector in Texas grew by 6.32% a year during the period, well above the national average of 1.98%, but below the annual rate of increase posted by five other states.

The other services category in Texas grew by 5.65% a year, which was the sixth best performance among all states. This category includes hotels and other lodging places, personal services, business and repair services, amusements, health services, educational services, and other services. The government sector, which includes federal, local, and state employees, grew by 2.14% a year, the third highest rate of growth among all states and well above the 0.59% a year national average. The only category where growth in employment in Texas was below the national average was the agricultural services, forestry, and fisheries sector, in which Texas growth was 4.79% a year and the national average was 6.92%. Indeed, only five states had growth rates below Texas in this category.

### High Technology

One area in which every state wants to excel is employment in the high-technology categories. Here, Texas has an outstanding record. Figure 3.1 shows the growth in employment in the high technology sector for California, Massachusetts, Texas, and the entire United States from the first quarter of 1975 through 1986. Texas has performed extremely well in this part of the economy, which is likely to prove critical to future growth well into the next century.

Texas has received wide admiration around the world for the foresight demonstrated by forging an admirable coalition of academic experts, business leaders, entrepreneurs, and politicians to ensure a bright future for the people of the state. This coalition has seen to it that the state has made significant contributions to research programs at colleges and universities in the state. These contributions have been matched several times over by grants from the federal government, foundations, and private citizens (Devereux et al., 1987).

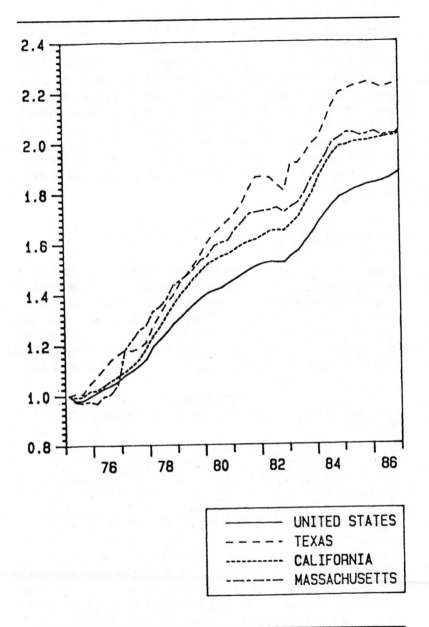

Figure 3.1    High-Tech Employment (1975, 1 = 1.0)

The result is that today Texas is at the forefront of new technological developments in aerospace, agriculture, artificial intelligence, biotechnology, chemicals, computers, enhanced recovery techniques for oil and gas, lasers, medical research, robotics, semiconductors, superconducting materials, telecommunications, and many other emerging growth areas. Indeed, the continuing breakthroughs in superconducting materials by Dr. Chu at the University of Houston have riveted the attention of thousands of scientists and the international news media on Texas. The Texas legislature has moved quickly to set up a Center for Superconductivity Research at the University of Houston with funding of about $10 million.

### Entrepreneurship

Employment growth in Texas in recent years has been helped by an extraordinary amount of entrepreneurial activity. H. Ross Perot is probably the most famous entrepreneur in Texas, a result of the growth of the company he founded with $1000 in 1963 being sold to General Motors in 1985 for over $2 billion. EDS is far from the only success story in the state, however. The company that most quickly (in four years) reached *Fortune* 500 status after being founded is Compaq Computers, which is based in Houston.

According to Dun & Bradstreet Corporation, there were 21,913 new businesses started in Texas in 1987. While this was a decline from the 26,073 new businesses started in Texas in 1986, it is still the second largest number for any state, being exceeded only in California.

Entrepreneurial activity may pick up even more in Texas as a result of publicity surrounding a recent study published by *Inc.* magazine of the best metropolitan areas in the country to start a new business. The maximum possible score on their analysis of factors making a successful environment for entrepreneurs was 100, and Austin, Texas, led all 154 metropolitan areas studied with a score of 99.22. Orlando, Florida, was a rather distant second at 73.37, followed by Phoenix, Arizona, at 72.72; Dallas-Fort Worth, Texas, at 72.23; Tucson, Arizona, at 69.31; and San Antonio, Texas, at 69.02. With three of the top six metropolitan areas on this list, Texas should see considerable benefits from people who want to start new businesses in the state.

## New Directions

### The Need to Change the
### Texas Homestead Act

There would undoubtedly be even more entrepreneurial activity in the state if the legislature were to allow voters to decide to change the Texas Homestead Act and if the voters then favored changes. This restriction on the freedom of homeowners to take out a second mortgage or to refinance their homes for any purpose other than home repair or remodeling is probably the only legacy from Andrew Jackson left in Texas today. When President Jackson closed the Second Bank of the United States in 1836, a shortage of credit rapidly developed, which led to the Panic of 1837. The direct result was that many farmers and ranchers in the fledgling Republic of Texas had their properties foreclosed, and the ensuing outcry led to a prohibition on such action by lenders that has lasted now for 150 years. Because all studies of the sources of capital for small business start-ups and expansions show that second mortgages are a significant factor in a large proportion of these cases, the inability of homeowners in Texas to tap this potential vast source of funds is not conducive to maximizing economic growth in the state (Duncan, 1986; Dunkelberg, 1985).

### Foreign Investment

Fortunately, Texas has been a magnet for foreign capital. Before Texas became a country temporarily, investors from England, Spain, and the United States were financing agricultural and ranching ventures. In the days of the Republic of Texas, the French and Germans became large investors. In the 1870s, European investors funded many of the large cattle and cotton operations in the state as well as providing much of the capital to harvest the enormous timber resources in East Texas. This influx of foreign capital and the growing realization of the wealth of natural resources in the state helped the population of Texas to grow by 94.5% from 1870 to 1880, a dramatic improvement from the 35.5% population growth rate of 1860 to 1870. To replicate the population growth rate of the 1870s today would require the addition of 11 million people to the current residents of Texas by the time of the 1990 census. Because that would be equal to nearly all of the residents of Florida, Ohio, or Pennsylvania picking up and moving to Texas, we will undoubtedly have to be satisfied with a lower growth rate of population in the 1980s.

Investors from the rest of the United States and other countries continue to find Texas an attractive place to invest. The change in our banking laws in 1986, which made Texas the first state to experiment with full interstate banking and limited branch banking simultaneously, has already attracted several major financial institutions to buy up Texas banks and thrifts and all observers expect much more activity in this sector of the economy in the future.

### The Mexico Connection

The foreign country of far more importance to the Texas economy than any other is Mexico. A recent study by the Federal Reserve Bank of Dallas found that for the 1970-1981 period, 20.7% of the variation in unemployment rates in Texas was directly attributable to variations in the rate of growth of the Mexican economy (Gruben and Phillips, 1986). Because Texas and Mexico share a border of over 1000 miles and have long had significant linkages in agriculture, retail trade, manufacturing, and services, this is not too surprising a result. A significant boost to employment growth in Texas in the past several years has come from the phenomenal expansion of the *maquiladora*, or in-bond twin plant industry. These are facilities that do all of the assembly and manufacturing in Mexico, usually using equipment and tools exported duty-free from the United States. Most of the distribution, engineering, research and development, and general management is in the United States.

Although the maquiladora industry has been in existence for over 20 years, it is only in the recent past that growth has expanded dramatically. In 1986, this industry surpassed tourism to become the second largest export industry in Mexico, after oil. There are well over 300,000 people directly employed in this industry in Mexico and somewhere between 50,000-100,000 people employed in Texas who are dependent on it. The major attraction to the companies involved, which are a large number of the world's leading firms in a variety of manufacturing areas, is that labor costs in Mexico are very competitive with those in Hong Kong, Korea, Singapore, or Taiwan. Obviously, for products designed to serve the North American market, transportation costs are much lower from Mexico than from those competitors. The visible growth and success of the maquiladora industry in the recent years has had much to do with the gains in total employment and manufacturing employment in the year ending in April 1987, in every border metropolitan statistical area including Brownsville-Harlingen, El Paso, Laredo, and McAllen-Edinburg-Mission. Indeed, total employment growth has been 5.6% in the El Paso area and 4.7% in the Laredo area in the 12 months ending in April 1987, leading the state.

### Population Shift

As the population of the United States shifts more to the South and the West, the role of Texas as a national and international distribution center is considerably enhanced. Two of the three largest air transportation companies of the world, Texas Air and American Airlines, have their headquarters in Texas. The recent announcement that one of America's largest retailers, the J. C. Penney Company, was moving its corporate headquarters to Dallas was further confirmation of the growing prominence of Texas as a distribution center. Many foreign trading companies have either their U.S. base or a major office in Texas and more such firms keep arriving in Texas on a regular basis.

The Texas market is a huge and growing one. According to the U.S. Bureau of the Census, Texas had 16,682,000 residents on July 1, 1986. This was up 2,453,000 people or 17.3% from the 1980 census count and was nearly three times the national increase. Only four states (Alaska, Nevada, Arizona, and Florida) have had a faster rate of increase in population than Texas in this period and all of them have far fewer people. The increase in population in Texas over the 1980-1986 period is more than the total population in each of 18 other states.

The growth in the number of households in Texas from 1980 to 1986 has been even stronger than the growth in total population. The Bureau of the Census reports that Texas had 5,916,000 households in 1986, an increase of 20% from 1980.

This increase in population and in employment has been associated with an even more dramatic increase in personal income. Total personal income in Texas in 1986 was reported by the Bureau of Economic Analysis of the U.S. Department of Commerce at $225.6 billion, up 60.6% from the $140.5 billion reported for 1980. Even adjusted for inflation in that period, the 1980-1986 increase is still 20.7%. In both nominal and inflation adjusted-terms, the increase in personal income in Texas in the 1980-1986 period has been well above the national average.

While Texas ranked only 26th in the nation in per capita personal income in 1986 at $13,523, only two states—California and New York—had more total personal income. Total personal income in California was slightly more than double Texas at $452.7 billion and New York was 34.8% above Texas at $304.2 billion. Total personal income in Texas, however, was $9.7 billion above that of all six New England states combined and was 26.7% ahead of Illinois, the fourth highest state.

The new Texas economy will continue to generate admiration from other states and other countries in the years ahead. Indeed, if Texas were still a country, it would have the ninth largest economy in the world, about 10% smaller than that of Canada, but about the same size as that of China—which has 50 times the population—and about triple the size of the South Korean economy.

### Prospects

The future of the Texas economy is very bright. Texas has an abundance of space for expansion, a large supply of industrial and office buildings that can be tailored to the specific needs of any organization, and a talented and highly skilled labor force attuned to the demands of coping with rapidly shifting markets. Texas also has a frontier, can-do spirit that encourages enormous numbers of entrepreneurs to try their luck at starting a business. Texas also has strong ties with Mexico, which is the third largest trading partner of the United States. In addition, a strong position in nearly every important high-technology area will continue to generate new economic growth for many years to come. Compared to other states, Texas has relatively low energy costs and a relatively low level of taxes. Only South Dakota and New Hampshire had lower levels of state tax revenues per capita than Texas in 1986.

# PART III


# Promoting Change

*4*

# The "Technopolis" Concept

RAYMOND W. SMILOR
GEORGE KOZMETSKY
DAVID V. GIBSON

*Technology transfer and growth is a critical analysis and planning issue for those interested in the information economy. The history of Silicon Valley and Boston Route 128 are rich examples of the growth of technology-based industries—many of which developed as "spin-offs" of one another. In the present intriguing report on the concept of a "technopolis," or technological city, the researchers report an analysis of high-technology growth in the Austin-San Antonio Corridor. Their efforts are assisted considerably by the concept of the "Technopolis Wheel," which accounts for the mediating forces of industrial development. David Gibson is a faculty member of the University of Texas Graduate School of Business; Raymond Smilor is Executive Director of the IC2 Institute, an organization devoted to researching and encouraging business development; George Kozmetsky, former Dean of the Graduate School of Business, is the Chairman of that Institute. We are grateful to the authors for contributing this chapter, which is drawn from their book,* Creating the Technopolis: Linking Technology, Communication and Economic Development *(Cambridge, MA: Ballinger, 1988).*

## Researching the
## Process of Development

### The *Technopolis* Concept

New kinds of institutional developments among business, government, and academia have been emerging to promote economic develop-

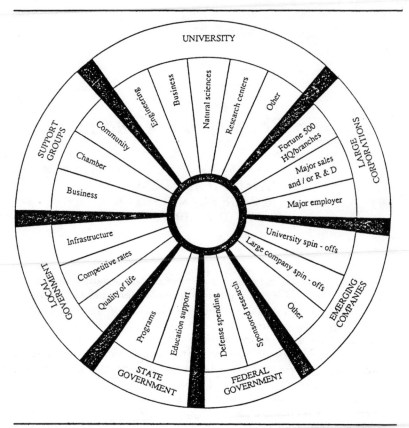

Figure 4.1    Technopolis Wheel

ment and technology diversification. Researchers have begun to analyze these new relationships and organizational structures. They have sought to evaluate the effects and ramifications of new kinds of relationships between business, government, and universities, particularly as they pertain to technology-based economic development and diversification.

This chapter develops a conceptual framework, which we call the *Technopolis Wheel* (Figure 4.1), to describe the process of technology development and economic growth in the Austin-San Antonio Corridor, an area we call an emerging technopolis. We believe this concept of the Technopolis Wheel has important implications for the development of an information economy. In the United States, the Wheel reflects the interaction of major segments that contribute to or inhibit the development of the technopolis. These seven segments include the university, large technology companies, small technology companies, state government, local government, federal government, and support groups. This chapter also considers important key individuals, whom we label "influencers," who link the seven segments of the Wheel.

### Defining and Measuring the Technopolis

Technopolis comes from the Greek term of *techno,* meaning technology, and *polis,* meaning city-state. In the United States, the modern technopolis is one that interactively links technology development with the public and private sectors to spur economic development and promote technology diversification. Three factors are especially important in the development of a technopolis and provide a way to measure the dynamics of a modern technology city-state. These are as follows:

*(1) The achievement of scientific preeminence.* A technopolis must earn national and international recognition for the quality of its scientific capabilities and technological prowess. This may be determined by a variety of factors including R&D contracts and grants; chairs, professorships, and fellowships in universities; membership of faculty and researchers in eminent organizations such as the National Academy of Sciences and the National Academy of Engineering; the number of Nobel Laureates; and the quality of students as measured by the number of national merit scholars. In addition, scientific and technological preeminence may be measured through newer institutional relationships such as industrial R&D consortia, academic and business collaboration, and research and engineering centers of excellence.

*(2) Development and maintenance of new technologies for emerging industries.* A technopolis must promote the development of new industries based on advancing cutting-edge technology. These industries provide the basis for competitive companies in a global economy and the foundation for economic growth. They may be in the areas of biotechnology, artificial intelligence, new materials, and advanced information and communication technologies. This factor may be measured through the development of R&D consortia, the commercialization of university intellectual property, and new types of academic-business-government collaboration.

*(3) Attraction of major technology companies and the creation of homegrown technology companies.* A technopolis must affect economic development and technological diversification. This may be determined by the range and type of major technology-based companies attracted to the area, by the ability of the area to encourage and promote the development of homegrown technology-based companies, and by the creation of jobs related to technologically based enterprises.

## An Analysis by
## Technopolis Segments

The developing Austin-San Antonio technopolis is a strip of land about 100 miles long in the heart of Texas. Interstate Highway 35 connects Austin on the north end of the Corridor to San Antonio on the south end. To the east side of the highway lies the Blackland Prairies, some of the richest farmland in the United States. To the west of the highway lies the famous Hill Country of Central Texas. There are other developing technopolis in Texas, namely the Dallas-Forth Worth Metroplex and the Houston area north to the Woodlands.

We next use the conceptual framework of the Technopolis Wheel to describe the development of the Austin-San Antonio Corridor. We consider each of the seven segments of the Wheel and show their role in and effect on scientific preeminence, the development of new technologies, and technology company formation.

### The University Sector

The nucleus in the development of the Austin-San Antonio Corridor as a technopolis is the university segment. In Austin, at the north end of the Corridor, the University of Texas at Austin has played the key role. In San Antonio, at the south end, the University of Texas Health Science Center and the University of Texas at San Antonio have played the key role.

An important point needs to be made about higher education in general in the Corridor. Other universities have also provided research, teaching, and training that contributed to the development of the technopolis. Some of these include Southwestern University in Georgetown (20 miles north of Austin); in Austin, St. Edward's University, Austin Community College, and Concordia College; Southwest Texas State University in San Marcos (20 miles south of Austin); in San

Antonio, Trinity University, St. Mary's University, and Our Lady of the Lake College, among others. Over 139,000 students are enrolled in these institutions.

The universities, especially UT Austin, UT Health Science Center, and UT San Antonio, have been pivotal in several ways:

- the fostering of research and development activities;
- perceptions of the region as a technopolis;
- the attraction of key scholars and talented graduate students;
- the spin-offs of new companies;
- the attraction of major technology-based firms;
- a large talent pool of students and faculty from a variety of disciplines;
- a magnet for federal and private sector funding; and
- a source of ideas, employees, and consultants for high-technology as well as infrastructure companies, large and small, in the area.

Indeed, the fundamental point can be made that if the major research universities were not in place, and had not attained an acceptable level of overall excellence, then the Corridor could not have developed as a technopolis. There would be little or no research and development funding, no magnet for the attraction and retention of large technology-based companies, and no base for the development of small technology companies.

Interestingly, the only other flagship university in the state, Texas A&M University in College Station, 100 miles northeast of Austin, also affected the Corridor through its major research activities. There is some speculation that the technopolis-shaped Corridor may eventually form a crescent by looping from Austin to College Station.

Several factors are important in measuring the scientific and technological preeminence of the region, all of which center on the role of the research university. In this chapter, we focus on the University of Texas at Austin (UT) and the University of Texas Health Science Center in San Antonio (HSC) as examples of the critical role that a research university can play in the developing technopolis.

The University of Texas at Austin now claims two Nobel laureates in physics and 38 faculty members who belong to the National Academies of Science and Engineering. In addition, the number of national merit scholar students has continued to rise from 361 in 1981 to 916 in 1986. In 1986, UT was second in total national scholarship graduates with only 87 fewer than Harvard. Grants and contracts awarded to the UT Austin campus grew from over 600 in 1977 to over 900 in 1986. This was an increase in dollar amount of over $50 million in 1977 to nearly $120 million in 1986.

In addition, the university has established major organized research units in the College of Engineering and College of Natural Sciences. In 1986, there were 18 research centers in the College of Engineering with a total funding in 1986 of $28,916,099. There were an additional 32 research centers in the College of Natural Sciences with a total funding in 1986 of $21,354,719. Many of these research units are in emerging, cutting-edge technological areas.The number of endowed fellowships, lectureships, professorships, and chairs in the University of Texas at Austin has increased significantly since 1981. (Details can be found in Smilor et al., in press.) Fellowships and lectureships in business have increased from 2 to 68. Fellowships and lectureships in engineering have increased from 0 to 67. Fellowships and lectureships in the natural sciences have increased from 2 to 50.

The University of Texas Health Science Center at San Antonio is a health professions university and a leading biomedical education and research institute in the Austin-San Antonio Corridor. The university has 700 full-time faculty members, 3400 employees, and 2200 students. The university offers degrees in medical, dental, nursing, allied health sciences, and the graduate school of biomedical sciences. A cooperative Ph.D. degree is offered with the University of Texas at Austin's College of Pharmacy.

Since 1975, the Health Science Center has more than quadrupled its grant-based research funds. It had more than $40 million in 1986 in sponsored research projects. These major research areas include cancer, cardiovascular disease, pulmonary and kidney disease, immunology, reproductive biology, aging, genetics, arthritis, nutrition, and psychiatry. The HSC has three centers that are nationally funded. These are the Multipurpose Arthritis Center, the Center for Research and Training in Reproductive Biology, and the Center for Development Genetics. In addition, it has received a five-year grant from NSF to develop an Industry-University Cooperative Center for Bioscience and Technology.

In Texas, the state government is responsible for the major proportion of funding for the budgets of public universities. The University of Texas component institutions have also benefited from a Permanent University Fund (PUF), with a current book value at $2.6 billion. The fund has been crucial to the development of the teaching and research excellence at UT, as well as in permitting the acquisition of modern facilities and laboratories. The PUF alone, however, is insufficient for the development of a technopolis.

Let this example drive the point home. In 1984, while oil prices were still about $30 a barrel and state revenues increased by $5.4 billion or 17% over the previous year, Texas was the only state in the nation to decrease appropriations for higher education, a decrease of 3%. In that same year, California increased its state appropriation for higher education by 31% over the previous year. It was at this point that UT's momentum toward teaching and research excellence—for example, being able to fill endowed positions—began to slow down.

Consequently, despite UT's recent phenomenal growth in endowed chairs, professorships, lectureships, and fellowships; despite the location of MCC in Austin; and despite national and international press claiming Austin-San Antonio a new center of excellence in education, the lack of sustained state support for higher education sent a mixed message to the best scholars and researchers whom the university was trying to attract.

### The Private Sector

One way to measure the growth of high-technology company development in the Austin-San Antonio Corridor is to track employment and high-technology incorporations by SIC code over time. Table 4.1 shows employment in high-technology industries in Austin and San Antonio as well as other Texas cities as of 1985 by SIC code. Figure 4.2 shows the incorporation of high-technology companies in Austin from 1945 to 1985. Figure 4.3 shows the incorporation of high-technology companies in San Antonio from 1945 to 1985. It is interesting to note that in 1984 and 1983, respectively, growth of these firms leveled off. These are manufacturing-related technology firms. They do not include service-related technology firms.

There are two other ways that we have tracked high-technology company development in Austin. One is the founding or relocation of major technology-based companies. The other is an evaluation of a selected list of emerging technology-based companies.

The location and homegrown development of major technology-based companies began in 1955. By "major" technology-based companies, we mean headquarters and branches of *Fortune* 500 companies, and/or those companies with annual revenues or annual R&D budgets

## TABLE 4.1

### Employment in High-Tech Industries in Texas, 1985

| SIC Code | SMSA Industry | Austin | DFW | El Paso | Houston | San Antonio | Total |
|---|---|---|---|---|---|---|---|
| 283 | Drugs | 962 | 1,413 | 0 | 435 | 303 | 3,113 |
| 348 | Ordnance and accessories (except vehicles and guided missiles) | 0 | 1,437 | 0 | 79 | 4 | 1,520 |
| 357 | Office computing and accounting machines | 4,334 | 12,610 | 391 | 3,979 | 3,441 | 24,755 |
| 361 | Electronic transmitting and distribution equipment | 175 | 1,478 | 0 | 1,996 | 16 | 3,665 |
| 362 | Electronic industrial apparatus | 1,094 | 4,947 | 449 | 3,330 | 99 | 9,919 |
| 364 | Electric lighting and wiring equipment | 104 | 5,277 | 0 | 1,734 | 189 | 7,304 |
| 365 | Radio and TV receiving equipment | 36 | 416 | 0 | 411 | 32 | 895 |
| 366 | Communication equipment | 605 | 21,348 | 537 | 3,396 | 282 | 26,168 |
| 367 | Electronic component and accessories | 4,929 | 13,941 | 4,768 | 896 | 482 | 25,016 |
| 369 | Miscellaneous electronic machines, equipment, and supplies | 487 | 2,792 | 404 | 380 | 3,395 | 7,458 |
| 376 | Guided missiles and space vehicles, parts | 0 | 5,282 | 0 | 75 | 750 | 6,107 |
| 379 | Miscellaneous transportation equipment | 122 | 2,096 | 4 | 524 | 227 | 2,973 |
| 381 | Engineering, laboratory, science and research instruments, and associated equipment | 406 | 1,021 | 250 | 1,675 | 115 | 3,467 |
| 382 | Measuring and controlling instruments | 862 | 3,499 | 629 | 13,842 | 398 | 19,230 |
| 383 | Optical instruments and lenses | 79 | 1,194 | 16 | 144 | 0 | 1,433 |
| 384 | Surgical, medical, and dental instruments and supplies | 523 | 1,489 | 391 | 1,439 | 213 | 4,055 |
| 385 | Opthalmic goods | 0 | 1,026 | 4 | 259 | 0 | 1,289 |
| 386 | Photographic equipment and supplies | 24 | 837 | 75 | 340 | 37 | 1,313 |
| 387 | Watches, clocks, clockwork operating devices and parts | 32 | 1,048 | 0 | 0 | 83 | 1,163 |
| | Total | 14,774 | 83,151 | 7,918 | 34,934 | 10,066 | 150,843 |

SOURCE: *Directory of Texas Manufacturers* (1986).

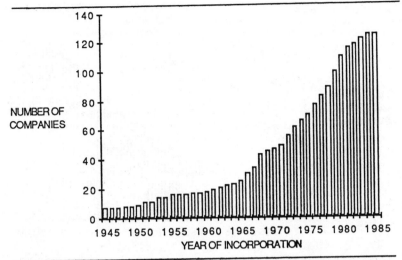

**Figure 4.2**    Cumulative Total of High-Technology Manufacturing Companies in Austin by SIC Code
SOURCE:    *Directory of Texas Manufacturers* (1986).

of over $50 million, and/or those companies with over 450 employees in Austin. As shown in the time line in Figure 4.4, Austin currently has 32 such major firms.

Six of the companies are homegrown, and all six have had direct or indirect ties to the University of Texas at Austin. In addition, the location of the other major firms in the area was dependent on two critical elements. These were the presence of the University of Texas at Austin, and the perception of an affordable high quality of life; that is, a place with high quality-of-life factors where a company could also make a profit. Two four-year clusters—1965 to 1969 and 1980 to 1984—are interesting to note. During the first, IBM located in Austin, and, during the second, MCC located in Austin.

In addition to these major firms, a second tier of small and emerging companies has been steadily increasing. We have been able to identify specifically 218 large and small high-technology-related firms in existence in Austin in 1986 (the list developed from the our database and the Austin Chamber of Commerce).

Of 103 small- and medium-sized technology-based companies in existence in 1986 for which the our Institute conducted a survey, 53, or 52%, indicated a direct or indirect tie to the University of Texas at Austin (Figure 4.5). These companies founders were UT students, graduates, faculty members, or employees. They demonstrate an

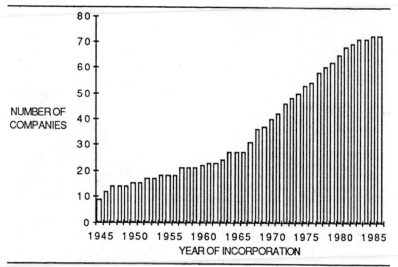

Figure 4.3    Cumulative Total of High-Technology Manufacturing Companies in San Antonio by SIC Code
SOURCE:    *Directory of Texas Manufacturers* (1986).

important requirement for a technopolis—the ability to generate homegrown, technology-based companies. These companies, in turn, have had a direct effect on job creation and economic diversification. Their tie to the university also enabled many of the companies to start their businesses with a contract that originated while they were involved in university research activities. In addition, the ability to continue their relationship in some capacity with the university was an influential factor in their staying in the area, along with their perception of an affordable high quality of life.

Another way to look at the tie to the University of Texas at Austin is to consider spin-off companies from selected departments and centers in the various colleges. Table 4.2 shows the type of diversity of new company development from research activities. Companies have spun off of computer sciences, physics, applied research, engineering, structural mechanics, and business.

These factors can be effectively demonstrated through a case study of Tracor, Inc., a homegrown company that is also the only *Fortune* 500 company headquartered in Austin. Figure 4.6 shows that, in 1955, from the College of Engineering and the Defense Research Lab at the University of Texas at Austin, came the educated talent to form the Associated Consultants and Engineers that led to the establishment of

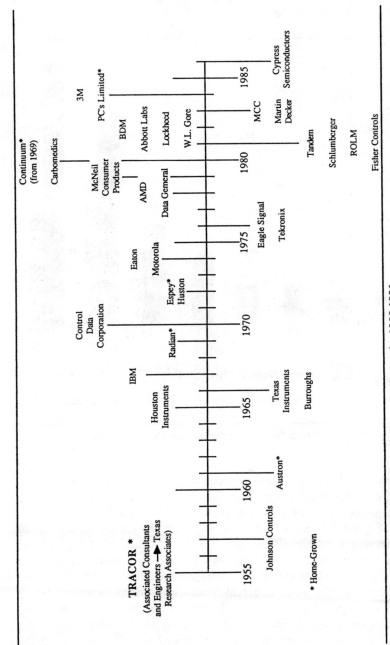

**Figure 4.4  Major Company Relocations or Founding in Austin, 1955-1986**

77

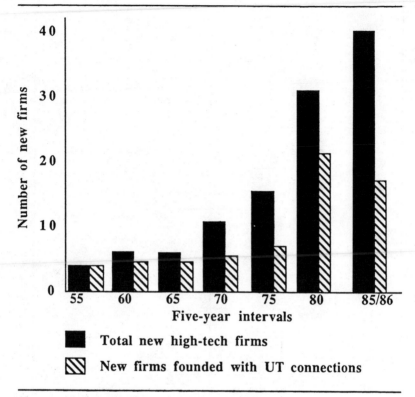

Figure 4.5    Small High-Tech Firms Founded with UT Connections

Tracor in 1962. Even more impressive, however, is the constant stream of entrepreneurial talent that came from Tracor itself. At least 16 companies have spun off from Tracor since 1962 and located in Austin.

Figures 4.7 and 4.8 dramatically show the job creation effect of Tracor and its spin-offs on the Austin area. A total of 5467 employees were employed in these companies as of 1985. Perhaps most impressive is that some of these spin-offs have the potential of becoming *Fortune* 500 companies as their parent Tracor did. All are also capable of creating spin-offs of their own. Radian Corporation, as one example, has spun off four companies. It must be remembered that neither Tracor and its spin-offs nor the jobs they created would exist without the University of Texas at Austin.

TABLE 4.2
Selected UT Spin-Offs by Department

| | |
|---|---|
| Computer Sciences Department | Applied Research Laboratory |
|   Information Research Associates |   Modular Power Systems |
|   MRI (since became a division of INTEL) |   Electro-Mechanics |
|   Statcom |   National Instruments |
|   Knowledge Engineering |   Tracor |
|   Cole & Vansickle | |
| | Engineering Department |
| Computation Center |   Mesa Instruments |
|   Balcones Computing Co. |   Geotronics Corp. |
| |   White Instruments |
| Physics Department |   Wight Engineering |
|   Lacoste & Romberg |   Execucom |
|   Astro Mechanics | |
|   Texas Nuclear | Structural Mechanics |
|   Columbia Scientific Ltd. |   Tekcon |
|   Scientific Measurement Systems | |
|   Eaton Corp. | College of Business |
|   Texion |   ARC |

SOURCE: Ladendorf (*Austin American-Statesman*, 1982); used by permission.

**Government Sector**

Federal, state, and local governments have also played an important role in the development of the Austin-San Antonio Corridor as a technopolis. Each level of government has affected the respective area economic development in different ways, however.

The federal government has affected the region in two key ways: through military involvement in the development and operation of U.S. military bases, and through federal funding for research and development activities on-site and at major universities in both cities. Table 4.3 shows the effect of military bases in the Corridor. All the bases provide a general economic stimulation to the region through their employment of civilian and military personnel. For example, a San Antonio chamber of commerce study determined that the bases have a $2.6 billion effect annually on the city's economy.

As noted, state government in Texas is the primary source of support for public universities, including the University of Texas at Austin, the University of Texas at San Antonio, and the University of Texas Health

80

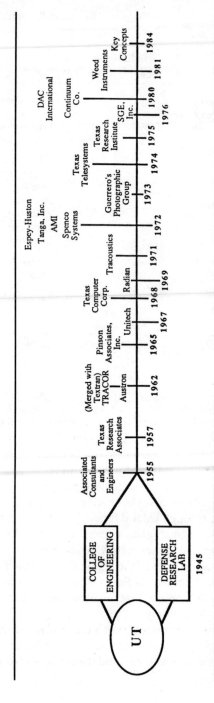

Figure 4.6   Development of Tracor and Its Spin-Offs, 1947-1984

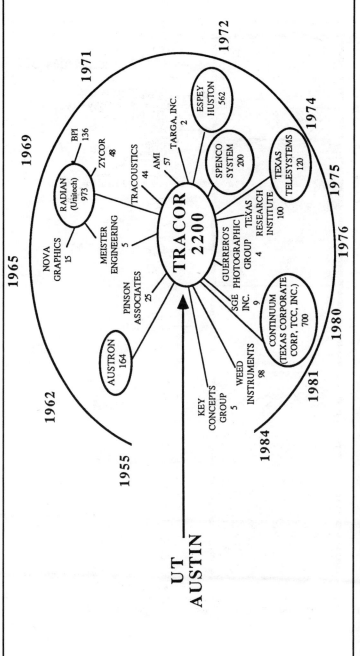

**Figure 4.7   Job Creation Impact of Tracor and Its Spin-Offs**
NOTE: Employees in Austin in company as of 1985.  Total = 5467.

81

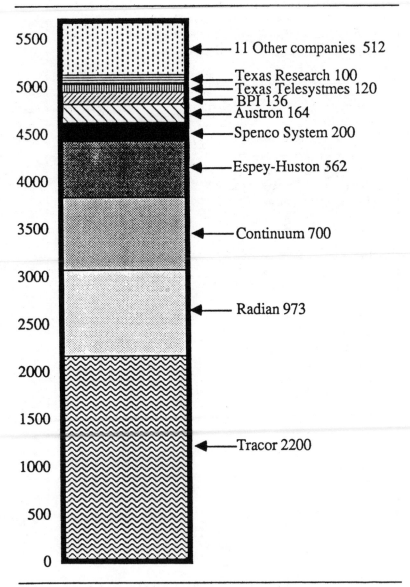

Figure 4.8    Job Creation Impact: Tracor and Its Spin-Offs

TABLE 4.3
Data on Military Bases in Austin-San Antonio Corridor

| Location | Founded | Personnel Civilian | Military | Annual Payroll |
|---|---|---|---|---|
| Austin | | | | |
| Bergstrom | 1942 | 1,000 | 6,000 | $167 million |
| San Antonio | | | | |
| Fort Sam Houston | 1876 | 6,000 | 12,000 | 42 million |
| Kelly AFB | 1917 | 15,000 | 6,000 | |
| Brooks AFB | 1918 | 600 | 2,000 | 72 million |
| Lackland AFB | 1941 | 8,000 | 11,000 | |
| Randolph AFB | 1930 | 2,500 | 5,500 | |

Medical Centers, Medical Training, and Research Programs
  Brooke Army Medical Center– 692 beds
                          – 200 on Gary Research Partners
  The Institute of Surgical Research–$1.3 million research budget
  Academy of Health Sciences – 32,000 resident students
                          –42,000 correspondence course students
  Wilford Hall USAF Medical Center – 1,000 beds
                          –   300 active clinical investigators
  Aerospace Medical Division–$120 million research budget

SOURCE:  San Antonio Chamber of Commerce and Military Bases Publications.

Science Center in San Antonio. State funding for higher education had been increasing until 1983 when Texas cut back on appropriations for higher education, just when every other state was increasing funding for education. The result was that, in 1984 and 1985, the image of Texas being committed to achieving excellence in education was questioned.

Spurred by general economic slowdown and a desire to promote economic development, the 1987 state legislative session took a more proactive role. New legislative proposals were presented to spur economic development and technological diversification. These included bills for business incubator support, state venture capital funding, a growth fund to spur product development, and other programs designed to assist new company development.

Although state government's primary role has been in relation to education, local government's primary role in Austin and San Antonio has focused on quality of life, competitive rate structures for such items as utilities, and infrastructure requirements. *Quality of life* carries different meanings given one's perspective and given the subjective attributes of the issues involved. In Austin, over the past years, quality of life has remained relatively high and relatively good in comparison to other technology centers. Perhaps the most dramatic statement in support of this view is that MCC, which listed an affordable quality of life as one of its four main site selection criteria, decided to locate in Austin. A quality-of-life survey done at the time rated Austin as exceptional (compared to San Diego, California; Atlanta, Georgia; and Raleigh-Durham, North Carolina) in terms of quality of primary and secondary schools, quality of parks and playgrounds, outdoor recreational opportunities, community cleanliness, and as a place to live.

A more important point is that perceptions vary within any region undergoing rapid economic growth associated with a developing technopolis. There is always the possibility that such growth will diminish the very qualities that caused the area to be so attractive to high-technology companies in the first place.

This fine balance between a sustained quality of life and sustained economic development has been most visible throughout the development of the Austin-San Antonio Corridor. One main reason Tracor located and grew in Austin and one main reason Tracor spin-offs were able and wanted to locate in Austin was the affordable quality of life. Nevertheless, with each new economic development activity, there was likely to be some community group that felt the loss of some aspect of Austin that made the city unique, desirable, and affordable.

Over the history of the economic development of the Austin-San Antonio Corridor, local government has tended to favor the "developers" or the "environmentalists," depending on one's point of view. The issue becomes more complex because many "developers" are Austinites who also want to preserve Austin's quality of life. An inspection of many of Austin's development projects supports this view. On the other hand, many "environmentalists" also favor economic development. Indeed, quality of life and economic development are two sides of the same coin; each has an important effect on the other.

Local government has gone through cycles of support for, or opposition to, perceived quality of life in the city. When local government supports economic development, then the development of the technopolis increases, that is, company relocation seems to be facilitated and obstacles to development seem to diminish. When local government believes quality of life is diminishing, then the development of the technopolis decreases, that is, company locations go to outlying cities, obstacles for development increase (such as high utility rates or slower permitting procedures), and the ability to work with diverse segments of the community declines.

One final point needs to be made about the quality-of-life issue. Although "environmentalists" and "developers" may disagree on what makes for sensible environmental/development policy, most would agree that overall quality of life suffers most when the people who inhabit the Corridor are out of work and cannot afford to pay the costs associated with further development, such as infrastructure or housing, or improved quality of life, such as expanded park land or recreational opportunities.

### Support Groups

Support groups have provided an important networking mechanism for the development of the technopolis. These groups take a variety of forms. Business-based groups in the Corridor relate to the emergence of specific components for high-technology support in the practices of big-8 accounting firms, key law firms, major banks, and other companies. These components provide a source of expertise, even when embryonic, and a reference source for those founding and/or running technology-based enterprises.

The growth of venture capital in the Corridor provides a good example. Figure 4.9 shows that venture capital increased significantly in the 1980s. The growth was due primarily to two factors, one external and the other internal. Externally, changes in federal tax laws in 1979 and 1986 on capital gains encouraged investments in venture capital pools. Internally, the perception of the Corridor as an emerging technology center encouraged the development of homegrown pools. The sources of the venture capital were a few individuals knowledgeable about the venture capital process as well as the major commercial banks in the area. Although funds in these pools increased, most venture capital investments continued to be made outside the Corridor and the State of Texas. Venture capitalists in the Corridor, while wanting a local window on technology and company development, still do not see enough good deals—that is, fast-growth company potentials—in the region.

The Chamber of Commerce is another important support group. It can provide a focal point for information about and support of technology-based companies. The Austin Chamber, for example, played a key role in attracting IBM in 1967. It has also helped to

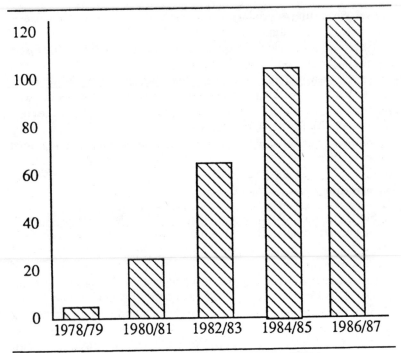

**Figure 4.9    Growth of Venture Capital in the Corridor (in millions)**
SOURCE:    Selected venture capital firms.
NOTE: Incubators, venture capital, and SBICs.

establish other efforts to expand further the high-technology network in the city. Such efforts included a highly publicized major study by SRI in 1983 that focused on Austin's potential as an "idea" city and one with real opportunities in specific high-technology industries; expanded programs to attract and retain Japanese companies; and new organizations to broaden networks among and between technology-based organizations.

In San Antonio, the chamber, with the mayor and city council, has proven to be a catalyst for cooperative activities to expand the south end of the technopolis. They have, for example, conducted annual economic development conferences to bring together various components of the city. They were instrumental in attracting the UT Health Science Center and UT San Antonio, and they raised the necessary private funds to ensure the creation of an engineering school.

Community groups have emerged to broaden the links and facilitate the communication process among and between technology-based organizations. The most notable development in the area was the organization of the Greater Austin-San Antonio Corridor Council in 1983. The Council has provided a high-level mechanism to link key individuals and organizations from both cities. It has significantly contributed to the growing perception of the area as one region with mutually beneficial opportunities and similar problems. Other community groups have served to try to bring together sometimes diverse and even opposing viewpoints to find common ground to address problems of mutual interest. Such groups include breakfast groups, policy-oriented groups, and special high-technology groups, such as the Greater Austin Technology Business Network, which was established in late 1986, and a risk capital network system that was established at UT San Antonio in early 1987.

### Influencers

Although each of the institutional segments in the Technopolis Wheel is important to the development of a technopolis, the ability to link the segments is most critical. Indeed, unless the segments are linked in a synergistic way, then the development of the technopolis slows or stops. In the Austin-San Antonio Corridor, these segments have been linked by first- and second-level "influencers"—key individuals who make things happen and who are able to link themselves with other influencers in each of the other segments as well as within each segment.

First-level influencers have criteria in common:

- They provide leadership in their specific segments because of their recognized success in those segments.
- They maintain extensive personal and professional links to all or almost all the other segments.
- They are highly educated.
- They move in and out of the other segments with ease, that is, they are accepted and consequently help in establishing requirements for success.
- They are perceived to have credibility by others in the other segments.

The second linkage is by second-level influencers within each segment, who interact and generally have the confidence of the first-level influencers. The role and scope of the second-level influencers is to act as gatekeepers in terms of their abilities to increase or decrease flows of information to first-level influencers. They also have their own linkages to other second-level influencers in the other institutional segments. In many cases, the first- and second-level influencers initiate new organizational arrangements to institutionalize the linkage between business, government, and academia.

Influencers seem to coalesce around key events or activities. They then play a crucial role in conception, initiation, implementation, and coordination of these events or activities. Once an event or action is successfully managed or achieved, they help institutionalize the process so that it can function effectively without them. Consequently, an important characteristic of a technopolis is to be able to develop first-level influencers and nurture second-level influencers in all segments of the Technopolis Wheel.

Both first- and second-level influencers build extensive networks. The larger the number of influencers, the more extensive their networks. The more they are able to interact effectively (i.e., be persuasive) with all the other segments, the more rapidly the technopolis develops. Influencers play a particularly important networking role through the support groups because these groups can provide convenient opportunities to interact across all segments of the Wheel.

San Antonio can be used as an example of the role of influencers. In 1947, the San Antonio Medical Foundation was chartered by a few prominent physicians. They realized that a large amount of land was critical to the long-term success of a Medical Center. Consequently, they acquired over 620 acres of land in the then uninhabited western area of San Antonio. Later they increased this to almost 1000 acres. Today San Antonio has the largest medical center in the United States in terms of acreage.

Situated on this acreage as of 1987 are eight major hospitals totaling 2893 beds, over six allied research services, and several specialized rehabilitation centers. The hub of this complex is the University of Texas Health Science Center. With more than 15,300 employees in the medical center, it is one of San Antonio's largest employers. The combined annual budget of the center's facilities is over $500 million.

Another example is the Southwest Research Institute in San Antonio. It was founded in 1947 as a not-for-profit research and development organization. The Institute works at any given time on more than 1000 engineering and physical science projects including biotechnology programs. There are currently more than 2000 employees. Their gross revenues are just under $149 million. A Southwest Research Consortium has been formed by the Southwest Research Institute, the University of Texas Health Science Center at San Antonio, the University of Texas at San Antonio, and the Southwest Foundation for Biomedical Research. These institutions participate in cooperative projects.

## Conclusion

Several key points emerged from the Austin-San Antonio Corridor study. They are as follows:

- The research university has played a pivotal role in the development of the technopolis by
    —achieving scientific preeminence;
    —creating, developing, and maintaining the new technologies for emerging industries;
    —educating and training the required work force and professions for economic development through technology;
    —attracting large technology companies;
    —promoting the development of homegrown technologies; and
    —contributing to improved quality of life and culture.
- Local government has had a significant effect, both positively and negatively, on company formation and relocation, largely from what it has chosen to do or not to do in terms of quality of life, and competitive rate structures and infrastructure.
- State government has had a significant effect, both positively and negatively, on the development of the technopolis through what it has chosen to do or not to do for education, especially in the areas of making and keeping long-term commitments to fund R&D, faculty salaries, student support, and related educational development activities.
- The federal government has played an indirect but supportive role largely through its allocation of R&D moneys to universities, on-site R&D programs, and defense-related activities.
- Continuity in local, state, and federal government policies has an important effect on maintaining the momentum in the growth of a technopolis.
- Large technology companies have played a catalytic role in the expansion of the technopolis by
    —maintaining relationships with major research universities;

> —becoming a source of talent for the development of new companies; and
>
> —contributing to job creation and an economic base that can support an affordable quality of life.

- Small technology companies have been increasing steadily in number and size in the area. They have helped in
  - —commercializing technologies;
  - —diversifying and broadening the economic base of the area;
  - —contributing to job creation;
  - —spinning companies out of the university and other research institutes; and
  - —providing opportunities for venture capital investment.
- Influencers have provided vision, communication, and trust for developing consensus for economic development and technology diversification, especially through their ability to network with other individuals and institutions.
- Consensus among and between segments is essential for the growth and expansion of the technopolis.
- Affordable quality of life, while subjective and hard to measure, is important in the development of a technopolis. It can be a major source of friction between advocates and adversaries of the growth of the technopolis.
- The very success of the development of a technopolis can lead to greed and many dissatisfactions. The result can be a shattering of the consensus that originally made the technopolis possible.

The Austin-San Antonio Corridor is a developing technopolis with promise. The area has been achieving scientific preeminence, developing and maintaining new technologies for emerging industries, and attracting large technology firms while creating homegrown technology companies. It still has a way to go before reaching maturity. There needs to be a broader vision of the future, however: a future that is not lost in local and state economic setbacks or interminable resolutions about affordable quality of life; a future that comes from using the Corridor's most important resource—its intellectual resources found within its institutional segments. It requires a future that provides a vision for effectively linking government, business, and academia.

# 5

# The MCC Comes to Texas

DAVID V. GIBSON
EVERETT M. ROGERS

*The stimulation of research and development, the transfer of technology from one sector to another, and the encouragement of industrial cooperation are all part of promoting the information society. But in Texas they were particularly dramatic events as represented in the recruitment of the Microelectronics and Computer Technology Corporation to Austin, Texas, in 1983. This consortium of U.S. information technology companies was organized to meet the threat of Japanese competition. Austin won the contract of the site of the MCC over 57 other cities, an effort that involved unusual cooperation among business, government, and educational leaders. The present chapter by David Gibson and Everett Rogers is the first of a series of publications by these researchers on this topic. David Gibson is with the Graduate School of Business at the University of Texas, and Everett Rogers is a Walter Annenberg Professor in the Annenberg School of Communication at the University of Southern California. Rogers is well known in this line of research for not only many articles on the diffusion of innovations, but for his book with Judith Larsen,* Silicon Valley Fever *(1984).*

## Researching the Microelectronics and Computer Technology Corporation

### The MCC Is Announced

On May 18, 1983, Texas Governor Mark White, the Chancellor of the University of Texas System, the Presidents of the University of

Texas at Austin and Texas A&M University, the Mayor of Austin, and
Bobby R. Inman, president and chief executive officer of the Microelectronics and Computer Technology Corporation (MCC), announced
the national research venture's decision to establish operations in
Austin. The governor predicted the MCC would "prove to be a turning
point in the economic history of Texas." Inman said that any of the
other three finalist cities—San Diego, California; Atlanta, Georgia; or
Raleigh-Durham, North Carolina—would have been an excellent
choice but "Austin was selected after an intensive, exhaustive analysis."
The MCC represented a unique effort to bring together the brightest
minds in the United States to keep this nation in the forefront of
advanced computer technology.

The MCC location decision was a most important economic
development event not only for Texas, but also for the resulting impacts
on the states that "lost" in this competition. A total of 57 cities
representing the East and West Coasts, the South, and the Midwest—27
states in all—eagerly pursued this R&D consortium. They valued the
MCC not just for its projected $75 million annual budget and the 400 to
500 scientific and administrative jobs that it would add to a local
economy, but, more crucially, for the high-tech firms that were expected
to spin off of the MCC over the long term. As the competition for the
MCC progressed during spring 1983, it became apparent that the
winning site would be identified as an important center of the
information age.

For Texas, the MCC was also seen as a means of diversifying the
state's economy from being so heavily dependent on agriculture,
ranching, oil, and gas. Soon after the MCC located in Austin, the area
experienced a spectacular land and building boom for two years, rapidly
followed by an equally dramatic downturn in the economic fortunes of
the entire state. It is not yet known to what degree the MCC location
decision helped establish Austin, Texas, as a center of high-tech R&D
and as a future center of the U.S. information society. In early 1988,
however, after another national competition, the main players in the
U.S. semiconductor industry chose to locate the industry's new research
consortium (Sematech), of 13 member companies, in Austin.

**Goal of the Research**

The purpose of this chapter is to describe the series of decisions and
events leading to the choice of Austin as the site for the MCC, and to
compare the economic, social, and political impacts of the MCC

location in Austin with the three other finalists in the site selection process. Our research pays special attention to the importance of the different perceptions that actors had of the same realities and events: (1) perceptions of what caused Austin to win and the other finalists to loose, and (2) perceptions of the impact of the MCC during its first four years of activity.

Our conclusions are based on 23 tape-recorded personal interviews conducted with key respondents most knowledgeable about the MCC location decision and its subsequent impacts, plus an extensive review of archival data. The present chapter is the first publication from our research on the MCC decision and its impacts.

## Chronology of the MCC
## Decision Process

### Meeting the Japanese Competition

By the early 1980s, it had become visible in the steel, shipbuilding, auto, and electronics industries what the Japanese were capable of doing to U.S. competitive advantage when they pooled their resources. Because of the advanced state of U.S. high-tech industry's R&D, many U.S. business leaders believed that the U.S. semiconductor and computer industries would be immune from the Japanese threat. Only six to seven years (during the late 1970s and early 1980s) were needed, however, for the Japanese to close the gap in technological innovation with the U.S. semiconductor industry. In fall 1981, the Japanese announced their Fifth-Generation Computer Project. This event caused the presidents of U.S. computer companies to think that "maybe we need to look at things a little differently" (as one company leader told us).

Control Data Corporation's (CDC) influential founder and chairman, William C. Norris, had long been a strong advocate of cooperative R&D by U.S. companies. CDC had favorable experiences with two small, cooperative R&D ventures: Computer Peripherals Inc. (CPI), founded in 1972, eventually including four companies; and Magnetic Peripherals Inc. (MPI) was founded in 1975 by three companies. These cooperative ventures were economically motivated. R&D and product development costs in the mainframe computer industry were escalating so that few individual companies could afford them. In an often-quoted 1981 speech, Bob Price, the President of Control Data Corporation, predicted that if present trends continued, within 10 years there would be only three computer companies: Japan, IBM, and possibly AT&T.

### Genesis of the MCC Idea

In February 1982, Norris and Price were able to attract the CEO or senior level executives of 15 leading U.S. computer companies to meet in Orlando, Florida. The objective was, in the words of one of the CDC planners, "to keep the discussion above the trivia about competition in the marketplace, and to discuss where the industry will be in 10 to 12 years. And, if we didn't like what we saw, to discuss how we might do things differently." From the Orlando meeting sprang the seeds of the Microelectronics and Computer Technology Corporation (MCC).

During 1982, the MCC was formed as a joint research and development venture of 10 major U.S. corporations: Advanced Micro Devices, Control Data, Digital Equipment, Harris, Honeywell, Motorola, National Semiconductor, NCR, RCA, and Sperry. Allied-Signal and Mosteck joined the MCC in early 1983. It was to have a budget of between $50 and $100 million per year. Initially there were four major areas of research in which the companies could participate: advanced computer architectures, component packaging, software technology, and computer-aided design and manufacturing (CAD/CAM).

### The Appointment of Admiral Inman

By late 1982, the crucial issue to be decided was who should lead this research consortium. All the member companies agreed that the chairman needed to be an independent, rather than one of the shareholder executives. The perception was that this revolutionary organization's chances of success would improve dramatically with the right leader. Such a man was found in Bobby Ray Inman, the recently retired Deputy Director of the U.S. Central Intelligence Agency, former Director of the National Security Agency, and retired U.S. Navy Admiral. Inman's reputation increased the shareholders' confidence in making substantial long-term commitments to the MCC.

Inman, on the other hand, noted that he was not really sure whether he wanted to get involved in this new venture. As he stated, "The suspicion among the member companies was absolutely palpable." Inman's past efforts to get NATO countries to think of the Soviets as their principal adversary, instead of each other, and to convince the U.S. military services that the enemy was the KGB, rather than the intelligence services of other U.S. military units, however, would be useful to him as head of the MCC. On January 21, 1983, Admiral Inman was appointed Chairman of the Board, President, and Chief Executive Officer of the MCC. Inman felt that he needed such absolute authority to contend with questions of equity and fairness among the shareholder companies.

## Avoiding Antitrust Litigation

Through its two previous cooperative R&D ventures, CDC had a history of dealing with the U.S. Department of Justice. CDC's strategy had been to employ full disclosure, telling the department: (1) what they were planning to do, and (2) why they were planning to do it (that it was good for the industry and the country). The antitrust issue loomed larger in the MCC case, though, because so many large electronics companies were involved. The timing for an MCC-type cooperative venture was excellent, however, due to concern, during the early 1980s, in the federal government about the competitiveness and long-term viability of the U.S. semiconductor and computer industries. These information technologies were considered central to increasing U.S. productivity and to maintaining the U.S. military's strategic advantage. On December 27, 1982, the U.S. Department of Justice gave a "yellow light" to the MCC, saying, in short, that they would not oppose the MCC on the basis of what they knew at the moment.

Throughout 1983, CDC's Norris and Price, their legal counsel, and the MCC Chairman Inman lobbied the U.S. government for the concept of cooperative R&D consortia. According to the leaders involved in this lobbying effort, "There wasn't much opposition once they [congressmen and senators] understood what we were proposing." In October 1984, the National Cooperative Research Act passed Congress and was signed into law by President Reagan. The law clarified the rules of the antitrust statutes to state that cooperative research companies such as the MCC were legal.

As a result of this act, U.S. industry no longer needs to fear third-party antitrust suits when forming research and development consortia. The MCC was the first research consortium to register for such protection. As of June 1987, over 60 other private sector-initiated and financed consortia have also registered under this act.

## Beginning the
## Selection of a Site

During March 1983, Inman and the representatives of the MCC shareholders visited Washington, San Francisco, and Chicago to hear 57 presentations from 27 states. Each state was given one hour for its one or several site presentations. After animated discussion among the MCC Board of Directors, the decision was made to limit the final competition to only four possible location sites. A short time frame of only two weeks was allowed for final site selection because the MCC could not begin employee recruitment until its location was decided. Participants at the four contending sites often interpreted this time constraint as the ex-CIA "crafty" Inman testing how they operated under pressure. Indeed, giving substance to this perception, Austin was the most able of the four sites to secure maximum cooperation from the business, academic, and government sectors during this two-week period.

Private views of the MCC Board (some strongly held) did play a part in what cities made the final four. Certain of the MCC shareholders stated that climate played a role although there was no explicit discussion of this issue. In 1983, the MCC was composed of about half northern and half southern companies. At that time, it was believed that the consortium would be staffed primarily by employees of the shareholder companies. It was also believed that it would be much easier to recruit employees out of companies in the northern United States to come to a southern location for a three to four year tour of duty, than to get southerners to move north.

According to Inman, however, the Sunbelt location of the four finalists was due to their lack of major problems that characterized the older industrial areas in the United States in 1983. Inman stated that many of the places that could have been on the list were in various stages of economic downturn and this limited what they had the potential to offer to do for the MCC.

There was general agreement by the MCC board that they did not want to locate the MCC where there were other high-tech "stars" to compete with, such as in Silicon Valley, California, or on Route 128 in the Boston area. This concern was based on the need to hire the best possible talent. As Inman stated, "We were concerned whether this brand new venture could compete with the big names [e.g., IBM, AT&T, Hewlett Packard, etc.] in attracting the brightest students." Over the past four years, this concern diminished in importance as the MCC has been able to attract bright graduates from Stanford and MIT as well as the University of Texas at Austin.

### The Finalists

On April 12, 1983, the four finalists—San Diego, Atlanta, Austin, and Raleigh-Durham—were announced by the MCC. Each was informed that they would have only 15 days before the final site selection visits. The four finalists were chosen for a broad range of reasons, but the primary selection criteria included

(1) ready access to universities that were leaders in graduate-level teaching and research in microelectronics and computer science;
(2) a good quality of life to facilitate the recruitment of technical personnel (such as primary and secondary education facilities and affordable housing);
(3) easy access by air from major metropolitan areas;
(4) supportive state and local governments that provided a favorable business operating environment; and
(5) the overall cost of operating the MCC at the proposed site.

Many of the other 57 candidate sites that were outstanding on most of these criteria missed making the final four because they lacked one fundamentally important resource, namely, a major research university with the promise of excelling in computer science and electrical engineering.

### Insights into the Selection Process

In order to understand the MCC site selection process, it is necessary to know the underpinning decision criteria of the MCC shareholder companies and of Admiral Inman. During the December 1982 negotiations leading to Inman's selection as Chairman of the Board, C.E.O., and President of the MCC, a second main condition that Inman levied was that he would have absolute authority in all personnel matters. The MCC board believed that all the necessary R&D talent would likely come from the shareholder companies, and that it was just a question of assembling it. Inman, thinking of his recent government experience, remembered when "I had to run to agencies and I was dependent on the people that the agencies wanted to send me. I said, never again." Inman felt that personnel issues were an especially serious constraint because it was imperative that the MCC get off to a successful, quick start.

From the beginning I focused on where MCC would get the talent. First, to what location could the MCC recruit existing talent? Second, knowing that this was a long-term project, I also was concerned with how the MCC was going to be able to replenish that talent. Even if we initially got quality talent from the shareholder companies, they likely would not stay for long. And the MCC would probably not get the same quality of personnel from the companies the next time around So I felt that we had better be prepared to grow our own talent.

The MCC member companies put together standard site selection criteria: cost of living, quality of life, tax climate, business climate, education systems (for the children of MCC employees), and transportation including (1) how long it would take for the MCC employees to commute between a likely place of work and a likely place of residence, and (2) airline connections for the MCC employees that would be traveling between the MCC and their companies. To this list, Inman added a seventh factor—access to a center or centers of academic excellence at the graduate level in computer science, electrical engineering, and related areas. As he stated, "I saw this as a way of growing talent to sustain MCC over the long-term."

A second issue that made the MCC site selection process so revolutionary compared to more standard corporate site-selection was that it was public, not private. Inman made the decision to go public for two reasons: one was announced, one was not. The announced reason was to be sure that possible locations fully understood the purpose of the MCC and what it might mean to continue sustained support for this R&D consortium. As Inman stated,

> I didn't want the MCC to be the victim of a quick honeymoon and then be dropped. I wanted to be sure that as MCC went through what could be a difficult growth period, it would get strong support from the local community and the state, that MCC would get the resources that it needed to operate.

The reason for going public that was not announced hearkened back to early MCC organizational meetings where Inman noted the palpable suspicion among the member companies. MCC site selection publicity, Inman felt, "would help 'nail down' the support of the ten companies who were then committed and the two others who were wavering but were probably going to join." Inman appreciated how companies (and governments) react to publicity. Publicity would open doors to executive suites that are usually closed, and it would help bind the member companies to what they had agreed on earlier. As Inman said, "If they were 'breeding in a fishbowl' they were less likely to go back to their old mode of operation."

A representative from one MCC shareholder company believed that Inman "quite wisely perceived that the way to get some credibility and some momentum and substance behind the MCC was to get a lot of ink in the national press. And one way to do this was to have a public site selection venture. There is always some excitement in a contest." He described the following scenario:

> I sat in his [Inman's] office one afternoon. It was about the middle of the site selection process and it was just incredible. About every ten minutes there would be a governor, a senator, a congressman, the president of some university, or the president of some big company calling. I sat in his office three hours and spent maybe fifteen minutes with him between calls trying to get some business done.

## How Texas Won the MCC and the Three Other Finalists Lost

### The Myths

Many reasons have been offered for the MCC's May 1983 decision to locate in Austin. Two reasons often suggested by observers outside Texas (and which we consider myths) are (1) that Texas "bought" the MCC with $62 million in incentives, and (2) that because Admiral Bobby Ray Inman was "a good ole boy" who had strong ties to Austin—he was born in Texas and is a graduate of the University of Texas—he influenced the MCC vote in favor of the area where he wanted to live, which was Austin. While Texas did offer substantial economic incentives, the package did not total $62 million in actual funding. State budget surpluses (which Texas enjoyed in 1983) were not used. Rather, the financial package reflected a Texas-wide funding effort based on the initiative of the private sector, as we detail later.

Concerning the second myth (Admiral Inman's ties to Austin), it could be argued that Inman had stronger ties to San Diego. He was raised in Orange County and Los Angeles, and his voting residence remained in this area as did his family and relatives. His son was a student at the University of California at Irvine. He continued strong ties with Navy colleagues living in San Diego, and he was on the board of directors of a company located in La Jolla, California. The vote on the part of the MCC site selection team was unanimous for locating the MCC in Austin, before Inman cast his vote.

MCC representatives stated that, based on the site selection criteria, any of the four finalists would have been a good choice. Each had the basics for the MCC to operate effectively. According to Inman, in deciding between the final four contenders, "It came down to momentum; how were they going to change or improve what they already had?"

**Why Austin Was Selected**

We believe that Austin won over San Diego, Atlanta, and Research Triangle because (1) the Austin team most accurately perceived the importance of "momentum," and (2) they were most effective in creating the impression that Austin was going to improve the desired qualities that it already had by effectively marshaling the business, academic, and government communities throughout the state of Texas. Indeed, networking across different types of organizations and geographical regions in Texas is a vivid example of the cooperation across normally competing groups that Ouchi (1984) believes is needed to rejuvenate the U.S. economy (which he labels the M-Form society).

Texas first demonstrated a feeling of statewide cooperation to the MCC Board during the preliminary presentations in March in Chicago. As one MCC site selection member (who was at the Chicago presentation) said,

> It was very interesting because in some of the states, the different cities were pretty much 'every man for himself.' You know, they'd make their pitch and they'd also make subtle innuendoes about how some other city in their state wasn't nearly as good as they were. But not so in Texas. Governor Mark White led the delegation of three very good presentations: San Antonio, Austin, and Dallas. And it came across as a 'Texas Presentation' with three options, but Texas wants you.

One MCC site selection representative was particularly struck that Texas lined up 40 top business and community leaders to sign the "Texas Incentive" for the MCC, which conveyed a sense of cooperation among business, academe, and government to build a better future for Texas. In other states, he felt, these three major sectors could be more accurately characterized as adversaries. "It was so refreshing to see the people say, 'Hey, this is Texas. This is a pro-business state; we're going to build a better future. We need you as part of that. We will help you and you can help us.'" This respondent continued:

It was interesting, at almost every other location, you would see the university people and they'd be introduced to the business people and they'd say 'Hello, Mr. so-and-so.' In Texas, on the other hand, the president of the university would motion to somebody—a banker or someone—and say 'Hello Charlie. How are your kids? Is Jane enjoying her trip?' You could just see that they were all part of a cohesive community . . . that they were used to working together, and that they had not just been pulled together to try and make a deal with us.

A task force of a dozen Texas leaders met daily in a "war room" in Austin for two intense weeks to design and enact the Texas Incentive for the MCC. These leaders represented a range of talent and professional skills: state government, local government, law, public relations, real estate developers, industry, consulting firms, and the University of Texas and Texas A&M University. Importantly, this Austin task force had the active support of such statewide leaders as Governor White, the Chancellors of UT and A&M, Henry Cisneros (Mayor of San Antonio), and Ross Perot (a Texas high-tech business leader). As Inman stated,

When I called White [to announce that Austin was one of the final four sites], he instantly zeroed in on Austin's presentation in Chicago. He got exactly what the strong points and weakness were. He then set out to create a statewide group to essentially duplicate and broaden Henry Cisneros's plan [the San Antonio plan presented at Chicago] plus adding the package for UT and Texas A&M.

The mayor and staff of San Antonio helped initiate the statewide spirit of cooperation for the MCC by supporting the Austin effort immediately after losing to Austin in the preliminary site competition. San Antonio's presentation at Chicago was judged one of the best of the 57 original presentations. The main shortcoming was that San Antonio lacked a major research university that excelled in electrical engineering and computer science.

Respondents at the other three sites mentioned the problem of getting top state leaders to devote the needed time and effort for the MCC recruitment effort. As one San Diego respondent stated, "While there was no starting Deukmejian [Governor of California], there was no slowing White [Governor of Texas] down." As a member of the Austin task force noted, "From the outset, Governor White continued to aggressively lead this state's effort." As are all such high-level influencers, Governor White, Mayor Cisneros, and Ross Perot had many other issues and concerns competing for their time and attention, but they elevated the MCC competition to top priority. This visible emphasis was crucial in attaining significant, action-oriented cooperation from the academic, business, and government communities in Texas.

**Importance of a**
**Research University**

In North Carolina, Governor Hunt was (as were his predecessors) a strong supporter of the state's research universities. Duke University, the University of North Carolina, and North Carolina State impressed the MCC Board as being excellent universities that had learned to work together. The Microelectronics Center of North Carolina also impressed the MCC team. One particular event, however, exemplifies the importance of the perceptions of the MCC site selection team concerning momentum and statewide support for education. During the MCC's visit to Research Triangle, Inman asked the head of one university's computer science department how he did in recruiting top-flight academic talent. The chairman paused and said that he had two vacancies that he could not fill at $68,000 per year. By lunchtime, he had the authority to offer $90,000, but it was too late. The impact, said Inman, was significant on the MCC site selection decision.

Georgia Tech was also considered an excellent research university and the MCC technologists were impressed with their tours of semiconductor and microelectronics research areas. Dr. Joe Pettit of Georgia Tech dazzled the MCC team with his commitment to launching another Silicon Valley in Atlanta. In California, an electrical engineering professor from UCLA made an excellent presentation for the University of California system. As one MCC site selection team member thought,

> Well, UC San Diego may not be that strong in all the areas we are interested in, but it's only a thirty minute flight to Los Angeles or San Jose and then we have access to Stanford, Berkeley, and UCLA. There are so many excellent universities close by that San Diego would have to get an "A" on universities.

The California team stressed the university aspect in their MCC bid. The Chairman of the State Board of Regents and major figures (deans and chancellors) from the most prestigious California universities participated in the MCC presentation, but (according to several MCC representatives) there was no feeling that they would (or could) work together. As Inman stated, "What they all said to us was how much they each would look forward to working with us bilaterally."

A second major education-related negative perception with California's MCC bid concerned the state's willingness to continue to support education adequately. During 1981 to 1983, California's state surplus had shrunk from $6 to $2 billion as a result of tax limitation (Proposition 13). The state had an excellent university system but the question was whether these universities were going to be financially hampered in their continued pursuit of academic excellence. According to the MCC site selection team members, "That issue was very unclear in the spring of 1983. At least it was unclear in our minds."

In Texas, on the other hand, the state government was making a major investment in education. Governor William Clements (who had preceded White) had initiated the Texas 2000 Plan, which the MCC site selection team had read. The plan talked about diversifying the state's economy by expanding existing bases of electronics and computer science. During the MCC competition, the state's commitment to education was demonstrated when Governor White and his high-level representatives coordinated, organized, and worked with the university regents and high-level administrators of the University of Texas at Austin and Texas A&M University to demonstrate strong statewide support (e.g., in terms of endowed chairs, professorships, and financial support for graduate students) for the Departments of Electrical Engineering and Computer Science. As one MCC site selection member said, "There was the feeling of Texas saying, 'We have the resources to really put UT in the first rank of world-class universities. Not only do we have the resources, but we will commit them.'"

This perception of continued support for higher education in Texas is especially interesting in light of the downturn in such support immediately after the MCC located in Austin. But in 1983, according to one MCC representative, "There was no doubt that in Texas you could get the right people in a room to write a check. And boom it was done." In other states (including those other than the final four) like Colorado and Arizona, the governor might have some ambitious program but the question was "Could he get the legislation to follow through? The feeling was maybe yes, maybe no."

Finally, in Texas, a spirit of university cooperation was demonstrated when the two chancellors of A&M and UT stood together and talked about how they would increase cooperation if the MCC were to come to Austin. As Inman stated, "That was a very clear moment of the commitment of the state to this process." Indeed, Inman stopped the Chicago presentation at that point and told the MCC members "what a historic moment this is when these two [UT and A&M] stand together."

### Financial Support

The Texas financial incentive of $62 million is often cited as proof that "Texas bought the MCC." This myth, however, obscures the central issue of the effectiveness of the statewide cooperation in Texas in conceptualizing and funding the incentives. Indeed, private sectors in the other three finalist sites could have enacted such a package of financial incentives. They did not. In Texas, the financial package was not funded by the state university oil revenue (the Permanent University Fund). The financial portion of the "Texas Incentive for the MCC" was an ingeniously thought out set of programs, which not only attracted the MCC but also benefited Texas businesspersons and universities.

For example, the Austin business community put together a package to subsidize mortgage loans for potential MCC employees to the amount of $20 million. A common perception is that this $20 million in incentives was contributed by Texas banks, savings and loans, and builders. This was not the case. Rather, 14 banks, savings and loans, and builders made mortgage loans available to MCC employees at favorable interest rates until such a time as the total of $20 million in lending had been reached. The amount that each lending organization was responsible for was determined by their 1983 market share. The banks and savings and loans absorbed a percentage point as did the builders. In this way, MCC employees got a loan at preferred rates, and the lenders could still realize a profit.

Some would argue that the banks and the builders participated in the Texas incentives for selfish business reasons (e.g., increased deposits and car loans, which often come with new customers, or to sell high-priced homes), but such concerns obscure that the program worked to the benefit of the MCC, Austin, and Texas. During its first year, the loan program was heavily used and the $20 million limit was reached. Some of the banks continued lending money at preferred rates past their assigned limit. After about two years, however, interest rates began dropping and the program became less enticing to both lenders and borrowers.

The "Texas Incentive" for the MCC did involve a statewide funding effort that was initiated and carried out by business leaders throughout the state. The money was used to fund the academic incentives of endowed chairs, professorships, and financial support for graduate students in the areas of computer science and electrical engineering. Such a program facilitated securing university cooperation because these resources did not have to be pulled from committed or planned departmental budget allocations. The University of Texas System and the state business community jointly provided funds for the construction of the building that MCC occupies, which is located on a 20-acre tract in UT's Balcones Research Park. The building is owned by UT, and the MCC will begin paying rent in 10 years. Private funding was also used to underwrite the cost of interim offices and MCC relocation expenses before the permanent facility was constructed.

In short, Texas' "financial incentives for the MCC" were viewed as an investment in the future—the future of Texas, its universities, and its businesses—not as an expenditure of funds to "buy" the MCC. According to San Diego's Economic Development Coordinator, "Once the numbers correlated with the spirit, there was no stopping Texas."

### Quality-of-Life Issues

Each of the four finalists advertised a distinctive state culture and exhibited a local pride in their quality of life. While the MCC site selection teams talked of the pleasant time they had in San Diego, they also were concerned with the financial cost of this life-style and were generally put off by the attitude they perceived, which implied, "Gee, you ought to be willing to pay to want to come to California." They noted that California offered the MCC some land and facilities, "but there was such a strong emphasis on what a wonderful place this is for recreation." Inman stated that he had to work to turn such negative perceptions around to keep the site selection team open for San Diego's presentation.

The cost of housing was a key indicator of an affordable quality of life. As one MCC site selection member said, "It's a cultural shock for somebody to move from an $80,000 home to discover that he has to spend twice to two and one-half times that much to get the same property in California." Another MCC member (earning about $50,000 per year) said, "If we go to San Diego, count me out. I'd like to be a part of this organization, but I just can't afford to live out there."

The Austin task force felt that what they viewed as a favorable quality of life in Austin was less well understood by outsiders. So they commissioned an independent quality-of-life survey to compare Austin with the other three sites on the quality of schools, parks, playgrounds, and outdoor recreational activities; the variety of entertainment activities and cultural events; and community ambience, safety, and cleanliness. The survey results documented that Austin, when compared to the other three areas, had the most desirable quality of life on most of the surveyed criteria. And when the MCC site selection teams arrived in Austin, they were flown over the clear blue lakes and lush green hills. Most important, as of 1983, Austin offered a very affordable, high quality of life, especially with housing prices.

## Texas Cooperation in the Bid for the MCC

### The Importance of Cooperation from Within

During the period between late April and early May 1983, why was Texas more successful than California, Georgia, and North Carolina in getting statewide government, industry, and educational cooperation for an MCC bid? One MCC respondent offered his explanation after living in Texas for three years, "That's the way 'we' [he now views himself as a Texan] do things here. You know, it's us against the world." While we believe that this simple explanation has some validity as well as some interesting implications for M-Form Society (Ouchi, 1984) concepts, other factors were also important.

In 1983, Mark White was a newly elected governor, aggressively looking for an issue with which to identify his administration. One key issue focused on was the development of economic alternatives to oil, gas, agriculture, and ranching. Because of the state's favorable experiences with Texas Instruments, Tracor, NASA, and IBM, high-tech industry with its modern, clean image was considered a premier route to economic growth and diversification.

Also in 1983, while high energy prices favored the economic fortunes of Texas, most other state economies were less promising. Houston, Dallas, and several small Texas cities were boomtowns. The state was celebrating its sesquicentennial, and UT and A&M were celebrating their centennial birthdays. Write-ups in the national media advertised the spectacular gains that Texas universities were making in endowed chairs, professorships, and the number of national merit scholars. Parochialism becomes less evident when there are enough resources to satisfy all interested parties.

Another less transient and less obvious reason for Texas' successful cooperative bid for the MCC concerns the spatial proximity of centers of academic, business, and government leadership. Austin had the advantage of having the governor and the state capital, one of the state's main research universities, and a considerable number of high-tech organizations and the supportive infrastructure all located at the proposed site for the MCC. This propinquity greatly facilitated communication and coordination among the government, academic, business leaders, and the Texas MCC task force.

In Austin, the "war room" spirit of a team of prominent individuals working together for the good of Austin and Texas was so strong that arguments over parochial issues were considered out of place. Personal interests may have resided beneath the surface, but for two weeks the "war room" team worked as one. Although representing different professional backgrounds, the Austin task force was homogeneous in many characteristics. All were young, highly successful professionals. Most were UT alumni. All were raised in Austin or had lived there for a long time. Most were old friends who respected one another and enjoyed instant rapport. They worked together on the MCC proposal and then returned to their successful careers (or launched new careers). All remembered the MCC competition as a high point of their professional lives.

Regionalism—north versus south, east versus west, city versus rural, city versus city—exists in all states. Traditionally, state universities compete with each other for resources. In California, UC Berkeley (in northern California) and UCLA (in southern California) have been the big winners in the resource war. The other state universities often are left with less. For example, there was no computer science program at UC San Diego as of 1983. San Diego is located at the extreme southern tip of California. UCLA is about a three-hour drive north, and Berkeley is about three more hours further north. If San Diego were to win the MCC, UC San Diego would receive a tremendous boost in the competitive resource war with UC Berkeley and UCLA. In Texas, battles for state funds also occur among the state's major universities. But until recently the rules for sharing the Permanent University Fund and other sources of state support were fairly set. In any case, the two premier state universities were both active participants in the MCC bid. Both were perceived to gain if the MCC came to Austin.

## The Contract Fulfilled

Given the package of Texas incentives, how did Texas live up to the promises it made to the MCC? A signed contract between the MCC and Austin, or Texas, or the University of Texas does not exist. The promises were sealed with handshakes. And, virtually all the private Texas contributors to the Texas Incentives suffered financially during the downturn in the Texan, and the Austin, economies. What was the result?

(1) Relocation assistance was provided, as one MCC employee stated, "beyond our wildest expectations." For example, Austin provided employment assistance for spouses of MCC employees. A coordinator, who was paid out of the Texas Incentive, worked with MCC spouses (male and female) to network them into local employment opportunities. The Austin community responded by making a special effort to hire these qualified people.

(2) Mortgage loans to MCC employees exceeded $20 million.

(3) Funding was provided for temporary office facilities for MCC operations in several modern buildings until the permanent location was completed in 1986.

(4) The University of Texas built a magnificent $23.5-million building for MCC on UT's Balcones Research Park.

(5) The University of Texas endowed 32 Chairs in computer science and electrical engineering, three times what was promised in the Texas Incentives.

(6) Access to a Lear jet was provided for one year, to overcome Austin's limited available direct routes to other cities.

Concluded one MCC respondent, "We think that Texas has exceeded everything that they promised us and, if anything, particularly the University of Texas has gone out of its way to assure that their promises were met."

Another measure of the success of the location of the MCC in Austin is the retention of MCC employees. During the first few months of operation, only a couple of employees left the MCC after they moved to Austin. The MCC still has little turnover. During the past three years, out of 400 employees, fewer than 20 professionals and 20 administrative and secretarial employees have left the MCC. As one MCC employee stated, "It's not the kind of organization people want to leave." Even when several shareholder companies decided to leave the MCC in 1986, their employees often elected to stay with the research consortium. For recruiting purposes, Austin is considered a definite benefit. There is a saying at MCC that "if we can get them off the plane, we've got them."

## Effects of the MCC on Business, Academia, and Government

### Immediate Impacts

Perhaps the most important immediate impact of the MCC was the perception that Austin and Texas not only joined but had become a potential leader of the U.S. information society. This perception resulted is some unexpected consequences in the academic, business, and government communities.

Before the MCC, few people perceived Austin, Texas, as a high-technology area. In reality, the MCC did not bring high tech to Austin. Indeed, one reason the MCC chose to locate in Austin was because it was already becoming a high-tech center. The beginnings of a high-tech research park in Austin was UT's Balcones Research Center, created in the early 1940s when the Federal government supported UT research in strategic resources to support the war effort. The grandparent of high-tech in Austin is UT engineering graduate Frank McBee, who founded Tracor in 1955. Tracor is Austin's only homegrown *Fortune* 500 company. After Tracor, and before the MCC came to town, the following major high-tech firms located in Austin (listed in order of their founding): Johnson Controls (1957), Houston Instrument (1965), Texas Instruments and Burroughs (1966), IBM (1967), Control Data Corporation (1970), Motorola (1974), Data General and Advanced Micro Devices (1978), Rolm, Tandem and Schlumberger (1981), and Lockheed and Abbott Labs (1982).

After MCC came to Austin in 1983, the following major high-tech firms located or began a major expansion in the area: In 1983 Martin Decker located in Austin, Lockheed's Software R&D operation moved from California to Austin, and Motorola made a major expansion in Austin. In 1984, 3M moved its R&D division (the first to locate outside

Minnesota) to Austin, and, in 1986, Cypress Semiconductors located in Austin.

Tracor has spun off 19 Austin-based firms with about 5467 employees. The MCC's direct employment impact is about 400. As of June 1987, two companies have spun off of the MCC. Products are just beginning to emerge from the MCC. The consortium began turning out technology to member companies in August 1985 and, as of early 1987, the pace has accelerated in most of the MCC's seven research programs. It should be remembered, and is often forgotten, that the MCC did not claim to be a quick fix for the Texas economy. The MCC is engaged in basic research, which has a long-time horizon until its application.

As of 1986, UT's Computer Science Department was receiving three times as many graduate student applicants (about 700) as it did before the MCC came to Austin. The department selects the top 30 Ph.D. candidates each year, who have an average GRE score of 1400, up from 1250 before 1983. About 30 UT graduate students and several faculty work part-time at the MCC. UT is constructing a $20 million microelectronics center with emphasis on electromechanical studies. The 1985 legislature created a UT Center for Technology Transfer, located in the College of Engineering. The Center is designed to serve as an incubator to facilitate the commercialization of university-developed technology and to bring these technologies to commercialization.

**Recent Events**

A popular Texas monthly magazine article reinforced the perception that Inman's January 1987 departure from the MCC, to become head of a new defense electronics holding company, certified the end of Austin's high-tech boom. Inman had symbolic value to the MCC. Indeed, the Lieutenant Governor of Texas stated to the press that "Inman is MCC." Inman had agreed to a three-year contract at the MCC. He stayed four years. MCC employees are comfortable with the structure that Inman left in place. Inman's personal qualities (such as being charismatic, personable, intelligent, and a go-getter who makes things happen) are characteristics commonly attributed to the founders of entrepreneurial, high-tech companies. While such qualities are often viewed as necessary to start a company, in about three to four years, these same qualities may not fit the needs of a growing, maturing organization.

The loss of three shareholders at the end of 1986 and the announcement that three more were planning to leave at the end of 1987 added to the public's perception of the MCC being in trouble. Such departures often had more to do with the companies long-term plans, corporate finances, mergers, and corporate buy-outs by foreign firms that preclude membership in MCC than with the operation of the MCC. Two of the 1986 shares were purchased by Hewlett-Packard and Westinghouse. The perception created in the press, however, was that the MCC was in trouble.

The MCC's second and current chairman is Grant Dove, a 28-year veteran of Texas Instruments. The MCC is currently composed of the following 20 shareholders: Advanced Micro Devices Inc., Allied-Signal, Bell Communications Research, Boeing Electronics, Control Data Corp., Digital Equipment Corp., Eastman Kodak, General Electric Co., Harris Corp., Hewlett-Packard Co., Honeywell, Lockheed, 3M, Martin-Marietta, Motorola Inc., National Semiconductor Corp., NCR Corp., Rockwell International, Unisys, and Westinghouse Electric. The company consolidated two of its research programs—parallel processing and data base systems management—into a single unit, the Systems Technology Laboratory, and is considering a new program in superconductivity. The MCC currently has 466 employees.

On June 23, 1987, a milestone was reached for the MCC when NCR Corp. announced the first commercial product born of research conducted at the MCC and transferred to a member company. The product was built around Proteus, a software product developed in the MCC's Artificial Intelligence Research Program. It will simplify the process of designing custom computer chips. Proteus was the first major piece of technology to emerge from the research consortium. The first version of Proteus was shipped to MCC shareholders in early 1985. A second more advanced version was shipped in 1986.

The growth of the information economy continues in Texas. It is constrained, however, by politics and public attitudes of Texans that are still wedded (in some circles more than others) to the traditional economy, and concerned by the slow recovery of microelectronics industry and the lead time it has taken for the MCC to have a visible impact on the state's economy.

### A Loss of Synergy?

Close academic, government, and business cooperation existed within Texas during the state's bid for the MCC in 1983. Although the other three sites also made impressive offers to the MCC, none came close to displaying cooperative spirit of Texas. In 1987, this academic-business-government synergy was less apparent in Texas due to the pervasive impact of a general statewide economic slowdown as a result of the steep drop in oil and gas prices, a ranch and agriculture depression, a decline of the Mexican economy, and a national downturn in the microelectronics industry. Such economic concerns underpinned the very fear that caused Texas to move in such a concerted way for the MCC in 1983. The cumulative shock of these economic impacts eroded the perception of Texas as a "can-do" state in two important areas.

First, there is the concern over adequate state funding to maintain the quest for education and research excellence. Shortly after the MCC announced it was coming to Austin, when oil prices were still about $30.00 per barrel and state revenues increased by $5.4 Billion (or 17% over the previous year), Texas became the only state to actually decrease appropriations for higher education (a decrease of 3%). During 1984-1986, Texas's universities were not competitive with other U.S. universities in terms of faculty salary. As of 1987, the gap lessened but UT system faculty salaries still trailed averages offered in the 10 most populous states. Also, during 1984-1986, the University of Texas lost some of the outstanding faculty it had previously acquired. As of 1987, many of the 1983-established university chairs and professorships remained vacant. The few qualified candidates for these endowed positions were attracted by more substantial offers from universities in other states.

Second, in 1986, there was a noticeable lack of synergy between the private sector and Austin's local government. Shortly after the economic boom of 1983-1984, certain community leaders argued that Austin was being "developed" too rapidly and that this fact was reflected in soaring land and housing prices. The boom led to speculative greed while local government became increasingly strident in its concern to protect Austin's affordable quality of life.

On the other hand, in 1986, business leaders and developers argued that Austin's city council had, either by action (e.g., increased electric rates, a web of building permits, or time and effort spent on countless meetings on "minor" issues) or nonaction (e.g., making no decision on important, needed projects such as a new airport and a convention center) had a chilling effect on high-tech development and economic growth in general. As of mid-1987, Austin was experiencing office vacancy rate of about 30% to 40%, an unemployment rate of 6.6% (compared to a national average of 6.1% and a Texas average of 8.6%), and a plethora of bank foreclosures and business bankruptcies.

As one MCC employee noted, "The unfortunate thing in this town is that Austin remains political and divided: pluralistic if you like it and fragmented if you don't." As another MCC representative said,

If we were looking at Austin in 1987 as opposed to 1983—we'd have to be concerned about a couple of things we were not concerned about then. Both revolve around one of the original strong appeals for the area in the first place—everybody working together to build a better future for Texas. The first concern is the question we had in California in 1983. Will the state [Texas] continue to fund higher education at the level it needs to be funded. Everybody says, "Yes, we want to do that." But there are now real budget battles to fight. Second, unfortunately the relationship between the business community and the city government has deteriorated. The city government is schizophrenic in that part of the people want Austin to look like it did in the 1950s.

## Those Who Won by Losing the MCC

When Austin won the MCC, government, academic, and business leaders in other states feared that Texas universities (principally the University of Texas at Austin and Texas A&M) had the momentum in developing academic institutions of excellence that they increasingly perceived as necessary for their state's economic development. They envisioned their flagship universities being stripped of some of their most valued resources: outstanding professors and their graduate students. They envisioned other companies following the lead of Lockheed, 3M, and Motorola in relocating established divisions and in locating new divisions in the developing technopolis of Austin, Texas.

The MCC decision jolted several states into acknowledging the fiercely competitive environment that exists among all 50 states in trying to attract high-tech industry.

According to Admiral Inman:

None of the reaction to the MCC contest was preconceived when I set out to do the site selection and went through the process, some of it was instinctive and some of it developed as it went along. It was not part of a "grand strategy plan." A lot of the things which were forecast were greatly blown out of context. But what was fascinating to me was that it picked up a life absolutely of its own. And that has continued.

The marketing of the MCC ended in having a fairly dramatic role in the many states concerning the importance of education and economic development. The governors of Arizona, Ohio, Michigan, and Illinois told Inman that the whole MCC episode caused them to begin to look at education and economic development issues in a much more organized way than they had done in the past. Inman noted that

> there was a good bit of soul-searching in California because people figured they had it in the bag. They were so comfortable. The news that Austin won really shook them up. Before the MCC, they really didn't see a need to work to keep what had been built over a long period of time.

After the MCC competition, California voted very substantial budget increases for the UC system.

In Georgia, Governor Harris used the "almost got it" psychology to work with the legislature to get them to dedicate substantial additional funds to do what Texas was planning to do, to promote high-tech development. His attitude was, "Well we didn't win it, but we learned what we have to do to win in the future." Subsequently, the Georgia state legislature allocated $30 million for a Georgia Research Consortium for centers of excellence. In North Carolina, ex-Governor James Hunt convinced his state legislature to ante up $32 million for the MCNC (Microelectronics Center of North Carolina), a state-of-the-art facility located in the Research Triangle. The MCNC is intended to attract high-tech industry to the Triangle area, and to facilitate interuniversity collaboration research in North Carolina.

In Arizona, the reaction to not being one of the final four contenders was one of shock. It constituted a rude awakening for many state leaders. The civic pride of business and community leaders was wounded. Influential leaders agreed that if Arizona wanted to become a high-tech state, then a better understanding of what private industry expected in terms of education excellence, quality of life, and cultural amenities was needed (Wigand, 1987). Two months after the MCC decision, Arizona's governor held a high-technology symposium attended by 150 business, academic, and government leaders in the state. Specific recommendations concerned the role of education, manpower training, venture capital, and university-industry research partnerships in attracting and nourishing high-technology industries (Wigand, 1987). Loss of the MCC greatly aided Arizona State University's Engineering Excellence Program, supported by state government and private industry funds.

## Some Concluding Observations

There is a means to conceptualize technological development. For example, as described in Chapter 4, Smilor, Kozmetsky, and Gibson designate seven sectors of what they label the "Technopolis Wheel": federal government, state government, local government, the university, large companies, start-up companies, and support groups. First- and second-level influencers network among these seven segments. During the two weeks of final competition for the MCC, the Technopolis Wheel was balanced and working in the state of Texas. First- and second-level influencers in academic, business, and government organizations pulled together to propose a "Texas Incentive" that set it apart from the other three areas. As Inman noted, "The visible collaboration between government, the academic community, and business was enormously important to the site selection team."

Participants in the Texas effort were driven by the spirit of competition with the other three finalist sites, and the vision of what the MCC meant for the Austin-San Antonio Corridor, the state of Texas, and for the competitive advantage of the U.S. high-technology industry. The spirit of interstate competition existed in the other states too, of course, but there it surfaced most noticeably only after Texas had won the MCC. For example, an article in the December 1984 issue of the *California* monthly was headlined: "The Eyes of Texas Are Upon Us" and described how some of California's top scholars "might soon be wearing cowboy hats."

The Texas/Austin experience with the MCC indicates how difficult it is to sustain statewide collaborative action. Perhaps, sustaining a team with the cooperative chemistry of the Austin task force is impossible. Duplicating such "chemistry" even on a focused, short-term basis in a community with a more transient population, where the participants are more heterogeneous on age, education, living experiences, and school and regional loyalties, also seems to be difficult to achieve. The MCC has maintained strong links with UT, but there has not been the expected cooperation between Texas A&M, UT, and the MCC. Since 1983, state government has constrained the quest for academic excellence, and local government and business leaders are at odds over what future is best for Austin. The synergy was fractured because of changes in state and local governments and the resulting changes in academic, government, and business participants, plus drastic changes in the economic fortune of Texas. But, for a brief period in 1983, the M-Form Society (Ouchi, 1984) existed within Texas.

# 6

# Urban Telecommunication Investment

## SHARON STROVER

*Until recently, telecommunications has been a nearly invisible component of the evolving information economy. Although computers seem very tangible and receive considerable press, we have mostly taken telecommunications for granted. One of the costs of this oversight is that we have not realized what major investment we already have in telecommunications and how critical that infrastructure is for economic development in the new era. Just as the waterways and highways and eventually the power grids were critical for industrial growth in the last century, the telecommunications infrastructure is a key environment for growth in the information age. Sharon Strover, an experienced researcher in this topic, provides an analysis of the urban telecommunications infrastructure in four Texas cities and their importance for development. Moreover, she stresses the need for city-based policy on the development and regulation of this infrastructure. Dr. Strover is currently completing a book on cable television for Sage Publications, Inc. This research was supported in part by a grant from the Policy Research Institute, University of Texas at Austin.*

## A New Growth Environment

Several chapters in this volume attest to the growth of the information economy in Texas. Much of that growth has occurred in urban areas, and that phenomenon and its policy correlates are the focus of this examination. Our thesis is that the newly developing information

117

economy in the United States has been guided and controlled in private sector institutions that are accountable to shareholders and investors rather than to the public at large, and that the public sector needs to surveil and more actively channel constituents of this economy.

The developing information economy encompasses recently deregulated industries (telephones), new computer networks and services, and various alternative message distribution services (VSAT's, other satellite services, cable and institutional networks, MMDS, and so forth) as well as intensified use of traditional services such as microwave links and broadcasting. (VSATs are Very Small Aperture Terminals, small satellite dish antennas operating at the 10-14 GHz range; MMDS refers to multiple multipoint distributions service, a microwave service capable of carrying several broadband channels of information. It is a common carrier, super-high frequency service that can transmit private TV programming, data, or facsimile transmissions to select locations within a metropolitan area.)

These industries or applications are regulated only minimally. This is in distinct contrast to the situation with traditional telecommunications. By that we refer to telecommunications industries that grew up during the first half of the twentieth century and were regulated as common carriers or as "public trustees." The latter phrase suggests the reliance of such industries on a public good or resource such as spectrum, and the consequent responsibility to safeguard its use for the public interest. (The "public trusteeship" model of regulation refers to broadcast media as promulgated in the 1934 Communications Act.)

With the deregulation philosophy espoused in this country since the late 1970s now in full swing, many analysts are beginning to wonder whether an infrastructure as important as telecommunications is becoming in our society should not have some fundamental direction by elected representatives or public policy planners.[1] With so many of these facilities and capabilities located in cities, the urban region becomes a logical arena for such policy to occur. As information technologies and systems are intensively developed in the urban area and then networked to other (urban) areas, devoid of oversight by federal or state government and absent any public interest standard, it is left to the local area to monitor and, as much as it can, direct telecommunications development in ways that are socially desirable.

Telecommunications planning on the local level is a new idea and one only poorly operationalized in most locales. The very notion of any city planning is still hotly contested in some areas. Houston is often held up as an example of what a city might become in the absence of planning. Whether for good or for bad, Houston is a disordered grouping of businesses and residences crossed by numerous highways.

Most cities have some control over major facilities such as airports, freeways, the location or construction of large buildings, sewers, and other such projects. The rationale in those cases is that the city should channel these endeavors to achieve the maximum good for all the citizens affected by such projects. Airports, freeways, and buildings significantly affect our day-to-day environments as well as our abilities to conduct business. Telecommunications facilities also have profound effects on the city's economic base, its further development, and the quality of life it can offer its citizens.

Cities, however, have been slow to recognize the importance of telecommunications facilities and opportunities. Consequently, the private sector—particularly recently, in Texas, the developer community—has been largely responsible for creating the local telecommunications base. Clearly, it seems that communications networks will proliferate in the coming decades, and that the demand for information processing, productions, and retrieval will escalate in business and in daily life. A necessary correlate is that local telecommunications infrastructures will become very important considerations to businesses when they evaluate their locations. This puts the developer community into a position of control and influence with critical resources.

The purpose of this chapter is to discuss the role of telecommunications in Texas cities and to explore some of the mechanisms available to cities to direct this critical resource. If we are to understand telecommunications services in this decade, we must understand the nature of urban systems and their role in an information economy. The data used in this study include statistics from various archival sources including federal government reports, local government reports, and some private industry studies. Additionally, interviews with city officials, members of the Public Utility Commission, the Texas Municipal League, and telecommunications service vendors provided information.

## Urban Telecommunications Systems

### Cities and Communications

The importance of communications to modern cities can be described in terms of large-scale economic shifts toward information processes

(Dunn, 1980). Cities are information-intensive social entities, their boundaries permeable to internal and external concentrated human effort. The agglomerated unit we call the urban region or the city is now a sort of command center, a locus for transfer and transformation activities. These transformation and transferal activities define the central activities of a city, be they warehousing or communications, or art or trade. Increasingly, the city's activities are of an "information processing" nature. We use that term to suggest managerial operations and all the communication activities of surveillance, regulation, feedback, and directing implied by them. Beniger (1986) correctly points out that postindustrial society will increasingly rely on the "technologies of control" because its subsystems—its industries, businesses, and bureaucracies—have become larger and more complicated. Telecommunications systems are the control instruments.

The urban area offers multiple points of access to alternative communication systems; because many types of information processing activities can achieve economies of scale when they provide the same service to various clients, most of whom are also located in urban areas, such operations will locate in or near a city. This explains the emergence of specialized information processing businesses such as computerized bookkeeping and payroll, auditing, marketing, accounting and legal services, environmental monitoring services, or sales brokers in urban centers. Communication systems are the critical transport systems of the 1980s and they are most intensively developed in urban centers. We can expect their impact on urban areas to be at least as significant as was the invention of the automobile.

## Constituents of
## Urban Telecommunications Systems

The modern urban telecommunications infrastructure is very different from that of even ten years ago. One might characterize the country as one large information grid, with the telecommunications infrastructure of key cities elevating points in the grid. The grid's base is the national telephone system, encouraged in its development during this century by its "universal service" code (telephone service to all regions of the country, rural as well as urban) and regulated monopoly status. On that base are several new "levels" of telecommunications services.

Connected to the phone network but more specialized are the

computer data networks that cross the country, linking banks, brokerages, businesses, universities, and other data users. Regional telecommunications systems in the shape of radio and microwave relays occupy the
next level of service, integrating the country with unique, often local,
information and services, although microwave relays may carry
messages many thousands of miles. Even more local are TV, Multipoint
Distribution Service (MDS), and Multiple Multipoint Distribution
Service (MMDS) technologies, delivering signals to only one or two
markets. MDS and MMDS can be specialized data services or they may
carry entertainment such as pay television. Local Area Networks
(LANS); cable television systems; smaller Satellite Master Antenna
(SMATV), or "private cable" systems; and cellular radio might occupy
the next level of service; their carriage is even more local, although they
can be tied into anything on the more basic levels. Private Branch
Exchanges (PBX), satellite dishes for C Band (TVRO's) or Ku Band
(VSAT's), and technologies located at the home or office might be at the
top of the telecommunications grid, tied to users via phones, televisions,
radios, or computers. This three-dimensional grid suggests telecommunications will be more intensively developed in the urban area.

Moss (1985) predicts that key "nodes" on the information grid
typically will be cities. As our economy intensifies its economic base in
the information sector, the role of cities will increase as important
economic centers. The city is a central switching center, a node linking
and filtering communications traffic of diverse origins. In their nodal
function, cities are developing and will continue to develop the
structures that are efficient for moving information—the offices, the
equipment, the jobs, the people, the networks. New technologies have
brought sophisticated capabilities into offices while also creating
entirely new service availabilities. Some businesses could not exist
without such telecommunications capabilities. For others, advanced
telecommunications adds a critical competitive edge to their operations.

Modern urban telecommunications systems pose a challenge to the
city planners who desire to mold telecommunications into a source of
regional economic development and social good. Certain communication
systems, such as local television and radio, are traditionally beyond the
control or influence of local city officials. Others, such as cable
television, have a history of local regulation. Still others are too new to
have any history or standards for local involvement.

### Texas Urban Telecommunications

#### Cities Studied

The Texas cities we have chosen to profile—Austin, San Antonio, Houston, and Dallas—are representative of other urban areas around the country in many ways. They represent several different economic bases, they are multiethnic, and they have had their share of problems as well as successes. Each has followed different growth curves over its history. Although Texas cities are now in a financially trying period, this is not unlike what other U.S. cities have gone through at other times (e.g., the "rust belt" cities during the 1970s, Detroit's declining auto economy). What differentiates them somewhat from circumstances in other cities is that Texas cities have experienced very rapid growth in the past 10 years. As we will see, this rapid, recent growth has affected telecommunications systems.

#### Population Growth

Austin, Houston, Dallas, and San Antonio experienced significant population growth in the past 10 years. Austin's 1970 to 1980 population growth rate was 4.1% per year, and the region's inhabitants roughly doubled during that time (from 363,300 to 542,200). Houston added about 1.1 million people from 1973 to 1982, roughly a 50% population gain. Its population in 1987 stands at approximately 3,378,300. Dallas went from 1,560,700 people in 1970 to approximately 2,294,700 in 1985. San Antonio had about a 20% increase in its population from 1970 to 1980, making it the nation's tenth largest city and the third largest city in Texas after Houston and Dallas-Fort Worth. Its population in 1987 is about 1,219,000. Each of these cities continues to grow, albeit more modestly in the second half of the 1980s than in the 1970s (Bureau of Economic Analysis, 1985). The percentage growth each has experienced over the 15-year period 1970 to 1985 is as follows: Dallas, 47%; Austin, 80%; San Antonio, 36%; and Houston, 78%. Houston and Austin experienced significant degrees of population migration in addition to normal patterns of local population increase (births exceeding deaths).

#### Employment Structure

As summarized in Table 6.1, each of the four cities has a unique mix of employment. Austin's employment centers on government and the

TABLE 6.1
Sectoral Employment in Texas Cities, 1986
(in thousands)

| | Austin | Dallas | Houston | San Antonio |
|---|---|---|---|---|
| Agriculture | 1.18 | 6.56 | 9.29 | 2.64 |
| Mining | 0.83 | 27.67 | 115.00 | 3.65 |
| Construction | 17.55 | 75.95 | 168.45 | 34.19 |
| Manufacturing | 40.16 | 246.41 | 254.28 | 61.89 |
| Transportation, communication, and public utilities | 9.30 | 83.95 | 119.98 | 21.45 |
| Wholesale trade | 13.17 | 133.12 | 150.40 | 29.61 |
| Retail trade | 56.78 | 224.61 | 291.02 | 93.34 |
| Finance | 19.78 | 126.12 | 118.45 | 35.68 |
| Services | 74.49 | 287.40 | 394.17 | 120.01 |
| Government, federal | 17.35 | 35.34 | 33.67 | 78.90 |
| Government, state | 90.00 | 119.60 | 166.65 | 67.96 |
| Total employment | 370.13 | 1467.37 | 1938.50 | 588.47 |

university. Dallas is known as a trade center. Houston's economy has emphasized oil and affiliated industries while San Antonio presents a mix of trade, services, and military (government) employment.

Employment in information industries alone cannot indicate the reach of the telecommunications infrastructure. In fact, employment figures can be misleading if incorporating telecommunications equipment and services into an industry results in reduced need for labor. That is, if an industry gains in productivity and falls in employment (the two may go hand in hand), then examining employment figures alone will mask the contribution of telecommunications, namely, using new technologies to accomplish more efficiently (cheaply) what (expensive) people used to do.

It would be ideal to examine the actual investment in telecommunications structures and services represented by the industries in each of the cities under investigation, and then integrate that statistic with employment statistics (which are reliably and regularly gathered by the federal government). Unfortunately, federal and state data-gathering do not lend themselves to this sort of disaggregation. Other crude but inferential methods can, however, be developed.

## Implications for Telecommunications Structures of Texas Cities

### The Urban Village Concept

Urban population growth and employment heterogeneity are accompanied by other subtle urban characteristics. According to the Department of Commerce, a great deal of the population growth in these Texas cities was taking place in center city areas, but even more of it was occurring in areas outside of the center city. These increases suggest a pattern of urban development some have called the "urban village." The urban village implies the growth of new minicenters around the city. Often anchored by a shopping mall and a set of offices, the village center is ringed by cheaper apartment houses and condominium living units, which are ringed in turn by more upscale suburban dwellings. Data for the four Texas cities under examination indicate extensive outer city development in each. Although it is tempting to read such non-center city growth as simply the expansion of suburbia, in fact, it is indicative of something else. Expanding population to these areas is accompanied by non-center city businesses as well, and most of these businesses are office-based. Construction statistics show nonresidential building in these cities to be nearly the equivalent of residential.

Leinberger and Lockwood (1986) provide an excellent example of information's impact on cities in their examination of the growth of urban villages. In their examination of urban population movements and office space growth, they point out that the information service jobs now proliferating require offices, the "factories of the future." These offices in turn are most cheaply constructed in areas where land and rents are cheaper (i.e., away from the central city), and where the most modern telecommunications systems can be installed, as in newly built units.

By examining office development in major cities around the country, these authors illustrate the link between information activities, urban sprawl, and the new urban village. Each of the four Texas cities under examination exhibits the characteristics of the urban village. These include magnet job/business centers on the outskirts of the city with concomitant shopping areas, condominiums, rental complexes, and subdivisions.

Telecommunications encourage urban sprawl by allowing people to conduct business through communications media (electronic mail and

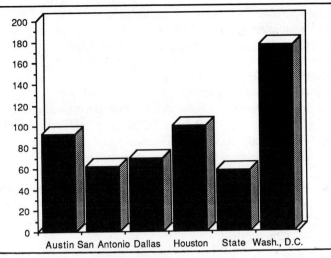

**Figure 6.1    Phones per 100 Population**
SOURCE:    Federal Communication Commission (1983).

modems or phones), thus obviating the need for physical proximity to other businesses and the city center. In other words, people can live and work further from central facilities if they can do their business electronically. The patterns suggest outer city growth of exactly the sort these researchers highlight. Discussions with the local major regional telephone company, Southwestern Bell, indicate that the individual urban villages in these city regions are priority areas for new optical fiber links. In fact, many of the developers of business complexes in those areas are installing sophisticated telecommunications for shared tenant services, proliferating "smart buildings."

**Telephone Utilization**

Numbers of telephone lines suggest the volume of communication activity in a location. Figure 6.1 illustrates the simple number of phone lines per 100 people in each of the cities under investigation, with Washington, D.C., used to illustrate the phone intensity of an information bureaucracy.

Austin and Houston rank highest in this list, suggesting heavier levels of phone utilization in these two cities than in Dallas or San Antonio. Southwestern Bell representatives report that each of these cities is the target of heavy investments in fiber optic lines. Austin received the first and to date the largest infusion of fiber optic and digital upgrades

(Interview, SW Bell representative, 1986). Roughly $100 million per year has been invested in Austin's Southwestern Bell phone plant over the last three years, compared to a maximum of $50 million per year in Houston and San Antonio. Consequently, Austin may be better poised than the other cities to accommodate large volumes of communication "traffic" (voice, data, and so on).

Additionally, Houston, Dallas, Austin, and San Antonio are all to be served with intracity optical fiber by MCI, a major interexchange carrier. The intracity network will certainly encourage bypass (which refers to linking the local loop caller with an interexchange carrier and avoiding the local operating company in the process). Houston and Dallas-Fort Worth are also on a separate fiber link constructed by MCI. Another vendor is also providing a five-city fiber network (Austin, San Antonio, Houston, Dallas, Waco) using the rights of way granted to the Missouri-Pacific railroad.

### High-Technology, Computer, and Data Processing Activity

Each of these cities is attempting to position itself as a modern, forward-looking city. In keeping with that, each has attempted to interest high-technology companies in locating in their region. San Antonio and Austin have probably been the most vocal in this effort, the latter winning considerable fame for bringing the research consortia MCC and Sematech to the area. Dallas has followed this course as well. With Trammell Crow's "InfoMart" building in the Market Center area and Southland Corporation's "Cityplace," Dallas could claim to be a national informatics trade, equipment, and service center. Examining how these cities stand with respect to their local computer and data processing services receipts, we might gain some insight into how deeply each city has entered the businesses they are trying to cultivate.

Figure 6.2 illustrates the average receipts for computer and data processing establishment for each area; the figures offer a measure of business volume. Dallas and Houston lead in receipts per establishment. If we consider those receipts in terms of the size of the community, however, Austin appears to be more computer-intensive than these other two cities.

The size, recency of expansion, development patterns, and degree of existing service sector business suggest that many telecommunications

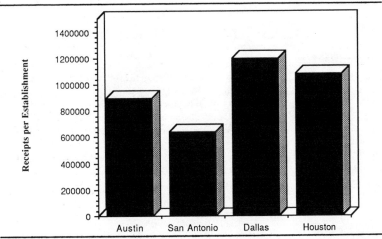

**Figure 6.2**  Computer Establishments Receipts by City, 1982
SOURCE:    Department of Commerce (1982).

systems would be useful for these cities. How the city interacts with service availabilities and needs is the subject of the remaining sections.

### An Inventory Approach

An approach to local telecommunications that may make sense from the city perspective is to examine local telecommunications services availability. With an inventory of local facilities in hand, the city might begin to assess where its goals in developing or utilizing local telecommunications can be best realized.[2] The "inventory process" could be a logical first step for the city planner attempting to become acquainted with the local infrastructure and its availabilities. Ideally a local telecommunications inventory will take stock of alternative facilities, regulatory and policy options, and service (business and citizen) priorities (Hanneman, 1986; Minneapolis Telecommunications Task Force, 1985).

Skeleton inventories for Dallas, Houston, Austin, and San Antonio are compiled in Tables 6.2 through 6.5. Much of the data needed to complete an inventory properly is fugitive, and much is of it is dynamic. Nonetheless, this listing can be a starting point in illustrating telecommunications capabilities and infrastructure in these cities.

Many of the entries on the tables are self-explanatory. For example, the quality of the local phone system, whether it has digital offices and

TABLE 6.2
Austin, Texas: Telecommunications Infrastructure

| Type of Service | Availability |
| --- | --- |
| Telephones | 1/4 lines served by digital; 323637 lines total (1984) |
| Fiber optic | SW Bell: 5300 fiber mi. |
| PBX | Some (govn.); large users considering bypass (e.g., IBM) |
| ISDN | Not available; being tested in St. Louis by SW Bell |
| CATV | 54-channel system with entertainment and information channels |
| INETS (Cable) | 225 miles serving hi-tech corridor and business district |
| Cellular radio | 2 franchises locally (GTE & CENTEX); 10 approx. dealers; |
| Digital termination | Under construction |
| ITFS | None |
| MMDS/MDS | One MDS System; 2 MMDS |
| LPTV | 3 systems, one in Spanish |
| Shared tenant systems | 2 "smart" buildings in business district; at least two more planned in hi-tech corridor |
| Radio and TV | 19 radio signals; 5 TV signals |
| Public access TV | 3 public access channels; also 5 government and educational channels available |
| Terrestrial microwave | Downtown: congested; other areas, available |
| Satellites | No uplink currently through one private teleport planned; several downlinks available |
| Subcarriers | Available |
| Teleports | None |

NOTE: All numbers for MDS, MMDS, and LPTV include permits.

the extent to which fiber optic cable has been deployed, is an indicator of telecommunications carrying capacity. The presence of PBXs, or private phone systems, is indicative of high-volume users who can afford their own internal systems (and whose volume warrants the economies they can achieve by a private system). "ISDN," integrated services digital networks, it not available in Southwestern Bell's region; it, therefore, is not a good discriminator for these cities. Nonetheless, it is sure to become important in future evaluations of telecommunications systems.

I-Nets or "institutional networks" are portions of cable systems dedicated to serving institutional traffic that may be voice, data, or video. I-Nets can be moderately important telecommunications carriers, offering competition to the local loop or to other local carriers. Cellular radio, requiring a franchise from the FCC, is allocated to all major markets in this country, although local competition among its retail

TABLE 6.3
San Antonio, Texas:  Telecommunications Infrastructure

| Type of Service | Availability |
|---|---|
| Telephones | SW Bell:  496,311 lines (1984 figure) |
| Fiber optic | 1/3 switching centers digitized; 37 downtown miles of fiber; fiber; more planned |
| PBX | No data |
| ISDN | Not yet available; SW Bell testing ongoing |
| CATV | 44 channels; addressable; interactive services; 3475 miles of plant; B trunk used for data services |
| INETS | I-NET available through cable system; limited use |
| Cellular radio | 2 franchises; several vendors |
| Digital termination | Nothing standardized |
| ITFS | 3 stations (2500 mhz) |
| MMDS/MDS | 2 MDS; 2 MMDS |
| LPTV | 3 LPTV stations |
| Shared tenant systems | Limited development |
| Radio and TV | 5 major TV stations; 29 area radio stations |
| Public access TV | Some channels available for public, educational, governmental use., mixed with local organization |
| Terrestrial microwave | Some path congestion |
| Satellites | Uplink available but limited (private); several downlinks |
| Subcarriers | Available |
| Teleports | SW Bell "telecity" plan alternative; one limited teleport |

distributors is fierce. (Although only two franchises per market are granted, these franchise-holders in turn allow different vendors to sell the service locally.) Digital termination services refer to the equipment necessary to make effective use of digitized lines. Such equipment is largely under development.

Instructional Television Fixed Service (ITFS) is a closed circuit television service using microwave. Its frequencies are allocated to nonprofit organizations (until recently, when the FCC allowed ITFS license-holders to sell frequency to Multipoint Distribution Services, MDS or MMDS). The latter uses those frequencies for various services, from paging to pay television. Low power television (LPTV) is also available with a license from the FCC. LPTV may have some small role in local telecommunications. (One of the first LPTV stations was an advertising service that operated as a "video greensheet" in Minnesota.) Public access television can be an important citizen communication medium, although it is not always provided channel space by cable companies.

TABLE 6.4

Houston, Texas:  Telecommunications Infrastructure

| Type of Service | Availability |
| --- | --- |
| Telephones | SW Bell: 1,572,087 lines (1984 figure) |
| Fiber optic | No data available |
| PBX | No data available |
| ISDN | Not yet available; SW Bell testing ongoing December, 1986 |
| CATV | Warner: 37 channels; addressable; no interactive services; Storer:  36 channels; addressable; no interactive services |
| INETS | No cable I-NETS |
| Cellular radio | Two franchises; several vendors |
| Digital termination | No standardization |
| ITFS | 8 stations operating (2500 mhz) |
| MMDS/MDS | 2 MDS; 2 MMDS |
| LPTV | 3 LPTV stations |
| Shared tenant systems | Some buildings; slowdown in mid-1980s |
| Radio and TV | 7 major TV stations; 35 area radio stations |
| Public assess TV | 4 access channels (2 operating) on Warner; 2 on Storer system |
| Terrestrial microwave | Inner city congested |
| Satellites | Uplinks available |
| Subcarriers | No data available |
| Teleports | One operating; one planned; one postponed (1986) |

Shared tenant systems refer to the facilities available for sharing in so-called smart buildings with advanced communication equipment designed into them. Such buildings are increasingly popular in urban settings, and Dallas is quickly becoming a national leader in shared tenant facilities. Shared tenant services offer the high-volume phone and datalink user cost advantages. "Subcarriers" are bandwidths on radio or television signals that are capable of carrying some additional information, typically data.

As the tables indicate, each city has a variety of telecommunications services available. One particular deficit in Austin, for example, is the absence of a satellite uplink facility, although many downlinks are available. San Antonio shares this problem although Southwestern Bell is positioning itself as an "alternative" teleport-capable operation with its optical fiber capabilities. The telephone system's recent upgrades and fiber deployment around the Austin as well as the other three cities (particularly in business areas) bode well for telephone-carrying capacity, although new users will be more pressed than ever to evaluate competitors to Southwestern Bell carefully.

TABLE 6.5
Dallas, Texas: Telecommunications Infrastructure

| Type of Service | Availability |
|---|---|
| Telephones | 1,800,000 lines (1986) |
| Fiber optic | SW Bell: 10,000 fiber miles |
| PBX | 3,200 systems operating |
| ISDN | Not yet available; SW Bell testing ongoing, December, 1986 |
| CATV | 80 channels, 76 operating, 3,008 miles |
| INETS | Local INET loops in Mesquite, Farmer's Branch and downtown Dallas; latter is 170 miles, 400 mhz cable |
| Cellular radio | 2 franchises locally; several vendors |
| Digital termination | Nothing standardized |
| ITFS | 9 systems operating in market area |
| MMDS/MDS | 2 MDS (2 more in Fort Worth); 2 MMDS, one for paging |
| LPTV | 1 in Dallas; 2 in Fort Worth |
| Shared tenant systems | Very active; largest facility in world built by Southland Corp. Most new buildings have form of STS, also many downtown |
| Radio and TV | 9 major TV stations; 33 area radio signals |
| Public access TV | 18 channels for all three types access, all operating |
| Terrestrial microwave | Inner city paths congested |
| Satellites | Uplinks available; several downlinks |
| Subcarriers | No data |
| Teleports | One public teleport; 5 local private teleports |

Austin, like other major Texas cities, has downtown microwave congestion, an unfortunate situation because microwave frequencies are useful for short-distance communications. Downtown or business-area microwave links can provide viable alternatives to local loop dependency on SW Bell, as can I-Nets or privately-built Local Area Networks (which need access to rights of way). The Austin I-Net's potential is barely tapped, as is the case in Dallas as well.

Shared tenant services, a small but growing industry, are becoming popular in Dallas. They will multiply in areas where new building occurs and where building lease rates are high. Houston, with its recent economic downturn and high office vacancy rate, is currently not as good a market for STS as is Dallas. Austin and San Antonio lag behind the two larger cities, although Austin's planned shared tenant services in buildings in the downtown and northwestern business corridor seem ambitious.

Each of these cities has several conventional television and radio broadcasting outlets, and one even owns its own radio station.

Subcarrier utilization (narrow bands "underneath" the primary broadcast, useful for data) on these media was not ascertained. Additionally, each city has a cable system with various levels of support for local access for public, educational, or government channels. Austin has by far the most developed cable access program to facilitate citizen-to-citizen communication.

## Problems and Opportunities in
## Telecommunications Planning

### The Traditional Approach

Local communications planning has been for many years the domain of telephone companies and city engineers. While the former established grids and switching centers, the latter made equipment decisions, advised on public rights of way and easements for telephone poles, and managed to get the right people the right quantities of telephones. With the advent of computers and their networking capabilities, competitive phone and data services, cable television and a host of new telecommunicating opportunities, however, urban telecommunication systems are now jungles of fiber optics, coaxial cable, and microwave paths, with several businesses competing to offer new services to a variety of consumer and business and government customers.

The urban planning component in the city has been remarkably ignorant of telecommunications. A survey of recent literature on cities and their growth and development shows planners and architects to be cognizant of cities' needs with respect to energy, to locational advantage, to the impact of spatial structure on local culture as well as individual behavior, but very little written work has addressed the need for planning communications systems (e.g., Panel on Policies and Prospects for Metropolitan and Nonmetropolitan America, 1980; Bingham and Blair, 1984; Bourne, 1982). It seems clear that the traditional scope of the urban planner's job must be expanded. Some of the blame for this oversight is tied to the nature of information itself. Few planners foresaw information as the commodity and as the control system it has turned out to be. Because it so easily slips into other transactions, its importance—its crucial addition or added value—was easily overlooked. Information activities now constitute too important and prominent an economic component of major urban centers to be overlooked. Moreover, they promise to affect directly numerous other aspects of urban life.

The urban planner's position is compounded by confusing jurisdictions over several telecommunications innovations. Federal, state, and public utility commission oversight and power in certain areas can quash the city's ability to work with a certain service provider or user. Clear delineations of authority are not always possible.

**New Attitudes
Toward Telecommunications**

The modern urban communications or planning person is now called on not only to manage the city government's own communications systems but also to consider the communication environment of the region. It is incumbent on the planner to have some familiarity with the above systems and their opportunities as well as constraints. Because of recent deregulation in the telephone and cable industries, coupled with rapid technological advances, this job is very difficult. Moreover, city personnel are frequently ill-equipped to understand these systems. The job of "communications planner" has a public relations legacy in too many settings. As one article reports, it is not unusual for the municipal public relations specialist to acquire a communications-oriented job title that over time is transformed into something related to telecommunications. Unfortunately, what the individual probably knows best is public relations, rather than telecommunications. We found some evidence of this legacy among our informants.

In interviewing city officials concerning local telecommunications, we found disinterest in the role of telecommunications in local economic development. Although most cities have cable offices to deal with the local cable TV companies, and internal communications divisions to handle the cities' own telecommunications uses, none of the Texas cities examined gives much thought to planning regional telecommunications development.

Austin's city hierarchy recognizes the role of communications insofar as there is a "Telecommunications Office," under which is the Cable Office. The official in charge of the office at the time of the study believed that the city has no role whatsoever in private telecommunication systems (personal interview, July 1986). He defined the city's communication role in terms of facilitating government communication (intraoffice communication), with the one exception to that being in the realm of cable television. In that instance, this official indicated that he felt the government access channel was providing a useful service that should continue to be supported, and that the local I-Net could be of substantial benefit to the community. Here again, however, the "community" involved with the I-Net is the city, and the primary use to date of that network is intracity office communication. This official stated that he would rather keep the government out of the local telecommunications arena, preferring to leave that entirely to the private sector.

We also examined the role accorded telecommunications in Austin's economic plan ("Austinplan") and in the workings of its Economic Development Commission. At this date, that role was nonexistent. We found that there had been little effort within the Telecommunications Office to engage in any planning meetings with regional representatives (i.e., nearby communities) or with the PUC. This city government's attitude was that the private sector should "take care of itself."

Dallas and Houston exhibit similar philosophies. Although Dallas operates its own radio station, that is an exception to a policy dictating "hands off" in areas where the private sector has a commercial role. It, like Houston, has an omnibus regulation office to regulate and watch over utilities and cable TV. In Dallas, no one specific city office handles telecommunications planning, although it, like other cities including Houston and Austin, has an office in charge of the city's own communications. Cable television regulation is combined with utility regulation duties in one office in Dallas, and it is staffed by five people.

The Houston Office of Revenue and Regulatory Affairs has two main functions. Half of the 70-person office works in collecting revenues, and the other half works in regulatory matters. That portion of the office dealing primarily with cable and the power companies (natural gas, electric), employs about 35 people and has three or four of them devoted to cable television matters. No other communications-related activities occur in that office, although some activities of other utilities and Southwestern Bell and the local electric company are tangentially related to communications. The Houston office is in charge of franchising companies that use the public rights of way, and phone companies would work with it on such matters.

One interesting benefit of this arrangement is that the staff is well acquainted with utility regulation and franchise provisions, which has apparently paid off in dealing with the cable companies. Although cable companies are not utilities and cannot be regulated as such under federal law, they do in fact operate much like utilities as far as their plant and use of rights of way are concerned. Staff understand rights of way and its utilization. They also understand the financial arrangements utilities make with each other for construction, and can coordinate when necessary. The staff in these offices is primarily concerned with franchising and compliance issues. In that sense, the staff does not operate offices that plan for the future but rather entities that respond to complaints.

The City of Dallas had a greater role in telecommunications regulation in earlier years when the State of Texas did not have a public utilities commission. In fact, Texas was the last state to create such an authority. In 1975, the Public Utilities Regulation Act was passed to create a new office with sole authority to regulate the telephone industry in Texas. One Dallas informant reports that the new state PUC ignored the cities and "treated them like intruders" when they tried to present their positions on telephone regulation to the PUC. With the PUC's authority over telephone business, there is a rationale for cities not to keep track of what telephone or other regulated utility companies are doing.

San Antonio's position is somewhat different; that city's efforts to attract the telecommunications businesses it desires have yet to be fulfilled. Nonetheless, it has adopted a collaborative position when it comes to developing local telecommunications. San Antonio actively promoted the idea of a teleport, a central facility for trunking various types of communications into other carriers, particularly satellite signals requiring downlinks or uplinks. Along with electronics, telecommunications is one of four areas that the Economic and Employment Development office within the city has targeted for attention. That office assists companies interested in locating in San Antonio, as well as companies already there and interested in expanding or changing their operations, in obtaining permits and necessary information. Some of the city personnel have a background in telecommunications. For example, one staff person working in the electronics and telecommunications area had technical training in cable, satellites, circuitry, and modems, although even she admitted she did not have time to keep up with the rapidly changing field.

San Antonio is probably best known for its efforts to obtain a teleport, originally thought to be a telecommunications business magnet. The city actively worked with a company interested in developing the teleport. According to one informant, however, it was "not the right time—all the parts did not come together." The intended provider went bankrupt and Southwestern Bell emerged with its "TeleCity" idea for an integrated network of optical fiber, digital facilities, and satellite transmission capabilities. TeleCity is embraced by the City of San Antonio, which promotes Southwestern Bell's facilities to local and incoming businesses. Most recently, another provider, USAA, has begun to offer uplink services to a limited range of satellites, functioning as a type of teleport.

There are limits to public intervention in local telecommunications industries. As the above description suggests, cable television has been the most notable communications system that allowed the city government planner to think about community communications (although in some states the pertinent regulator is the state utility commission). Traditionally, the local franchise authority for cable television has had rights over fees and rates, certain service categories provided by the system, construction loans, construction progress and locations, and service quality. But that industry won substantial deregulation in 1984 and, as of the end of 1986, rate regulation in most cities is no longer allowed. At the end of 1986, cities in markets where there is "effective competition," defined as being able to receive three over-the-air TV signals, are no longer able to regulate the rates cable systems charge for "basic" service.

Telephone systems are regulated by state and federal law, the decisions of judges in some cases, as well as state-level PUCs. Texas, for example, has recently passed certain bills affecting Southwestern Bell and interexchange carriers. Some states have pricing restrictions or access restrictions for certain services. A host of other technologies rely on the FCC for regulation of some sort, or they may be entirely unregulated.

Nonetheless, there are certain actions or policies cities can consider that would allow them to control or direct the development of some telecommunications systems. It behooves planners to understand their local or regional telecommunications infrastructure so that they can creatively channel or control its development to enhance the interests of *all* the city. In some states, governments have taken an active interest in developing and even funding local telecommunications facilities or services in order to encourage selected businesses.

## *Telecommunications Policy Options*

Particular services suggest different policy options. The city has no regulatory role at all with certain technologies, such as television and radio. It can exercise some indirect as well as direct control on the total infrastructure, however, through carefully planned activities. The policymaker can consider the following:

### Franchises

Franchises are contracts the city strikes with a variety of service providers. Utility companies, phone companies, and cable companies are but a few of the industries utilizing franchises. Although franchises granting use of the public right of way to phone companies are fairly brief documents, a franchise for a cable television system can be an inches-thick document. Cities have many opportunities to use the franchise to tailor a service in one way or another. The franchise could be used much more creatively than is currently the norm. For example, a grant of right-of-way use to a phone company might carry with it a restriction on the type of cable to be used, or some reservation to grant use of the *same* rights of way to competing service vendors (assuming sufficient space for more than one service provider). Although cable television franchises come under attack by cable companies all too frequently, such documents offer models of what cities might begin to think about with respect to obtaining the most value for their franchising authority.

### Collaboration with the Private Sector

Private telecommunications services often use city-provided conduit and easements. The city would be able to encourage optimal use of the limited space in conduit or in public rights of way by maintaining adequate inventories of the locations and capacities of both (particularly electrical and communications conduit). They can consider providing maps showing their locations and making those maps available to all. A franchise could be constructed granting preferred treatment to those who promise to lease conduit, pole space, or both, to others. More aggressive collaboration is illustrated in the New York City Teleport, operated by the Port Authority. In that case, the city joined forces with private entities to fund a much-needed central facility that can handle the large amounts of telecommunications traffic in the New York area. Collaboration can take the form of loans or investment, preferential construction permits, or joint operating authority over a project, to name a few examples.

### Sale of Excess
### Microwave Channel Space

Urban microwave frequencies are increasingly congested. Under a recent FCC ruling, licensees can resell unused capacity and should be encouraged to do so. The city should identify private microwave permit-holders and urge them to lease extra capacity, possibly providing a "clearinghouse" function for potential users in the process. Microwave paths are particularly useful in the downtown or heavy business corridors of the urban region, and every effort should be made to use these carriers to their fullest capacity.

### Integrate Telecommunications Planning

Our examination of city communications offices showed that they have little cognizance of the importance of telecommunications facilities to extant or new businesses. As cities consider proposals for new buildings or new developments, they should consider what communications facilities will be needed, including their impact on employment, local aesthetics, and the likelihood that other businesses or industries will be affected by the proposal. This includes being able to use the same facilities, or considering them sufficiently attractive to influence a decision to move to the provider's location. Given the current bottleneck on local loop transmission (most local telephone-operating companies dominate the local loop and its interconnects), cities should encourage competition lest one provider eventually obtain too much control with no regulatory oversight.

### Revise Codes and
### Inspection Procedures

City codes can effectively enforce planning for future needs by establishing appropriate standards for communications wiring. These might be codes pertinent only to buildings in certain areas or of a certain scope—selective codes that can be applied in such a way that buildings in certain locations are required to be equipped for telecommunications services.

## Encourage Information Sharing

Much more attention can be given to encouraging information sharing between businesses and communications vendors so each knows the other exists. All too frequently, organizations with specific telecommunications needs are unaware of "the solution" or of alternative solutions to their needs. To the extent that the city can play an information role—making known what is available as well as what is needed or planned in the way of telecommunications—it will be doing its telecommunications users and services a substantial favor.

## Engage in Joint Planning Efforts

Cities should collaborate as multicity or multicounty units in the planning process so that the region gets the best telecommunications agreements possible. Additionally, it would behoove them to become acquainted with the operations of the Public Utility Commission and the FCC as both these bodies make and enforce rules that ultimately affect the city's telecommunications infrastructure. Cities have been remiss in lobbying such agencies with their viewpoint on regulatory matters.

## Consider Zoning and Tax Laws

There needs to be more consideration of zoning and tax laws as ways to channel communications growth into desired directions. Cities can give preferred status to certain projects (e.g., teleports) in zoning or in financial assessments. (Indeed, this was the case in terms of land initially allocated for the San Antonio teleport.) Zoning laws could also be used to establish office development or sites of potentially heavy telecommunications use in an appropriate area, one with the proper cabling already in place, for example, or one where ancillary facilities (transportation) are already present.

## *NOTES*

1. To some extent, one can legitimately argue that public policymakers have neither the expertise nor the resources to establish a national "information policy." Indeed, simply

dealing with AT&T rate cases before divestiture occupied years of the government's time. How can policymakers be expected of come up with a viable game plan for national telecommunications? Others argue that if sufficient resources and mandate were given to policy planners, the expertise would, in time, come. They point to the extensive information policy planning efforts of other industrialized countries and conclude that, without planning, our situation will be hopeless in a world economy. There is no question that as things stand in this country, the national telecommunications infrastructure will be developed and structured according to the priorities of the business enterprises allowed to control it.

2. We refrain here from an extensive discussion of what a city's best advantage might be. For some cities, simply making use of local facilities for governmental purposes might be deemed sufficient. For others, active planning for efficient use of local telecommunications facilities might enable the city to aid local businesses. It could allow them to profile local telecommunications vendors for potential customers, or it could be a tool in their arsenal of incentives to new businesses. Some cities are taking steps to make local telecommunications facilities as available to users as possible.

# 7

# Science and Technology Policy

## BRIAN MULLER

*As stated by Daniel Bell in* The Coming of Post-Industrial Society *(1976), advances in science and technology are the raw materials of the postindustrial economy. Although the United States leads the world in many aspects of science and technology, its policies have been mostly a response to international competition such as when the Russians launched Sputnik or when President John F. Kennedy made a commitment to take us to the moon. Another twist has been that, during the years of the Reagan administration, states have been increasingly under pressure to take responsibility for their own policies, including those in science and technology. The state role in such policies was the topic of a special research project and seminar in the University of Texas Lyndon B. Johnson School of Public Affairs conducted by Professors Jurgen Schmandt and Robert Wilson. The present chapter was contributed to this volume by Brian Muller of that project, whose responsibilities centered upon the study of science and technology policy in Texas. Brian Muller is now associated with the Texas Department of Agriculture. A longer version of this chapter appears in* Promoting High Technology Industry: Initiatives in Policies for State Governments, *edited by Jurgen Schmandt and Robert Wilson (Boulder, CO: Westview Press, 1987).*

## Questions for the
## Study of Science and
## Technology Policy

Science and technology policy has been discussed widely in Texas as a way of diversifying the state's economy. Since 1982, the downturn in markets for the state's mineral and agricultural products and the increase in levels of unemployment and poverty have added urgency to the need for diversification. The Texas legislature debated research and economic development issues intensely in the 1985 and 1987 sessions.

Interest in technology-intensive growth stems from the perception that the technology sector in Texas has two competitive advantages. First, the state over the last two decades has begun to build a strong university system and, therefore, possesses a growing capability to assist technology industries. Second, the fastest-growing industries in Texas during the 1970s were based on new technologies and may engender additional growth.

In light of this interest in science and technology policy, a group of students and faculty at the LBJ School of Public Affairs conducted a study during 1985 to 1986 of related programs in eight key states around the country. The study was designed to provide a comparative view of the effectiveness and the political and economic foundations of science and technology policies in the various states. This present chapter reviews the history of science and technology policy in the state (up to the 1987 legislative session), and outlines major issues for science and technology policy.

Given an analysis of Texas demographic and economic background and trends, three questions emerge for science and technology policy:

(1) Can science and technology be directed to assist traditional Texas industries? These industries have experienced significant international competition but might be made more viable through application of new technologies.

(2) What incentives can be employed in science and technology policy to stimulate the growth of new industries? These range from sectors, such as microelectronics—which have established an important presence in Texas over the last decade—to sectors that are small but rapidly growing, such as instruments.

(3) How does science and technology policy relate to these secondary service, finance, insurance, real estate, construction, and related sectors? This question concerns the service sectors of the economy. While not producing substantial exports like the manufacturing sectors do, they represent a rapidly growing source of employment in Texas.

## An Overview of Science and Technology Policy

### History Prior to 1980

The setting for the development of technology policy in Texas is shaped by the unusual political history of the state, in which a strong probusiness tradition is combined with anticorporate populism. A laissez-faire attitude coexists with active state intervention in certain economic sectors.

One dimension of Texas populism, the attitude that state institutional power should be dispersed, is manifest in the sharply constrained powers of the governor and in other aspects of Texas government, such as the election of commissioners to head six state agencies. This approach tends to weaken state government and make it difficult to coordinate policies for economic intervention.

On the other hand, Texas state government has taken an active role in some areas of economic policy. Texas has strictly regulated industries such as oil and gas to achieve specific development goals. In addition, the state has provided funding at a high level for research in agriculture and medicine.

The Texas Railroad Commission is an example of a regulatory agency that has played a key role in the economic development of Texas. The pattern of decisions at the agency has represented the effort to balance technology with economic development policy. A guiding principle in decision making has been that technical concerns about oil field conservation should be balanced with a state economic interest in capturing profits from the industry.

Another traditional focus of state technology policy has been agriculture. The state for many years has provided substantial funding to a system of land grant universities, experiment stations, and extension offices. Texas A&M University, the heart of the research and extension system, has played an important role nationwide in the evolution of agricultural technologies. Innovations in biotechnologies and the use of growth hormones in cattle feeding were pioneered at A&M.

Scientists at A&M developed high-yielding hybrid strains of grain that have revolutionized agriculture worldwide. These innovations were transferred to Texas farmers through the agricultural experiment stations, the agricultural extension service, and by private companies.

The Texas Energy and Natural Resources Advisory Council (TENRAC) is a third historical example of technology policy in Texas. A product of the energy crisis of the mid to late seventies, TENRAC was created in 1979 through merger and expansion of earlier programs. Its purpose was to plan, coordinate policy, and administer research grants related to energy and natural resources in Texas (TENRAC, 1980). During its existence, approximately $8,500,000 was expended by TENRAC. Each dollar leveraged another $1.06 of external funding.

Research was performed in a range of energy technologies from lignite gasification to alcohol fuel production (TENRAC, 1983). TENRAC had a short life, however. After 1980, the energy crisis was perceived to be less urgent; the agency was terminated by the legislature in 1983.

## The Environment for
## Recent Initiatives

In about 1980, emphasis in science and technology policy debate began to shift. New goals emerged to stimulate growth in emerging industries and to improve the position of Texas in international competition. A new set of political actors and rationales were introduced. This shift, still ongoing, was also influenced by two critical changes. First, the decline of the oil and gas industry made economic diversification an imperative. Attention was drawn to the high-technology export industries, such as Texas Instruments, that had expanded dramatically in the late 1970s and early 1980s.

Second, the funding base for the Texas university system expanded substantially during the 1970s. Major universities were better able to attract faculty with national reputations. Almost 800 endowed chairs were added to the University of Texas during the 1970s and early 1980s. Texas A&M also created significant new programs. Texas colleges and universities became aggressive supporters of legislation encouraging development of new technologies.

The first major public forum for technology policy was the Texas 2000 Commission. The commission's original research agenda had emphasized natural resources, but science and technology emerged during the research (Interview with Meg Wilson, former staff member, Texas 2000 Commission, Austin, October 5, 1985). The commission issued recommendations in its final report related to science and technology policy. These included providing universities with "sufficient financial, physical, and human resources" to support research; establishing a science and technology council; developing technical assistance programs for small businesses and individual entrepreneurs; improving legal, regulatory, and financial incentives to private sector research; and creating a communications program to expand awareness about the potential benefits of technology.

Also during the early 1980s, the Microelectronics and Computer Technology Corporation (MCC), after surveying communities around the country for suitability as a location for computer research, chose

Austin. The selection produced great excitement within Texas and publicity nationwide about the opportunities for technology businesses in the state.

Technology policy played only a minor role in the 1982 gubernatorial campaign, but emerged again in 1983 after the new governor, Mark White, began defining priorities. A staff slot in the Office of Economic Development was dedicated to policy coordination in this area.

Other new actors emerged. Individual universities, particularly the University of Texas at Austin and Texas A&M at College Station, became powerful advocates for technology programs at their institutions. Other governmental and quasi-public organizations began to assume roles, including the City of San Antonio, the Metroplex High Technology Task Force in Dallas-Fort Worth, and the Houston Economic Development Council. Private industry also became involved in policy discussion. This sector has been represented by the Texas Computer Industry Council, the American Electronics Association, the Texas Venture Capital Association, and the Texas Industrial Development Council, which represents organizations such as chambers of commerce.

This new wave of interest in technology policy differed from previous state involvement in several respects. First, it addressed a new set of industries—the high-technology firms—rather than traditional resource sectors. Second, it had a broader conceptual scope, namely, high technology intended as a vehicle for statewide economic and job generation rather than as a narrow incentive for an individual industry. Third, it tended to focus on entrepreneurship and the front end of the product cycle—that is, the creation of new products—rather than on increasing productivity and efficiency in established businesses. Fourth, it was given urgency by the evidence of increasing international competition and the decline of resource industries.

### New Initiatives in
### Science and Technology Policy

The major components of Texas state government science and technology policy were instituted during the 1983 and 1985 legislative sessions. So far, the steps taken are largely piecemeal and not incorporated into an overall state plan. Areas of emphasis include funding levels for university research, funding and structure of secondary education, patent problems and other issues related to university-

industry cooperation, and funding and design of programs for investment and assistance in new-product commercialization.

Two concrete actions were taken by the 1983 legislature. First, the
legislature appropriated $1 million for INVENT, the Institute for
Ventures in New Technology, located at the Texas Engineering
Experiment Station at Texas A&M. In addition, authority was
provided by the legislature for the creation of the Senate Interim
Committee on Business, Education, and Technology. The committee's
most important charge was to produce a report that outlined technology-
related issues in Texas and proposed legislation to address these issues.
Proposals included encouragement of closer collaboration between
universities and industry, increased organized research funding, flexible
policies dealing with intellectual property, and improved methods of
project solicitation funding. This report had an important influence on
the 1985 legislative session (Texas State Senate).

In 1984, Governor White appointed the Science and Technology
Council, which was staffed from the governor's office. Composed of
representatives of universities, high-technology corporations, the business service industry, and others, the council's mandate was to develop
policy recommendations and advise the governor on a broad scope of
issues ranging from university-based research and development to
capital availability (Texas Science and Technology Council, 1984-1985).

During the summer of 1985, a special legislative session was held to
consider reforms in the Texas educational system. Technology development was never an explicit goal of this legislation, but debate during the
session was informed by a general perception that Texas needs a
technically trained labor force, strong in math and science, to advance
its international competitiveness.

The 1985 legislative session was active in the area of technology
policy. A variety of persons and groups initiated proposals, among them
the Science and Technology Council, the major universities, and the
lieutenant governor. The Senate Business, Education, and Technology
Committee and the House Science and Technology Committee (created
by speaker Gib Lewis during the 1985 session) introduced over 30 bills.
The Senate Education Committee and the House Higher Education
Committee also played important roles in considering technology
legislation under their jurisdiction. In all, 14 technology-related bills
were passed by the legislature, although most did not include
appropriations.

Two bills were passed during the 1985 session that may have important short-term effects on science and technology policy in Texas. One was the creation of the Texas Advanced Technology Research Program, a $35-million fund awarded through a competitive grant process. The other was the formation of the Select Committee on Higher Education, which is mandated to hold hearings throughout the state on the future of public education and to prepare proposals for future legislation. Technology policy is an explicit area of concentration for the Committee.

### Science and Technology Programs

Participation by Texas state government in science and technology programs has taken a variety of forms. For example, the Houston Area Research Center (HARC) was created in 1982 as a research consortium of business executives and representatives from four Texas universities: Rice University, Texas A&M, University of Houston-University Park, and the University of Texas at Austin. The consortium's goal is to transform scientific and technological advances into practical and commercial applications.

A number of research centers attached to public universities receive state appropriations. The University of Texas system supports 26 centers, 9 of which were on the drawing board in 1985. Texas A&M University, the University of Houston, North Texas State University, and Texas Tech University sponsor the bulk of non-UT centers. Only about 20 of the state's 80 centers emphasize high-technology research topics. Even fewer are involved in joint efforts with industry or receive private industry funds.

The 1985 legislature appropriated $35 million for a new initiative, the Texas Advanced Technologies Research Program (TATRP). This program was designed to support individual research projects in the fields of microelectronics, energy, telecommunications, aerospace, biotechnology, materials, and other areas of science and technology that hold "substantial promise of great benefit to the people of Texas" (General Appropriation Bill, 1986-1987, pp. 111-122). Rather than disburse funds based on a formula, the legislature chose to award the funds on a competitive basis.

## *Funding for Research in Science and Technology[1]*

The enthusiasm about new initiatives in Texas science and technology so far has found only moderate expression in financial support. State research appropriations overall are dwarfed by both federal and public funding and are also small in comparison to state monies provided to traditional research efforts in agriculture and medicine. Most current state support for science and technology goes to research and graduate education, as opposed to commercialization and manpower development. Exceptions include the appropriation for INVENT and for the agricultural extension service.

### Research and Development Funding in Texas

According to the National Science Foundation (NSF), in 1983, Texas ranked sixth among the 50 states in terms of federal obligations for research and development, but only about 24th on a per capita basis (NSF, 1984). Table 7.1 shows that in 1983, federal agencies performed relatively less R&D in Texas than the national average, partly because there is no national laboratory in Texas. On the other hand, industry performed relatively more federal R&D than the national average.

Table 7.2 shows that in 1983 Texas received on average more federal funds from the Departments of Transportation and Agriculture and from NASA. The state receives substantially less from the Department of Energy and secures relatively few funds from the NSF.

Data on industrial R&D spending are incomplete and difficult to obtain. The most recent survey of industrial R&D spending did not release data for Texas because the operations of a single company would have been disclosed. In 1979, the NSF estimated that Texas industries spent $1.2 billion in the state on R&D, compared to the federal government's $1 billion (NSF, 1981, 1983).

Currently the only state government funding for R&D is for the state institutions of higher education including universities, medical schools, health science centers, research institutes, and extension services. Public higher education is funded in two ways, including by direct appropriations from the legislature and by the Permanent University Fund—a pool of state revenue earmarked for members of the University of Texas and Texas A&M systems. The interest income from the invested

TABLE 7.1
Federal Obligations for R&D by Performer in Texas
and Share Compared to the United States, 1983
($ million and %)

| Performer | Funds | Share | U.S. Share |
|---|---|---|---|
| Federal facilities | 229.1 | 16.2 | 27.1 |
| Industry | 903.4 | 64.0 | 49.1 |
| Universities | 235.1 | 16.6 | 18.8 |
| State and local government | 36.8 | 2.6 | 4.5 |
| Other | 8.3 | 0.6 | 0.5 |
| Total | 1,412.7 | 100.0 | 100.0 |

SOURCE: National Science Foundation (1984, vol. 33, p. 142).

TABLE 7.2
Share of Federal Obligations for R&D in Texas
by Agency Source Compared to the United States, 1983
(in percentages)

| Agency | Texas Share | U.S. Share |
|---|---|---|
| Agriculture | 3.1 | 2.2 |
| Commerce | 0.4 | 0.9 |
| Defense | 60.2 | 61.0 |
| Energy | 1.8 | 12.0 |
| Health and Human Services | 10.7 | 11.5 |
| Interior | 0.4 | 1.0 |
| Transportation | 1.7 | 0.9 |
| EPA | 0.8 | 0.6 |
| NASA | 19.2 | 7.0 |
| NSF | 1.8 | 2.8 |

SOURCE: National Science Foundation (1984, vol. 33, p. 150).

Permanent University Fund makes up the Available University Fund,
which is distributed to the eligible universities for plant and equipment
purchases and in support of certain programs.

**State Funding of
University Research**

State funding of research at colleges and universities in Texas
(excluding TATRP) takes two forms: organized research and special
line item research. Organized research funds are nonspecific and are
distributed among all the state's senior colleges, universities, and health

TABLE 7.3
Research Funding at Texas Senior Colleges
and Universities, 1972-1987, and Total Change
(in $ thousands and %)

| Biennium | Organized Research | Special Items | Total | Change |
|----------|--------------------|--------------:|------:|-------:|
| 1986-1987 | 13,590 | 35,780 | 49,370 | −6 |
| 1984-1985 | 18,218 | 34,474 | 52,692 | 13 |
| 1982-1983 | 17,339 | 29,384 | 46,723 | 31 |
| 1980-1981 | 14,327 | 21,458 | 35,785 | −10 |
| 1978-1979 | 14,573 | 25,280 | 39,854 | 2 |
| 1976-1977 | 18,696 | 20,190 | 38,886 | 38 |
| 1974-1975 | 16,342 | 11,905 | 28,248 | 22 |
| 1972-1873 | 14,588 | 8,643 | 23,230 | − |

SOURCE: Texas College and University Systems, Coordinating Board (internal document).

science centers according to a Coordinating Board formula with special weight given to the number of master's and doctoral students in science and engineering programs. The funds are then allocated by the administration of each institution to individual programs or to the deans of particular schools and colleges within the university.

In addition to the organized research funds, the legislature also appropriates, on a line item basis, special funds for particular research institutions and programs, such as the University of Texas McDonald Observatory or the Texas A&M Cyclotron Institute.

Table 7.3 shows that funds for organized research have remained relatively constant over the last 15 years, but have declined in real terms. Funding of special item research in the same period, however, has increased dramatically, over 400%. This growth is primarily due to an increase in the number of special items. A review of the appropriations bills shows that in the 1986-1987 biennium, 54 programs or institutes were funded by special line item appropriation, as compared to 25 in 1972-1973.

### State Funding for Health Education and Research

In addition to the funding of research at senior colleges and universities, the Texas legislature has strongly supported education and research at state medical schools and health science centers. Nearly $1.3 billion was appropriated for health education during the 1984-1985

TABLE 7.4
State-Funded Health-Related Research,
1972-1987 and Percentage Change
(in $ thousands and %)

| Biennium | Organized Research | Special Items | Total | Change |
|---|---|---|---|---|
| 1986-1987 | $34,621 | 15,581 | 50,203 | 8 |
| 1984-1985 | 28,930 | 17,689 | 46,620 | 12 |
| 1982-1983 | 24,432 | 17,117 | 41,549 | 46 |
| 1980-1981 | 19,244 | 9,134 | 28,377 | 47 |
| 1978-1979 | 15,627 | 3,638 | 19,265 | 46 |
| 1976-1977 | 11,037 | 2,177 | 13,213 | 7 |
| 1974-1975 | 8,107 | 4,241 | 12,348 | 13 |
| 1972-1973 | 6,819 | 4,106 | 10,925 | — |

SOURCE: Texas College and University Systems, Coordinating Board (internal document).

TABLE 7.5
Other Research Funds at Experiment Stations and
Various Research Institutes, and Percentage Change,
1972-1987

| Biennium | Research Funds ($ thousands) | Percentage Change |
|---|---|---|
| 1986-1987 | 136,773[a] | 17 |
| 1984-1985 | 117,303 | 10 |
| 1982-1983 | 106,636 | 45 |
| 1980-1981 | 73,427 | 13 |
| 1978-1979 | 64,731 | 12 |
| 1976-1977 | 57,660 | 40 |
| 1974-1975 | 41,097 | 22 |
| 1972-1973 | 33,625 | — |

SOURCE: Texas College and University Systems, Coordinating Board (internal document).
a. Includes the $35 million for the Texas Advanced Technologies Research Program.

biennium and $1.2 billion during the 1986-1987 biennium. The universities received twice as much funding, but had over 30 times as many students (Legislative Budget Board, 1984-1985; General Appropriation Bill, 1986-1987).

Table 7.4 shows that both organized and special research funding for health have grown rapidly over the last 15 years. Total funding for

TABLE 7.6
Source of Research Funds at Public Senior Institutions
and Agencies of Higher Education, Fiscal Year 1984

| Source of Funds | Amount ($ millions) | Percentage of Total |
|---|---|---|
| Public | | |
| State appropriated | 102.5 | 25.1 |
| Institutionally controlled | 17.9 | 4.4 |
| Federal government | 209.3 | 51.4 |
| Private | | |
| Profit | 19.7 | 4.8 |
| Nonprofit | 42.8 | 10.5 |
| Other | 15.3 | 3.8 |
| Total | 407.5 | 100.0 |

SOURCE: Texas College and University Systems, Coordinating Board (1984, p. 2).

health research was half of total university research funding in 1972-1973. In the 1986-1987 appropriation, it has surpassed university research funding. Clearly, high priority is placed on health-related research in Texas.

**State Funding for Other Research**

A significant amount of additional research is performed at various state institutes and extension services. The most important of these is the Texas Agriculture Experiment Station at Texas A&M University, which received over half of all the funds in the 1986-1987 appropriation. Also included are the Texas Engineering Experiment Station, the Texas Transportation Institute, the Texas Forest Service Research Program, and others. Table 7.5 shows that this funding category has increased over 400% in this period, and is now greater than the combined funds for university and health-related research.

**Other Sources of
Funding for University Research**

The state is not the major source of funds for university research. An annual survey of research funding conducted by the Coordinating Board's Educational Data Center is summarized in Table 7.6 (Texas College and University Systems, Coordinating Board, 1984). Most research funds in higher education come from federal agencies like the

NSF or federal departments such as the Defense Department. Private sources such as industry and foundations also support a significant amount of research.

At individual universities, the proportion of federal government support can be much greater than the state average. For example, the University of Texas at Austin has reported that, for the 1984-1985 academic year, its researchers secured $106 million for sponsored research projects, with $82 million, or 77%, coming from federal agencies. This is almost 10 times the approximately $11 million the university receives per year for research from the organized research formula and for special line items (Interview with Dr. Kenneth Tolo, Associate Vice-President for Academic Affairs and Research, University of Texas at Austin).

## Implications for Science and Technology Policy in Texas

Existing state initiatives in science and technology do not represent a coherent body of state government policy. No firm consensus about policy goals and organization emerged from the 1983 or 1985 legislatures. Appropriations for post-1980 programs are relatively low compared to other states in our survey. Comparatively few innovative programs have been adopted by the Texas government. Those programs that have been undertaken—in state agencies, universities, local public organizations, and the private sector—are only loosely coordinated.

The relatively low profile of Texas as a funder, initiator, and innovator of science and technology programs corresponds in principle to the roles of state government in California and Minnesota. The private sector and universities have taken the policy lead in those states, with state agencies and the legislature acting as junior partners.

The constitutional structure of state government in Texas may prevent the governor, legislature, or state agencies from aggressively directing science and technology policy, the role Governor Hunt performed in North Carolina. An effective science and technology policy, however, will require concerted legislative actions and arrangements for a high level of coordination among publicly funded programs and between those programs and the private sector.

Government and the private sector have been cooperating actively on the local level in Texas, where much of the momentum for science and technology policy has developed. The city of San Antonio, for example, is helping to organize a biotechnology research program and industrial park based at the University of Texas and Southwest Research Foundation. Other local public-private programs include the North Texas Commission and the Houston Economic Development Council.

On the state level, however, the private sector has taken a lower profile in policy development than in the other surveyed states. For example, the Milrite Council in Pennsylvania, and comparable private-sector organizations in Massachusetts and Minnesota, play a highly visible role in defining and supporting public-private programs.

There is no firm evidence to support a comparison between states of private-sector contributions to joint public-private research and commercialization programs. Several states such as Pennsylvania, however, have established large matching funds programs in which state appropriations are used to leverage private research dollars. Texas has not used this policy tool as extensively. Overall, private contributions to joint public-private programs, excluding agricultural research, are probably at a lower level in Texas than in states such as Pennsylvania.

The ability of policymakers in Texas to define a framework for both public and private coordination and concerted action—which works effectively within the unusual institutional structure of state government and education in Texas—is a major challenge to science and technology policy in the state.

Although there is no established science and technology policy in Texas, recent legislation reflects a number of principles that may provide a direction for policy development.

(1) Improved research activities foster new industries and new jobs (expressed in TATRP legislation).
(2) Research is a legitimate university activity (expressed in Senate Concurrent Resolution No. 118).
(3) Universities require aggressive intellectual property policies (expressed in 1985 legislation).
(4) A well-educated work force is necessary for sustained economic growth (expressed in 1984 education reforms).
(5) More emphasis should be directed to homegrown industries (expressed in INVENT legislation).
(6) State government should fill some strategic gaps in the marketplace such as technology information-sharing and assistance in R&D for prototype development (expressed in INVENT legislation).

(7) State-sponsored research can help solve development problems of resource sustainability and infrastructure provision including declining water supplies, inadequate transportation facilities, and soil erosion (expressed in the Texas 2000 Commission Report).

Even if these principles are used, the state legislature will still face many allocative decisions. Allocative issues in Texas relate to the following four areas: sectors, regions, populations, and institutions.

One allocative problem is that of distributing state monies for research, development, and commercialization among industrial sectors. In Texas, this problem concerns the balance among the three major industrial groups. These include the emerging, largely technology-based, industries; the traditional, largely resource-based, sectors; and the secondary sectors, particularly finance, insurance, real estate, and other services.

There is evidence in other states of growing competition between traditional and emerging industries for R&D resources. Mature industries in some states are complaining that their research needs are being neglected in favor of the high-technology industries. For example, Governor Martin of North Carolina appointed an Assistant Secretary for Traditional Industries in the Department of Commerce to assist such industries with innovation and other development needs.

Most of the discussion about science and technology policy in Texas has focused on the so-called high-technology industries like micro-electronics, robotics, and biotechnology. Research efforts are not completely absent in the state's traditional industries. The Geotechnology Research Center, a part of HARC, directs research efforts toward oil and gas, and agriculture is a longtime focus of research policy in Texas. But these and other traditional industries like textile and apparel manufacturing could benefit more fully from new science and technology initiatives. Production innovations, improved resource extraction processes, and new-product development could all help make these industries more competitive. In particular, the market and resource problems facing agriculture are massive. International markets for bulk commodities, such as grain and cotton, are becoming more competitive, reducing prices. At the same time, falling water tables, soil erosion, and other factors are increasing production costs.

In addition, the tertiary sectors, such as FIRE and services, are critical to the Texas economy because they represent the largest source of absolute job growth. The experience of MCC in Austin suggests that most employment growth resulting from research-intensive industry location occurs in the service sector. Many secondary industries provide technology-based producer and consumer services. A disparate group of businesses, from software companies to hospitals to construction companies, can benefit from innovation.

Texas encompasses a number of economic regions with different interests. Legislative representatives of these regions can be sharply divided over technology policy. Particularly, representatives of districts outside central Texas and the major cities are suspicious that their districts will not receive benefits from science and technology policy.

The University of Texas has begun to address regional inequities within its system by funding regional industrial development centers. Apart from this effort, little state funding goes to R&D outside the major universities. For example, Pan American University, the largest university in the South Texas region, receives only a few thousand dollars a year in organized research funding.

There are several problems inherent in the effort to distribute R&D resources broadly in Texas. Regional economies in the state are not equally equipped to host research-intensive industries, and regional institutions are not equally qualified to support such activity. Moreover, the basic research process tends to benefit from agglomerations around major institutions. In any case, economic benefits from research in one region of Texas can overflow into, and be oriented to, other regions.

In short, policymakers in Texas are faced with a quandary. On one hand, the research process may be more successful if concentrated among major institutions. On the other hand, demands for regional equity argue for a broader distribution of resources.

Demographic studies show that Hispanic populations in Texas will grow more rapidly than other groups and that the state may experience increasing rates of poverty and unemployment. The role of science and technology in addressing these social problems is not clearly reflected in the state's activities. Nationwide, the growth of high-technology industries has probably done relatively little to reduce poverty and structural unemployment. Employment in some states, such as Massachusetts, however, has increased rapidly due to the growth of technology-based industries, and structural unemployment has been reduced. It can be argued that research-intensive development policy is not the appropriate instrument with which to address poverty and unemployment. Incentives may be too long-term and results too indirect to be effective for this purpose. On the other hand, the potential for using science and technology policy to address specific problems of community and regional economic development has not been explored fully.

The issue of targeting resources to population groups—both income and ethnic—did not emerge in most of the state debates surveyed in this project. Failure to target could develop into a deeper controversy in Texas because of the state's large Hispanic populations and rising unemployment rates.

Several institutional questions have emerged in Texas that are also raised in other states. The most important of these are as follows: Should private universities receive resources for technology policy? And what is the relationship between newer technology-related programs and older research programs created to aid economic development?

States with major private research universities—California, Massachusetts, and New York, in particular—have experienced relatively little conflict about funding research in private universities. In Texas, however, private colleges have not yet achieved the status of those in California and the Northeast. The policy issues in Texas concern whether the state should devote resources to strengthening institutions such as Rice and Baylor.

The agricultural land grant university system in Texas, based at Texas A&M, illustrates some difficulties encountered between traditional and new science and technology programs. This system has undoubtedly been effective in the commercialization and dissemination of certain new technologies, leading to increased productivity. But it can also be argued that the system has been sensitive only to a narrow range of research needs in agriculture. According to this view, priorities for agricultural research do not correspond to statewide economic objectives, such as resource sustainability and employment generation. Traditional agricultural research might benefit by incorporation into a comprehensive science and technology policy directed toward broad state economic objectives.

## NOTE

1. This section was written by Michael Dowling, Graduate Student, Graduate School of Business, the University of Texas at Austin.

# 8

# The Governor's Science and Technology Council

## LARRY D. BROWNING

*There was a movement toward state development of science and technology across the United States in the early 1980s and Texas wanted to be a competitor. This was one reason that Texas Governor Mark White appointed a blue-ribbon council on science and technology. Group researcher, Larry Browning, had the good fortune to attend many of the meetings of this council and to analyze their deliberations. We are shown from his analysis of a crucial meeting of the group that many of the problems Texas would face in making a transition to the information age would surface early in the deliberations of this council, especially the commitment of Texas political leaders to change. The major figure in these deliberations is Rear Admiral Bobby Inman, then chairman of MCC, who also figures prominently in Chapter 5 of this volume. Professor Browning teaches in the Speech-Communication department at the University of Texas at Austin, where he specializes in the qualitative study of group communication processes in business and industry.*

## Aim of the Research

Among the many strategies for promoting economic and social change is to empower a group of leaders or change-makers to establish an agenda for action. This was one of the major efforts of Governor Mark White of Texas who had been earlier impressed by William C. Ouchi's, *The M-Form Society* (1984). Ouchi gives much credit for the

Japanese success in business to cooperative planning among the academic, governmental, and business communities. Accordingly, in September 1984, Governor White appointed a 28-person council to "recommend ways Texas can improve its position as a national leader in science, technology, research and development" (Governor's press release, September 14, 1984). The initial aim was to develop a science-oriented agenda for Texas education, government, and industry. The council was to meet quarterly.

In many ways, the meetings of this council epitomized the challenges of promoting rapid change—not just the legislative and budget issues, but the problems of definition, commitment, and priorities reflected in the interactions among council members. This chapter examines several samples of these interactions taken from transcriptions of proceedings to illustrate that, even among the most talented of individuals, planning for change does not come easily. In another respect, this chapter serves as an example of a type of qualitative research that can lend insights into the change process. Most of the analysis is centered on transcripts taken from a key meeting of February 14-15, 1985, where the council was forced to confront problems of priority and commitment of Texas leadership to change.

## *The Council*

The council was made up of 28 individuals selected primarily from government, business, and education. The group was to convene quarterly beginning with the September meeting. The initial structure was open, which meant that the interactions allowed for any number of individual or group interactions, agreements or disagreements, to be discussed. The climate of the meetings was like a board room of a large business with a relaxed style of exchange. Interspersed with the serious discussion were moments of laughter, as with references to an individual's recent accomplishments, or responding to the ups and downs of the business world. The group was positive, spontaneous, and forward looking. Patterns of deliberations reflected strategic planning tactics, where decision makers examined the competition as one basis for establishing their own priorities. The visible behavior from the council was task-oriented. How can we move forward with a science and technology plan?

The governor knew that most of his power with the council existed before it convened and through his appointments to it. The selection of participants went through 13 lists of revisions to get the "proven doers, top notch educators, big gun industrialists, and visionary futurists" from geographic regions of the state onto the council. As the analysis in this chapter will show, missing were policymakers or representatives from the Texas legislature, who would have been helpful to carry the word of technology development to that decision-making body.

For most meetings, items of business and the amount of time to be spent on each were identified at the beginning of the council workday. The agenda also tended to determine the strategies available to the individual members of the council. They could attempt to choose among alternatives, but the agenda determined the outcomes among which they might choose on any given meeting day. A list of policy proposals was often laid out in summary form for the council to discuss, amend, reject, or approve. The results were recorded for use with other legislative committees.

The initial open structure of the council was a match with the previously undefined opportunity to carve out a purposeful agenda for science and technology development, and with the collection of blue-ribbon members to sit on the council. The mix of government, business, and research talent selected for the council meant that they would advise the governor and give direction to the aim he had established.

The two most active figures at most council meetings were Henry Cisneros, the mayor of San Antonio, and retired Admiral Bobby Inman, the chairman of the Microelectronics and Computer Technology Corporation ("MCC"), the company whose recruitment to Austin was a major milestone in the "high-tech" boom in Texas.

## Selected Analyses

### Importance of the
### February 14-15 Meeting

The present analysis focuses on the third meeting of the Science and Technology Council on February 14-15, 1985. They had an organizational meeting in September 1984, and a second meeting two days before Thanksgiving of that year.

The third meeting of the Council was pivotal because it was overshadowed by a recent public statement that the state budget was suffering a financial shortfall, which raised the possibility of cutting salaries of state employees by 11% and imposing a hiring freeze on all state positions. The salary cut was the bigger issue, but the hiring freeze at a time when the universities, especially the University of Texas and A&M, were recruiting new faculty to give energy to the movement, was a serious drawback.

The governor's first science and technology coordinator, Meg Wilson, and Art Hansen, the current chairperson, had met with the governor earlier in the day to set the agenda for the meeting. As the financial and educational crisis the state was facing were immediate issues for the governor, he suggested at the planning meeting that he talk to the council. Wilson agreed and made changes in the agenda, thus setting the stage for an immediate consideration by the council of these pressing issues.

Although the council was composed of leaders accustomed to working with others of prominence, the presence of the governor, his press secretary, and other functionaries, had a visible impact on the mood of the committee. Texas was in competition for the General Motors' Saturn Project and the governor raised practical questions such as "Do you realize that employee medical benefits weigh so heavily in the Saturn decision they may tip the scale?" The governor was impatient and his focus was more on pursuing specific opportunities rather than solving the problem of a salary cut for state employees. George Mitchell suggested the possibility of a one-cent per barrel tax on oil with the proceeds going directly to research and the governor responded positively to the tone and specific suggestion made by Mitchell.

The governor talked in ways to reduce the perception of the seriousness of the salary cut: "Don't holler till you're hurt." He had pressed the council to provide evidence that anyone had been rejected for hiring or that there was a problem in hiring the talent necessary to fuel the science and technology initiative. This may have been effective talk with the press, but the oversight of the problem to this group only gave them something else to work around. Bobby Inman, the President and CEO of MCC, was not at the first part of meeting during the governor's visit, which avoided the possibility of a direct ideological clash between the two over where there was a hiring problem. (As a subsequent discussion indicates, the governor's political response to the problems caused by the salary freeze and reduction being planned was at odds with the vision of development articulated by Inman.) The governmental relations director of MCC, Bill Stotesbery, was at the meeting and was later to brief Inman on the earlier proceedings.

The usually visible Cisneros could not attend the February 14-15 meeting, however, his actions at the immediately previous meeting had set some of the stage for deliberations. In that meeting, he had obtained a tentative agreement to support a research center to study the effects of petrochemical by-products, including toxic wastes, at Lamar University in Beaumont Texas. This action represented Cisneros's "technocrat" philosophy well in that it showed regional involvement, and the use of technology to solve problems and to create new business opportunities. Cisneros's decision-making style in groups was also integrative. He drew the best of individual contributions together and moved toward a solution quickly, which produced a feeling of action and accomplishment. His absence was conspicuous from the February 14-15 meeting. His presence and actions had provided part of the growing order and structure of the group.

**Reconsideration of Goals**

One of the first challenges discussed at this critical meeting was the reconsideration of goals because of the recently announced budget shortfall. Although the council's mission statement was clear enough, its real meaning in practice had not been stabilized in the short tenure of this group. There was a general feeling of *What are we doing now?* This was introduced by one member in the following statement:

> I'm a little bit concerned in listening to the governor this afternoon. It's clear to me he is looking for a number one specific suggestion. As a matter of fact, I think George you have an excellent one and he jumped right on top of that because it was specific. And he's looking for something right now, and we're still dealing with setting a science policy. And it appears to be our timing with the governor is way out of synch here. He is clearly looking for some specifics and he's looking for them pretty quickly. And we're still dealing with policy and I don't know that we're ever going to bring that together.

The council had focused in the earlier two meetings on general direction, but the budget crisis emphasized the immediate and critical nature of the financial problem. Because the council was appointed by the governor, it was natural to interpret their task in relation to his remarks at this meeting: "What is the boss looking for?"

A response by George Mitchell (Energy and Development Company) continued to focus on goals and added information on how to interpret the governor's wishes. He based his evidence for direction with recent personal contact with the governor. He redirected the council back to long-range planning:

> In an earlier conversation this morning with him [the governor], he once spoke of where will Texas be down the line. He's aware of the problems that have joined us such as water, all of that. So he is saying how do we plan for the future? In having said that, he also was saying this legislature has got to be addressed. We have some current sharp problems that you on the Science and Technology Council need to respond to—specifics. He also, I think, is looking at the long-range policies that we ought to be implementing today to pay off tomorrow. At least that's the impression I had in talking to him.

At a point later in the discussion, Jurgen Schmandt, a council member from the LBJ School, attempted to summarize and draw together the need to address both short- and long-term directions. In this statement, Schmandt suggested a mixed agenda of both short- and long-term directions. He also used his speaking time to add to the goals of the council by supporting a commission to review higher education and higher education resource allocation. The goal would be to redirect resources. While the council was reconsidering goals, it was also simultaneously making specific suggestions on how to meet the financial crisis. Schmandt's comments summarized the search for goal clarity and the desire to use meeting time effectively.

George Mitchell then puts the planning role in perspective:

> I think the most specific comment we can make . . . is if you don't do something and do it right on the majority of funding in higher education, there isn't going to be any damn future. They need to learn that. They have already torn into part of it—MCC.

While planning was the goal of the council, the pragmatic leadership of Mitchell was resistant to acting "as if" the funding problem would be solved and instead focused on the immediacy of the emergency. His "there isn't going to be a future" moved the discussion from goals to survival. In doing so, he changed not only the direction of the discussion, but the level of seriousness of the problem.

## Will Texas Leadership
## Honor the Commitment to Change?

In discussion leading up to the analysis, the speaker had mentioned educational planning in Kansas. This was a reflection of the council's tendency to compare Texas with "the competition." The evaluation of other state's initiatives was often critical information to the council. At the time of the following exchange, Admiral Inman had arrived at the February meeting. He joined in the use of strategic planning arguments to reemphasize the urgent and critical nature of the funding problem. To a query about what he had heard about the damage already caused by the funds shortfall, Inman responds:

> Not much yet. Some phone calls asking is it real, how big, how far is it going to spread, and was it really significant? But these are not companies that are thinking right now about major installations in Texas, that's five/six years down the way, when they are at that point. As technology begins . . . [Inman is interrupted here with some seeming disbelief, to which he changes his direction.] Some are already looking at it. To be very candid, there are two that are looking where to locate major research centers, three, I'm sorry. And this is certainly . . . it couldn't have been a worse set of signals to send. And a lot of these people sat around and listened to repeated strong assurances about ten years of dedicated effort and we are on our way and we are never going to turn back.

As the meeting progresses, the question of direction—what are we doing?—is dispersed and unresolved. The topic switches through Mitchell's comment to a more sober question of survival: Will there be a future? This is answered with a "not likely" unless drastic measures are taken. Inman moves to question whether "we have honor and conviction?" The group took his words like a beating, looking embarrassed and responsible for the financial issues the council faced. Council participants knew his analysis and the legitimacy of his discontent compounded the bad news and moved the crisis in funding from the position of strategic intelligence "out there" into the meeting room.

This event moved the meeting to a level of emotion above strategy. Men (and women) known for keeping their word, accepted and wore on their faces a real and collective guilt for letting him down. Inman, one of the two active members of the council, was now expressing active doubt and discouragement about the willingness of Texas leadership to commit to the grand design of technological development for which he stood. Inman had chosen Texas as the site for MCC two years earlier and in doing so had put in place the flagship that was needed to galvanize the research and entrepreneurial talent that had been collecting in recent years. He had made the decision to move to Texas based on continuing support, a commitment well known to the council. As one member later said, "They knew he would have been justified in pulling MCC out of Austin at that moment."

## What Is the
## Role of the Council?

The discussion of the commitment of Texas leadership to change turned to an example by the governor's representative, Meg Wilson, as to what might be expected from the council. We pick up toward the end of Ms. Wilson's statement:

Let me do (this). We're going to discuss this tomorrow so I don't want to get very far into the SSC [superconductor-collider project]. Now we've got to decide, I say "we" meaning the Council, as to the continuing role we play for support or review of the SSC. Along that line, the questions that I think the governor or somebody can answer are the following: Should we continue in this game? All of us are in this, so far we have to. Well, what are the things we should be sensitive to as the governor speaks for the state vis-à-vis a very big federal program? Potentially very big. Can you, of the Council, give me some advice and help? And, if so, I [speaking as the governor] would like some specifics. Second, are there other opportunities that might come along like an SSC? I don't know what they might be. The whole thing is space. Give me advice. Should we be looking at problems of this type? Along with that and I'll pick space to get off of SSC, what should we be doing at the universities? What other policies should we have? Whatever. Now, the follow-up on that, however, is that we've got very near term important problems which, again, I need advice on if this legislative session goes by (and this is what we were saying), and all of a sudden DOE comes along or NASA comes along or somebody comes along and says we'd like this proposal from the states to put a center of "X" there and we say "that's a great idea, except for one problem; we don't have any money!" and we say, I don't want to get caught in that kind of a trap so I need something from this Council that will give me some assurance that I can play in the game if we have to. The fundamental, overarching question is, "What role do we play in advising you?" "What role do we play in analyzing what the frontiers might be like?" All of that, he is saying, "I don't know the answers, governor, I'm looking to you for a fundamental overview, of policy, of opportunities, and right today, some very short-term legislation that I need to have enacted if we're going to play this game a few years from now." What do you think?

[voice from off-mike:] So at the end of this session tomorrow, we should be able to answer some of these questions for him, then?

[Meg Wilson:] Exactly. That's the message I get from him.

[Inman; interrupts speaker:] Mr. Chairman, the recent events have been made clear. What we have failed to do is to get a clear understanding of either the factors involved in creating technology or those in commercializing it. The roles that are played by industry, by the academic community, by government, both at the federal and state level. [At this point the group becomes remarkably silent and grants Inman their undivided attention, something not given to any previous speakers.]

[Inman:] I have found . . . you know I have listened to a lot of assurances two years ago about an unwavering commitment to quality in higher education. Yet as soon as there was a squeeze on the budget, rather than going back to redo the whole process, the easiest place was to take all the cuts that had to be done when the comptroller pulled the plug on revenues out of the projected higher education budget. Now I've gotten all kinds of assurances that that's going to be repaired. I understand that there was an earlier "don't cry until you're hurt." The hurt was immediate. The recruiting of top flight talent, which this state badly needs, has already been severely impacted by the sense that we are going to return to a period when there is not a sustained investment in creating technology.

The . . . I'd hold the floor for an hour, and I promise you I won't, but it seems to me that as we look at the objectives this Council can undertake, that we ought to focus on what are the things that are going on? What are the things that we ought to urge for acceleration for creating technology? And secondly, what are the things that we can do to accelerate the commercialization of it? Attracting other industries to the state all becomes part of that. When you break it apart, you can begin at least to get at areas that you can deal with. There has already been some good work done on the emerging technologies; what do you need to focus on?

But if you look at the breakdown by state, Texas has never had a significant percentage of the federal funding for research. We have never gone after it in any kind of targeted way. Much of the spin-offs that have helped create growth in creating technology have come from the industries that are defense contractors . . . are the ones that have been recipients of defense research funding. You know a lot of the start-ups have been from them. But there hasn't been any concentrated effort to look at accelerating the flow of federal research dollars in this state. We are talking about the higher education part. Clearly there are voids now as you look out. Shepherd's paper on the information age of the 90's. Where's the work that's ongoing in manufacturing technology? Where's the work that's ongoing to assist agriculture, to assist energy? The existing economy, the existing base economy to be modernized with their emerging technologies? We aren't going to have a . . . we aren't going to recover the damage that has already been done in the announcements of the projected cuts in higher education. They hopefully will be restored. But unless one can build in a long-term sense that we aren't going to government as usual—and I've had the graduate-level course in government as usual in my previous thirty-one years—that every time there's a problem that everyone takes an equal cut, because it is easier to administer . . . you can sort of deal with the squawks. So what we really have to deal with ultimately in looking at both these fields is priorities. What are the priorities? And where are the areas where we do not believe, even in a crunch, that the government can look to find immediate solutions to budget problems.

At this point, there was an awkward silence that lasted nearly 15 seconds. Inman had openly expressed discontent about the progress being made. He was known for his anger when systems were sluggish and he was impatient with a political system that makes it hard to leverage for decision making that supports the science and technology agenda. He was unhappy with the legislative allocation process that gives general, rather than specific, funds to support programs. His questions of persistence and character are followed by offering means for meeting the crisis: take risks, avoid safe decisions, deal with the squawks if you want to get anywhere.

### How to Force the Commitment

Another major problem was that of meeting immediate challenges, especially of convincing Texas leadership (mainly the legislature) of the need for commitment and funding for change. In a discussion that the science and technology initiative cannot begin to be successful with the current conditions of funding for education, the group affirms Inman's analysis that there was a commitment problem.

Inman then offers more support for this position by commenting on strategy that may or may not affect the Texas legislature.

[Inman:] The problem is that they see you as looking after your own constituency. And the heart of the problem is that there has not been a dialogue outside to attach the economic importance to the investment.

[George Mitchell:] That is why it is so important for this council to, for this group of people, who represent the finest educators and the finest industries in the state. We're the people who have to carry the ball. We're certain that you have a certain degree of credibility, as do newspapers, but they are not going to listen.

[Inman:] Well, for my colleagues in industry, if they've not been out scenting the same thing, then I would simply give you two data points that in the universities around the country, with great glee, the reports of what's happened to the news coverage have been widely circulated to the faculty to discourage them from taking any of the offers to come. I can give you a chapter in verse of some extraordinarily bright people who were poised to take some of the endowed chairs, who have now pulled back, not to do so. For the other note, I am being warmly congratulated by chancellors in California, Georgia, in Illinois, for bringing MCC to Texas because I have brought them money, in their judgment, on a scale that they have not had in years, as their states look at the impact. I would not like to be compared as an albatross here! [Inman's last remark brings out a chuckle in one of the other speakers and Inman seems to respond with disdain to that reaction; he adds:] Well, it's a little discouraging in the face of all of the assurances that were given.

After discussing strategy for communicating with the legislature, the council decided to appoint a smaller group of its members to polish a more refined statement of the position that Inman had written out on his legal pad during the meeting. This refined statement was communicated to the governor, the lieutenant governor, and the speaker of the house to show the policy direction the council supported. The statement developed from the meeting also served as the lead item in the Science and Technology Council's annual report the following September. The references to "boldness" and "risk taking" in these reports are oblique references to reviewing the educational system—which was later undertaken—and also getting the funding necessary to support educational excellence in Texas—which was positively addressed in 1987.

## Some Generalizations

### Group Characteristics

Generalizations from these analyses reflect what one might expect from high-level planning groups in the information age. As such councils are formed in other places at other times, we should anticipate certain characteristics to shape their performance.

*(1) The council acted very much as an "emergent organization,"* with all the ramifications. Rather than having a product on the shelf, and a collection of leaders who had the experience together of making that product successful, the council was a new organization with new members setting out on a newly charted direction. Science and Technology development was new to Texas. Although the council was chosen for their previous leadership experiences, and their personal histories of success, they were boarding a train that was laying track in front of it rather than moving on a completed track. Much of the analysis of their early experience is understood best as a group with "zero history," as an emergent rather than a stable organization.

*(2) The council had the advantages of a heterogeneous group.* The rich mix of governmental, academic, and business types selected to follow the *M-Form Society* model is widely accepted as what it takes to make a statewide economic development initiative happen, but there are strengths and weaknesses in the model. The strength comes from the group decision-making dictum that one must have a complex decision-making group to solve complex problems (Bavelas, 1968).

*(3) The council had the limitations of a temporary organization.* Fifteen years after Warren Bennis and Phil Slater suggested in *The Temporary Society* (1968) that future organizations would be characterized by groups of specialists coming together for short periods of time, accomplishing tasks, and disbanding to take on other projects, the council was organized to follow this model. The council met two days quarterly and although the subcommittees composed of council members were assigned to work on specific subtopics between meetings, membership was a limited, "part-time" involvement. There were long periods of time interspersed with other commitments and interests, which made each meeting a renewal. When there are three-month lags between meetings, major problems are more difficult to overcome.

*(4) The council struggled to find a leadership style to match the problem at hand.* Art Hansen used laissez-faire leadership with the council, which was effective on days when individuals like Cisneros were generating alternatives that gave direction. But when the problem called for joint action by the group, as was the case on February 14-15, the overly democratic style left too many spaces and called for a more active role in setting the agenda. Hansen did not display a personal vision and energy, which sometimes meant the meetings he led were sluggish. The chairman the following year, Mike Waterman, shaped the council with a more active version of what he thought it should be doing.

## The Special Role of
## Admiral Inman

Admiral Inman represented the role of an individual leader in shaping the direction of an organization, the way others showed respect and deference toward him and looked to him for policy guidance. Other observers at the meeting, when interviewed over a year later, still marvel at the uniqueness and boldness of his actions. He broke rules. He did not follow social roles. Technological leaders are usually seen as Young Turks who are dependent on champions above them to get their ideas accepted. Inman is a unique combination of technological knowledge and position power. It is rare to see both in the same persona.

Still, the meaning of data changes over time, and, by the time this chapter was written, Inman had announced his resignation from MCC. An article identifying an end to the microelectronics boom had been published in *Texas Monthly*, and the state was suffering through cheap oil and double-digit unemployment. State policy had adjusted and paired back—for the time being at least—its aspirations. Although microelectronics and high technology are still seen as a part of a diversifying Texas economy, ways of supporting the basic industries of oil, gas, and agriculture are returning to a central position on the agenda. During the year in which the February 14-15 took place, the legislature did lift the hiring freeze, limit the budget cut to 2%, fund a $35-million dollar research pool, and pass a sales tax increase and a series of legislative programs to streamline a bureaucracy that had been a roadblock to research and commercialization of scientific findings. The policy statements by the council had helped to foster these changes, but at best these actions were damage control rather than the progress for which the council had hoped.

Admiral Inman resigned from the Science and Technology council in its second year. Current governor, William Clements, who both preceded and succeeded Mark White, and whose "Texas 2000" report had suggested a science and technology council, did not choose to continue with a council. Nor is there much talk of "the commitment."

# PART IV

# *Attitudes Toward Change*

# 9

# Modeling Change from Survey Data

### JAMES DYER
### DON HAYNES

*In a democracy, attempts at major socioeconomic change will have to be consonant with the attitudes of the large bulk of the population. Put into research terms, it is important to study the readiness of a particular population for change in a state or national economy, and how all of such change fits within the general cultural context. The present study capitalizes upon the availability of several decades of survey data obtained from the Texas population, making it possible to create a longitudinal picture of change. One of the questions stimulating the research report in this chapter was the degree to which change over this period in Texas has positioned the population as ready for an information society-type existence. James Dyer and Don Haynes present just such an analysis in this chapter, including the ideas for a preliminary model of the types of demographic and attitudinal variables that may identify persons who are candidates for success in an information society. James Dyer is a political scientist at Texas A&M and for the last several years has directed the Texas Poll, a quarterly survey of the population of Texas. His associate, Don Haynes has served as a faculty member at Texas A&M and a research associate on the poll.*

## New Perceptions or Myths?

The common perception is that Texas has undergone profound social, economic, and political change in the past 20 years. Symbolically, the Texas of Hud and Jett Rink has given way to the Texas of J. R.

Ewing and Ross Perot. The underlying sociocultural conditions that produced the extreme individualism and parochialism of a Jett Rink have been superseded by a sociocultural system that produces the corporate, high-tech, and more mainstream values of contemporary heroes. At least this is the conventional wisdom.

But to what extent does the reality of social, economic, and political change conform to the mythology? Has a new, more modern Texas emerged? And, if so, to what extent does the new Texas retain the cultural ties to its recent past?

These are the kinds of questions we want to address in this chapter. Specifically, we explore the changing attitudes of Texans in recent decades. We are particularly concerned with looking at the changes in attitudes that are important to the political, economic, and social life of the state both in terms of understanding the present, and in terms of what they portend for the future.

In order to study Texas attitudes, we make use of survey data and use comparisons over time, when such data are available. The most direct way to measure change is to look at shifts in responses to the same or similar questions. A less direct way to look at attitudes so that we can make inferences about change is to compare data from Texas with data from the rest of the United States. There is a general argument that through migration and as the state has developed economically and socially, attitudes tend to homogenize with the rest of the country. By looking at attitudes and observing which are similar to those in the rest of the country and which remain different, we can gain an idea as to the nature of the change that may have or may yet take place.

Texas is fortunate to have an archive of survey data that dates back into the 1950s. Belden and Associates conducted the Texas Poll from the 1950s through the mid-1970s. Beginning at the end of 1983, Harte-Hanks Communication has sponsored a quarterly survey of 1000 Texans conducted by the Public Policy Resources Laboratory at Texas A&M University. This survey is also called the Texas Poll. These two sets of surveys provided a way of looking at change in Texas as measured by responses to hundreds of questions over the years. The information goes well beyond that available from the U.S. census and from other aggregate statistics. It reflects the systematically collected responses of cross sections of Texans for a long period of time.

In this chapter we look at four major areas in which change has occurred: economic, political, racial/ethnic relations, and religious and moral attitudes. We observe the forces underlying these changes:

migration, historical events, and evolutionary development. A major conclusion is that in many ways public sentiment in Texas has changed from being different from national opinion to tracking national opinion closely. And yet, in some areas, Texans remain distinctive.

## Dimensions of Change

### Social Attitudes

Probably the most significant social attitudinal change that we have observed in Texas has been the change in attitudes of Whites toward Blacks. Less than 20 years ago, the majority or near majority of Whites disapproved of interaction with Blacks in a variety of settings. Today, there is nearly universal acceptance in most of these settings. Although we must suspect that the change in willingness to agree verbally with racial integration outdistances actual behavior, it still shows a major shift.

In 1968, the Texas Poll conducted by Belden and Associates asked a series of questions of "Whites" about involvement with "Negroes." We adapted the questions used in that earlier survey. We made it easier to ask the questions on the telephone, eliminating several categories of activities that seemed less important or redundant, and asking about "having a (Black) as a close relative by marriage" and "having as president," which were not asked in the earlier survey. We also collapsed the original 20-point numeric scale to a four-answer response: "accept completely, accept somewhat, reject somewhat, and reject completely."

The percentage who said they accepted each of the situations is presented in Figure 9.1. A person is counted as accepting if he or she responds "accepts completely" or "accepts somewhat" on the current questions or is on the positive side of the 1968 scale. Although the level of acceptance is high, there is variation among the items. The two areas in which there is the least acceptance is having a Black as a close relative by marriage, and, although considerably more acceptable, having a Black president. The marriage question is a traditional indicator of group acceptance. The continued reluctance to accept this suggests that a wide social gap still remains.

In order to continue the analysis of the responses to these questions, we coded "completely reject" as a −2, "reject somewhat" as a −1, "don't know" (a volunteered response) as a 0, "accept somewhat" as a 1, and

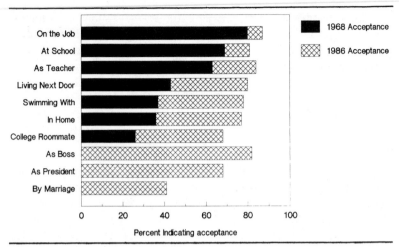

Figure 9.1    Black Acceptance: 1968 and 1986
NOTE:    Bars represent total percentage in all categories of response indicating acceptance of Blacks in the situation. Anglos and Hispanics are combined. (Note that an earlier draft of this chapter included only Anglos for 1986.)

"accept completely" as a 2. Thus, the higher the score, the greater the acceptance. To create an overall measure of social acceptance, we averaged each person's responses over all 10 items. A principal components factor analysis of the items indicated that they form a single dimension, suggesting that such a combined measure is appropriate.

In Table 9.1, we display the differences of means by the categories of the following variables: income, education, whether a newcomer to the state, and age. An analysis of variance of these factors shows that except for income, each shows a statistically significant relationship to social acceptance controlling for the others. Acceptance increases the younger the person is, the better educated, and the higher the income. (Although the latter is probably spuriously related because of education.) Those not being born in Texas are more accepting of Blacks as well.

Although we cannot use the data to determine the cause of the change, we can see from this analysis of present attitudes where the change is likely to have occurred. The state has become better educated, increasing the numbers of accepting people. Newcomers are more tolerant and the influx of new residents has undoubtedly made a difference. Finally, the age difference suggests a generational change. Those growing up in integrated schools and workplaces are more accepting. Without data on cohorts, however, we cannot rule out life cycle changes rather than generational differences as the reason for the observed age differences. That is, life cycle changes would relate

TABLE 9.1

Social Acceptance of Blacks by Anglos Within
Categories of Education, Income, Age, and Birthplace

|  | Mean Acceptance* | N |
|---|---|---|
| **Education** | | |
| Less than high school | .80 | 82 |
| High school graduate | 1.28 | 367 |
| College graduate | 1.46 | 192 |
| **Income** | | |
| Less than $10,000 | .83 | 70 |
| $10,000-$30,000 | 1.23 | 264 |
| Over $30,000 | 1.41 | 307 |
| **Age** | | |
| 18-29 | 1.45 | 146 |
| 30-44 | 1.41 | 226 |
| 45-61 | 1.21 | 147 |
| 62- | .86 | 122 |
| **Birthplace** | | |
| Newcomer | 1.59 | 111 |
| Texas born | 1.21 | 530 |

*−2 = "completely reject"; +2 = "accept completely."

declining acceptance to an individual's getting older than to a socializing experience of the era in which he or she grew up. We suspect that at least some of the age differences are because of generational change.

The change in racial attitudes is important and will remain important as Texas continues to modernize. The prospects look reasonably good for continued increase in acceptance. As older cohorts die and are replaced by the more tolerant generations, and as the general level of education increases, we can expect further increases in acceptance.

## The Political Party System

Probably the most obvious way in which political change has occurred in Texas has been through changes in the party system. Texas has moved from a one-party state dominated by the Democratic party, to a state in which the Republican party plays an increasingly large role. That change has taken place is demonstrated by the increasing tendency of Republicans to win in the Texas races for the president, senatorial seats, house seats, and governor. Perhaps more important, Republicans are winning or making closer races in less significant offices, including those at the local level. This factor reflects a change in the organizational

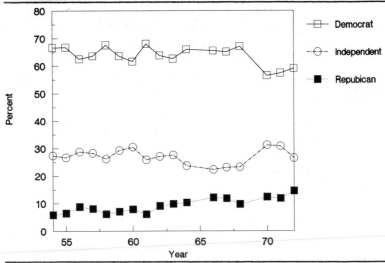

Figure 9.2    Party Identification in Texas: 1954 to 1972
SOURCE:    Belden Poll.

status of the Republican party, but also a change in the identification by voters with the party, a change that makes them willing to support the party candidate even without a special incentive.

It is the shift in the attitudes of the public that interests us here. Partisan alignment in the electorate is reflected in the identification of individuals with each of the parties. In answer to the question "Do you tend to think of yourself as a Democrat, Republican, an Independent, or what?," people indicate a basic orientation toward the party that has been found to be relatively stable. This is an important determinant of behavior, particularly in low saliency elections. Partisan identification provides a predisposition to vote for candidates of the party and it also provides a basis for screening information so that partisans tend to receive information reinforcing their partisan choices.

What we have seen in Texas has been a major shift toward the Republican party. In Figure 9.2, we plot the data from the Belden Texas Poll from the 1950s into the 1970s. In Figure 9.3, we plot the same data from the beginning of the Harte-Hanks, Public Policy Resources Laboratory (PPRL) Texas Poll beginning early in 1984. There was some erosion of Democratic party identification and growth in Republican identification between 1952 and 1972. Democrats had declined from 66% to 57% and Republicans increased from 6% to 14%. Between then

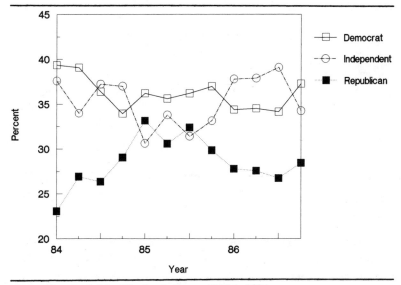

Figure 9.3    Party Identification in Texas: 1984 to 1986

and the first Harte-Hanks, PPRL Texas Poll, the proportion of
Democrats dropped to 39% and Republicans increased to 23%. What
happened during fall 1984 was dramatic. Republican strength grew until
it was only several percentage points away from the Democratic
strength.

This partisan division stayed relatively constant throughout 1985, a
stability we interpreted as supporting the argument that a lasting
realignment of partisanship had taken place. Recent changes, however,
cast some doubt on that interpretation. Beginning in the winter quarter
of 1986, Republican strength resided somewhat, the number of inde-
pendents rose, and there was little change among the Democrats.
Currently, the trend seems unclear, but it looks more now like a
dealignment has occurred, the weakening or sundering of old party ties
in favor of independence, rather than a realignment where new party
identifications are made relatively permanently.

In either case, the change is important. Democratic strength has
declined and Republican strength has increased greatly since the early
1970s and the change has continued into the present period.

The primary causes of this change are due to the effects of new
migrants and the shifting orientation of younger voters. Aggregating the
data between October 1984 and October 1985 to provide a large sample

TABLE 9.2
Logit Analysis Explaining Party Identification in Texas:
Chi-Square Results

| Source | Degrees of Freedom | Chi-Square | Probability |
|---|---|---|---|
| Intercept | 1 | 85.15 | 0.0001 |
| Education | 2 | 1.54 | 0.4627 |
| Income | 2 | 52.79 | 0.0001 |
| Ethnicity | 2 | 121.44 | 0.0001 |
| Age | 1 | 113.00 | 0.0001 |
| Residency | 1 | 26.17 | 0.0001 |
| Educ-ethnic interaction | 4 | 18.63 | 0.0009 |
| Ideology | 2 | 160.95 | 0.0001 |
| (Likelihood ratio) | 254 | 255.01 | 0.1650 |

during a time in which the partisan division was relatively stable, we looked at the party distribution within age groups. The youngest age group (18-29) was the most Republican (39% Republican to 28% Democrat). The oldest group (over 62) was the most Democratic (49% Democratic to 26% Republican). Using the same aggregate sample, we found that those living here less than 10 years were most Republican (39% Republican to 24% Democrat). The lifetime Texans were the most Democratic (41% Democratic to 27% Republican).

On the summer Texas Poll in 1985, we asked people to report previous party affiliation, if any. From these results, we could look at the characteristics of those who had changed. The two biggest shifts were the self-identified conservative Republicans shifting from the Democratic party to the Republican party (31% shifted), and the Anglo Democrats shifting to the Republican party (26% shifted).

To provide a multivariate analysis of party identification, we used a logit statistical model to predict party identification with education, income, ethnicity, self-identified ideology, age, and place of birth. The analysis is presented in Tables 9.2 and 9.3. The analysis indicates that all of the factors except education contributed to the explanation of party identification. In relative terms, ideology, ethnicity, and age are most important. Income and place of birth were less important but still significant.

Although it is beyond this chapter to discuss the impact that the partisan shift might have, we can briefly suggest some changes. The shift from a one-party dominant system to one in which significant competition occurs has implications not only for the electoral process, but also

TABLE 9.3
Logit Analysis Explaining Party Identification in Texas:
Parameter Estimates

| Independent Variable | Parameter Estimate | Standard Error |
|---|---|---|
| Income | | |
| Low | −0.48 | .096 |
| Medium | −0.07 | .067 |
| High | −0.55 (derived) | |
| Ethnicity | | |
| Anglo | 1.27 | .116 |
| Black | −1.37 | .192 |
| Hispanic | −0.10 (derived) | |
| Ideology | | |
| Liberal | −0.78 | .084 |
| Moderate | −0.09 | .065 |
| Conservative | 0.87 (derived) | |
| Age | | |
| Younger | 0.59 | .055 |
| Older | −0.59 (derived) | |
| Residency | | |
| Newcomer | 0.24 | .048 |
| Native | −0.24 (derived) | |

for the way in which policymaking proceeds in government. For elections, one of the implications is that the importance of the primary has declined while the importance of the general election has increased. For policymaking, the parties will become more important in the internal organization of the legislative houses. Also the rise in importance of party competition may provide a force to make the party organizations more cohesive, with implications for competition over policy and the way in which legislative leadership and committees are chosen. Furthermore, there is some evidence that the shift might have an impact on representation. Interests that do not find expression in a one-party system may find it in a competitive system.

To some extent, the change in partisanship in Texas is a reflection of changes that are going on generally in the South and the remainder of the United States. Although there is uncertainty as to whether we are seeing a temporary change, a dealignment, or a true realignment, there is evidence of widespread change.

Perhaps as important as party competition is the change in the composition of the Democratic party in Texas. Once conservative with a liberal wing in the distinct minority, the Democratic party is now nearly evenly split between liberal and conservative interests. About a quarter of the party earns above $30,000; a quarter less than $10,000; and the remainder in the middle. About a quarter say they are liberal, and a quarter say they are conservative, with the remainder in the middle. Of the Democratic party identifiers, 40% are either Black or Hispanic, two traditional sources of Democratic strength whose relative importance has grown with the defection of Anglos to the Republican party.

The composition of the Democratic party identifiers can be expected to have an impact on the primary elections and on the organizational structures of the party. With the increasing strength of the minority factions of the party, the possibility of conflict over policy directions of the party may be increased. Holding the coalition together may prove to be a problem. Additionally the increasing domination of the more liberal part of the party may reduce the party's appeal to the more conservative Texas electorate as a whole.

Although the ultimate impact of the partisan shift is not clear, it is a major feature of the change in attitudes of Texans that will undoubtedly make Texas politics much different in the future decades than it has been in the past decades.

## Other Political Issues

In fall 1985, we asked a series of questions about trust in government, whether government pays attention to people, whether government wastes money, and whether the government or the individual should be responsible for maintaining a decent standard of living. These reflect some of the basic issues that identify an individual's view of government and his or her relationship to it. Here we do not have comparative data with an earlier period of time, but we do have comparative national data.

What we find is consistent with the description of Texas as a traditionalist-individualist culture. In a traditionalist political culture, there is the acceptance of an elitist social order that controls the political system. We find Texas as "trusting" of government as people are nationally. As can be seen in Table 9.4, the distribution of responses to how often a person feels they can trust government is nearly identical between Texas and the nation. At the same time, 30% of Texans think government does not pay much attention to them, compared to only 10% in the national sample. Texans fit the traditionalist culture to the extent that they trust government, even though they are less likely to think it pays attention to them.

TABLE 9.4
Texas-National Comparisons on Basic Political Attitudes
(in percentages)

| | Texas[a] | National[b] |
|---|---|---|
| Trust in government | | |
| Trust none of time | 3 | 1 |
| Some of the time | 48 | 45 |
| Most of the time | 38 | 34 |
| Almost always | 7 | 3 |
| Government pays attention | | |
| Not much | 30 | 10 |
| Some | 48 | 32 |
| A good deal | 18 | 33 |
| Provide standard of living | | |
| Individual | 65 | 42 |
| Both | 12 | 32 |
| Government | 18 | 26 |

NOTE: The percentages total to less than 100% because the don't knows were omitted.
a. Data are from the fall 1985 Texas Poll.
b. Data are from the 1984 Presidential Election Survey conducted by the Center for Political Studies, University of Michigan, October 1984.

The individualist culture is clearly reflected in the responses to the question as to whether it should be the government's responsibility to provide a decent standard of living or whether it should be up to the individual—65% of Texans say the individual, compared to 42% of the national sample.

On the other hand, the image of the typical Texan as some kind of reckless libertarian does not seem to be supported in other data. In several different contexts, Texans have been accepting of the need for increases in taxes. They express support for government activity designed to promote economic development and the infrastructure for such development. There is evidence that they want and expect good quality-of-government services. There is no evidence of a "low tax over everything else" mentality that is sometimes depicted.

## Religion and Moral Issues

Attitudes on religious and moral issues have changed some in Texas, but this is an area in which Texas is still distinctive from the rest of the nation in a number of ways. In spring 1985, we asked Texans if they had ever "tried to encourage someone to believe in Jesus Christ or accept him as his or her savior." Texas were nearly 20 percentage points more likely to say they had evangelized than a national survey taken in 1980 (64% in Texas, 45% in a Gallup poll). It is interesting that almost the exact same percentage indicated in 1957 that they had asked someone to visit a church (66%). There is a similar pattern on attendance. Nationally, one-third reported going to church at least once a week; in Texas, 44% say they do. Nationally, 20% say they go to church less than once a year, only 11% say they do in Texas.

Data from a Belden Texas Poll from 1957 indicated that 65% attended church "every week" or "almost every week." In 1968, 48% said they went to church "about every week." This indicates considerable change in the 1960s, but little if any change from the present where 48% responded "nearly every week," "every week," or "several times a week."

Age differences and the length of time in Texas indicates that some of the same forces for change may be working in this area that are operating in other areas—52% of lifetime residents said that they attend church at least once a week, while only 40% of those living here 10 years or less do. Younger Texans are more likely to report attending church, although this is undoubtedly due at least in part to life cycle changes as it is to generational differences.

Looking at political issues that have moral implications, we find evidence that Texans react somewhat more moralistically than others. An interesting example is paramutual gambling in horse races, an issue that was asked about in the 1960s as well as the present. In winter 1985, we found that 62% favored local option paramutual horse racing. This is a 10-point shift from a Belden Texas poll done in 1968, when only 52% favored it.

On a related issue, we find that in 1964 only 39% favored a lottery, while in 1985, 71% said they favored. (The questions were asked differently and this probably exaggerates the change. The 1985 question was asked more clearly in the context of raising money in some way other than increasing traditional taxes.)

Drinking is another area that moral issues become involved in policy. Liquor by the drink and the maintenance of dry areas was a central issue on the agenda during the time of the Belden Texas Poll, but drinking has not been an issue in recent times. It is evidence that a change in attitudes has taken place and that there is no serious effort made to limit alcohol consumption on a widespread basis. Prohibition in Texas has disappeared with the exception of a few local areas.

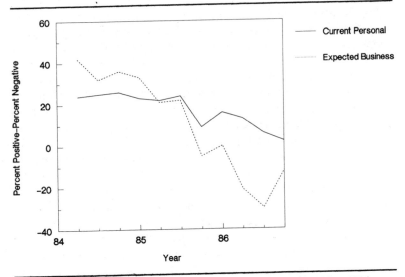

Figure 9.4    Texas Personal and Business Economic Confidence: 1984 to 1986

## The Economy

We have been measuring Texans' response to the economy since near the beginning of the Harte-Hanks, PPRL Texas Poll, in winter 1984. As would be expected, attitudes reflect the boom-bust changes that have occurred during this time. In Figure 9.4, we plot an index computed by subtracting the percentage negative from the percentage positive. The perception of how well off you were a year ago remained fairly stable through the summer of 1985. It plummeted in the fall, recovered a little in winter 1985, then began a decline that continued through the most recent survey. Even more precipitous a decline is seen in the index based on the responses to the question on business conditions during the next 12 months. Both fluctuate with the rise and fall of the Texas economy, but respondents are more pessimistic about the future business economy than they are their own economic position. On another question reflecting well-being, when asked to rate Texas as a place to live, 67% said excellent in winter 1984, which dropped 16 points to 51% in winter 1986.

What these figures will ultimately mean is not clear. An important question is the extent to which the malaise represented by these numbers is a momentary reaction to the economy that will quickly change once the situation improves, or will have consequences extending beyond economic recovery. Undoubtedly, the reaction to the economy had much to do with the replacement of Governor White with Governor Clements. What is not clear is whether the figures represent an underlying pessimism and loss of confidence that will affect the future of the Texas development. Speculating somewhat, the change of conditions for Texas could have been especially painful because previously things were going so well here while the remainder of the country was doing poorly. There was a widespread feeling reflected in public statements that something was being done right in Texas that was not being done in the rest of the country. The realization that much of the success was not related to some superiority could undermine collective self-confidence. On the other hand, perhaps a more realistic view of the world will prove useful to public reactions to policy issues in the future.

### Attitudes of the New Texas

Social scientists have speculated on the impact of underlying cultural values on the type of politics associated with certain areas. Daniel Elazar (1984), for instance, argues that three principal subcultures, a moralistic, an individualistic, and a traditionalist, defined by underling attitudes toward politics and society, have been instrumental in shaping the political culture of the United States. Elazar's ideas provide us with a way of understanding the types of changes that have taken place in Texas and speculate on the future.

Moralistic subculture, descended from early Puritans and later-arriving Scandinavians, places great emphasis on the promotion of the common good. Persons and organizations are evaluated in accordance to their role in securing collectively held benefits. Government is expected to be actively engaged in the production of collective benefits. Moralists place a high premium on public service as opposed to individual gain. Individualists, on the other hand, place high value on limiting government functions in a way that allows the pursuit of private gain. Politics is a business untainted by notions of common goals and relegated to professionals with wide latitude to govern. Elazar argues that this individualistic subculture arose primarily from the German and non-Puritan English settlers migrating from the East coast.

Last, Elazar defines a traditionalist subculture that views politics as the purview of an elitist, precommercial class. The primary function of the political class was to preserve the underlying social order partly by discouraging active participation by nonelites when necessary. The roots of the traditionalist subculture were found in the plantation economy of the old South and were based on an economic and political elite formed long before the Civil War and whose influence survived long past Reconstruction.

Based on analyses conducted 20 years ago, Texas was viewed as a combination of individualistic and traditionalist political cultures. Texas, Elazar (1984, p. 133) argues, "has tended to adopt individualistic elements as its traditional social bases have eroded." Historically, then, the pattern of social change has been one of an individualist culture competing with the traditionalist.

For Elazar, the single greatest factor in producing cultural dynamism has been migration, but clearly economic modernization has been an important factor as well. The early conflicts between traditionalist and individualist were produced in part by the early migration from the upper South. Most of these migrants had been excluded from the plantation culture of the tidewater, and in Texas they interacted with a traditionalist culture that had been reinforced both by the Spanish and Catholic heritage in Texas and by the compliance of Blacks. The result was a dynamic intermingling of political ideas and values that reinforced limited and often-times exclusionary politics.

But the analyses we have presented suggest that previous patterns are changing, a large part of the change fueled by the influx of migrants in the last decade and changes in the economic structure of the state. Some of the factors that underlie these changes are a breakdown in cultural barriers between ethnic groups. This increases competition between political elites represented by changes both within and between parties, and changes in political attitudes and ethical values. One of the consequences is that, in Elazar's terms, a moralist perspective— represented by attitudes toward taxation and spending on the one hand, and by the increasing complexity of political organizations on the other, which asks for a larger role for public officials in guiding future changes—has been previous patterns. For the new Texas, this means assuming more responsibility for managing the process of change rather than allowing change to be defined by the interaction of individualists.

If our analyses is correct, then Texas is at once becoming more like the political mainstream of the United States on some dimensions, but retaining a distinctly Texas air. For the future, this portends more conflict over the basic values of society and directions of government, rather than less.

# 10

# Gauging Public Attitudes Toward Science and Technology

## JAMES DYER
## FREDERICK WILLIAMS
## DON HAYNES

*Because science and technology will play an ever-increasing role as Texas makes a transition to an information-based economy, it is important to understand the underlying public attitudes toward these concepts. Using a survey of Texans conducted by the Texas Poll, this report both describes the distribution of attitudes in Texas and explores reasons why certain people adopt positive or negative attitudes toward science and technology. James Dyer and Don Haynes were mentioned in the preceding chapter; again Dyer directs the Texas Poll, and both are faculty members at Texas A&M University. Frederick Williams is director of the Center for Research on Communication Technology and Society at the University of Texas at Austin, and was the originator of the New Texas Project that spawned many of these studies.*

## Measuring Attitudes
## Toward Science

The study of public attitudes about science and technology is not a new undertaking. In the post-World War II years, there have been systematic surveys undertaken in Western Europe (Rabier and Inglehardt, 1977, 1978; Inglehardt, 1977) as well as in the United States (Pion, George, and Lipsey, 1981; Etzioni and Nunn, 1974; LaPorte and

191

Metlay, 1975; Marshall, 1979; Yankelovich, 1982). The rationale underlying such studies is generally as follows. A positive attitude about science and technology is a necessary value in the cultural and political milieu of a nation undergoing modernization. Not only must political attitudes support leaders favoring the advancement of science but public expenditures for such advancements must be made. Moreover, in the sense of Daniel Bell's (1976) postindustrial society, increasing numbers of individuals will be employed in a techno-economic system dependent on advances in science and technology. In the largest view, therefore, a gauge of a population's attitudes about science and technology is in part a measure of their commitment to modernization.

The researchers are well aware of important distinctions between science being a way-of-knowing and technology being a tool or tactic. But in the general public, these concepts are often part of a global attitude, especially in regard to modernization. We were especially interested in exploring for factors related to these public attitudes. What role is played in the formation of this attitude by education, occupation, or even personal or professional involvement with technologies?

Finally, there is the question of who will enjoy the benefits of change in a techno-economic system. Relative to employing the advantages of science and technology, are some individuals "users" while others are being "used"? Does this current mode of modernization have its winners and losers?

These questions were the motive for a survey of public opinion in Texas regarding individuals' sense of change, attitudes about science and technology, and the relationship of these attitudes to the sense of change. There was also an attempt to study individuals' attitudes about their own knowledge of science and technology, as well as involvement with technologies, particularly information technologies such as use of computers.

### The Survey

#### Questions

In late July and early August 1986, the Texas Poll asked approximately 1000 Texans how much they thought peoples' lives had changed since 1960 and whether that change was for the better or worse. Additionally, they were asked a cluster of questions about the role of science and technology relative to society, as well as a question about their own knowledge of science. These questions are given verbatim in the Appendix to this chapter.

After responses to the questions were evaluated using usual survey analysis procedures, we next created several indices to serve as a basis for a more detailed statistical model of the relations between characteristics of individuals and attitudes toward science and technology.

**Plan for Analyses**

The analysis proceeds in four parts. First, we present a descriptive analysis of public responses to questions. Second, we describe how indices representing level of involvement, perceived knowledge, attitudes, and evaluation were created, and describe the distribution of each. Third, we present a series of regression analyses using each of the variables as dependent variables. Fourth, we present a regression analysis of overall evaluation of change using the first three indices as independent variables along with demographic characteristics.

## Basic Attitudes

### Change

Figure 10.1 shows that about 77% of the sample felt that their lives had changed a great deal in the last 25 years. Only about 6% viewed their lives as static. Moreover, as shown in Figure 10.2, about 70% of those offering an evaluation viewed the changes as making their lives better and about 30% felt their lives had gotten worse.

The latter groups cite different reasons for their evaluations. Bivariate analysis (not shown) of evaluations with a question about the reason for their evaluation shows that those who say their lives have gotten better also cite economic and technological reasons for their evaluation, while those who say that their lives have gotten worse tend to cite moral reasons. Simple bivariate analyses also suggest that demographic variables related to responses to these questions are occupation, income, and education.

### Science and Technology

Again, the Texas Poll asked individuals whether they agreed or disagreed with a series of questions about the role of technology in

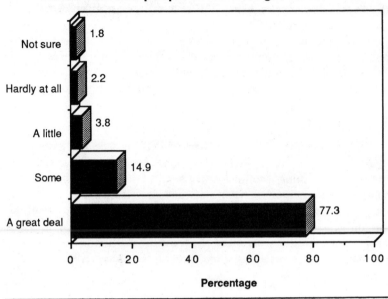

Figure 10.1   Attitudes About How Much Life Has Changed

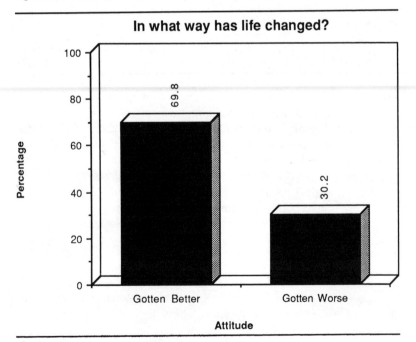

Figure 10.2   Attitudes About the Quality of Change

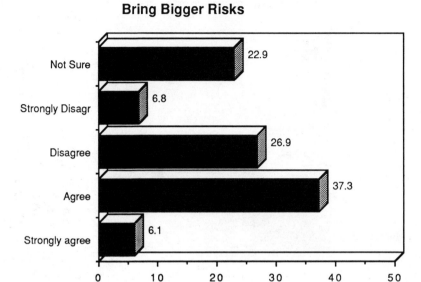

Figure 10.3    Does Science Bring Bigger Risks?

society. Respondents were asked whether they thought that science and technology brought bigger risks for society (Figure 10.3), whether science and technology had produced more and better jobs (Figure 10.4), whether computers benefited society (Figure 10.5), and whether they felt that they were knowledgeable about science and technology (Figure 10.6).

In general, although respondents were favorably disposed toward science and technology, they thought that they posed risks for society. Some 44% felt that science and technology produced bigger risks for society and 34% felt that it did not. About 23% were unsure about the risks associated with science and technology.

Some 75%, however, felt that despite the possibility of extra risks, science and technology produced more and better jobs. Only 16% gave a negative response to the question. Similarly, 76% thought that the use of computers benefited society. In both cases, respondents showed a much lower degree of uncertainty about concrete benefits. About 52% of the sample felt they knew very little about science while about 41% disagreed with the statement.

In general, then, Texans view concrete applications of technology

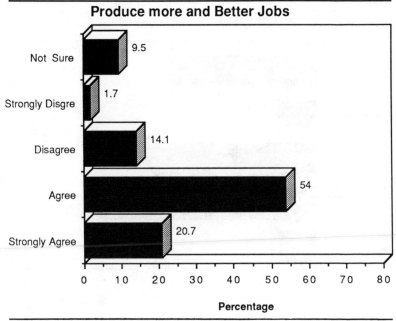

Figure 10.4   Does Science Produce More and Better Jobs?

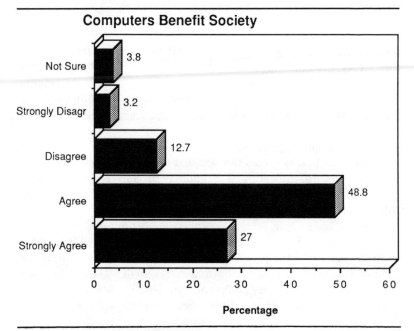

Figure 10.5   Computers Benefit Society?

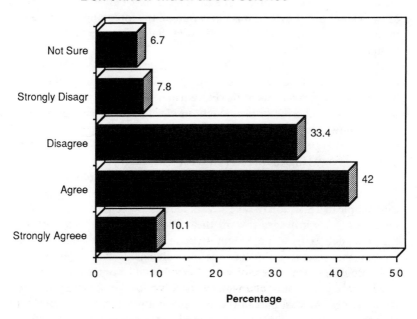

**Don't know much about science**

Figure 10.6    How Much Do You Know About Science?

favorably, agreeing that computers benefit society and that more and better jobs have been produced. On the other hand, when asked questions that might be understood to be tapping an evaluation of the larger role of science and technology in society, Texas were more uncertain and felt less equipped to deal effectively with those changes.

## *Relations Among Attitudes, Involvement, Knowledge, and Evaluation*

### Rationale

What contributes to attitudes and evaluations related to science and technology? Our exploratory model proposes two interacting lines of influence: For one, attitudes, involvement, and knowledge are inter-actively related. The level of knowledge about science conditions one's attitudes toward science, and both, in turn, are a product of involvement with science and technology. Conversely, evaluations and attitudes can condition the level of one's involvement with science. That is, the relation can work both ways. Individuals who are involved with technology are likely to have a greater range of experience from which to draw evaluations. Further, it is likely that all the foregoing are, in part, influenced by demographic characteristics that define one's place in the techno-economic system.

Recent empirical evidence suggests social factors that help structure attitudes toward science and technology. Two of the most important have been income and education (Etzioni and Nunn, 1974). Age has also been argued to be a factor in evaluations of science and technology but exactly how age conditions attitudes has been subject to dispute. Contrary to arguments that the young are more skeptical about science and technology (Inglehardt, 1977), most U.S. surveys have found that young people are more positive toward science and technology (Etzioni and Nunn, 1974; Pion, George, and Lipsey, 1981). Other studies suggest that people in a position to take advantage of new technologies develop more favorable attitudes toward them (Winner, 1977). This suggests that occupation is an important structuring variable as well. Other factors that might influence one's involvement with science and technology are race and sex. Minority groups and women are, because of cultural conditioning, often not in a position to take advantage of new technologies. At least part of the available empirical evidence suggests that one's position in the techno-economic system accounts for attitudes toward science and technology. In the following, we will use variables that we think give indications of this positioning.

Again, our model suggests that an individual's evaluation of science and technology are a product of both his or her place in the techno-economic system and the levels of involvement and perceived knowledge about the system. Further, as discussed at the outset of this report, we may be able to use this model to describe stratification of individuals in terms of their locations and evaluations within a techno-economic hierarchy—that is, the users versus the used, or winners and losers. As related with attitudes toward, and uses of, science and technology, demographic characteristics may imply whether selected individuals are winners versus losers in this process of techno-economic change. Ethnographers (e.g., Pelto and Pertti, 1973) have identified a pattern of reaction to the introduction of new technologies into a traditional culture. They argue that the evaluation of change is determined by whether one is in a position to take personal advantage of the new technologies. Winners use new technology to advantage; losers cannot. Each is a product of one's strategic location with the socioeconomic hierarchy. We expect that similar patterns will be observed in the current process of techno-economic change in Texas.

## Construction of Variables

Four variables were constructed for the poll data to reflect the attitudes, evaluation, involvement, and knowledge components of the model. Their construction is summarized as follows.

*Attitudes*: The index of attitudes toward technology was created by summing the positive responses for the questions about risks, jobs, and benefits of computers. Disagreement was taken as a positive response for risk, and agreement for jobs and benefits. Each positive response was assigned a 1, all other responses were assigned a 0. Summation yielded an index ranging from 0, representing the least positive attitude toward science and technology, to 3, representing the most positive evaluation of science and technology. A factor analysis of the three questions suggested that there was indeed a single underlying dimension structuring responses.

*Involvement*: The index of involvement was created using a series of additional questions from the Texas Poll that asked whether respondents used computers at work and at home. If the response was yes, respondents were scored a 1, otherwise, they were scored a 0. Summation yielded an index ranging from 0, representing the least involvement with technology, to 2, representing the highest level of involvement.

*Knowledge*: The variable representing level of knowledge about science and technology was created by recoding the question about scientific knowledge. The transformation created an index ranging from 0, representing both lack of knowledge and high uncertainty, to 5 representing high levels of knowledge.

*Evaluation*: The evaluative index was created by transforming the original evaluation question to 0 and 1, with 1 representing an evaluation of "better."

## Prediction of Involvement, Attitudes, and Knowledge

The first step in analysis was to use each of the indices as a dependent variable and to use other indices and the demographic variables as independent variables. Three separate regression equations were calculated. To facilitate comparisons between and within models, standardized regression coefficients were used.

In general, the amount of variation explained by each of the equations was not high, ranging from about .26 for level of involvement, to .14 for perceived knowledge about science.

For level of involvement with science and technology, each of the regression coefficients were in the expected direction and all except gender were statistically significant at the .05 level. The analysis shows that the greatest contributing factor to level of involvement with science and technology is level of income. Persons with higher levels of income were likely to be more involved with science and technology. This is not surprising, as the measurement of involvement employed indicators of use of costly items such as home computers. Only about 7% of the population scored the maximum value, claiming possession of the technologies. The slope for occupation (.15), a dummy variable dividing the sample into professionals and administrators, and others, bolsters this because they are more likely to be involved with computers in some way on the job. Education, as well, figures more prominently than other variables (.10).

Attitudes play a significant and independent role in level of involve- ment (.13) suggesting, it would seem, mutual conditioning rather than causation. Positive attitudes result from involvement and, it seems likely, that positive attitudes toward science and technology increase the likelihood of employing sophisticated technologies in the home. Neither gender or race figured prominently in the model.

In determining level of perceived knowledge about science and technology, four variables were significant at the .05 level—involvement, attitudes, education, and gender. The strongest relationship was between perceived knowledge and education (.19), followed closely by technological attitudes (.13) and involvement (.11). The slope for gender suggests some slight but significant gender differences with males reporting themselves to be more knowledgeable about science and technology.

As could be assumed for relations with education, college graduates are more exposed to science and technology courses and, therefore, are more likely to possess more knowledge about science and technology. The strong relationship between attitudes and perceived knowledge and between involvement and perceived knowledge conforms to our notions that these are interactively related and mutually conditioned. Again, because of the way these interact, we want to stress interdependence rather than causation.

The interesting finding here is the relative strength of the gender variable (.08) compared to its insignificance in the previous model. After controlling for education, occupation, and involvement with science and technology, real differences in perceived knowledge remain between males and females. Changes in the composition of the work force and the introduction of new technologies into the home have not washed out these differences. While the previous model shows that gender differences in the level of involvement disappear with cultural changes, this model indicates that culturally conditioned differences linger. Given the role of education, we can speculate that the difference is the result of continuing distinctions in the way that males and females are tracked through the education system.

Of special interest to us was the equation predicting attitudes about science. All the regression coefficients were in the expected direction. All except income, occupation, and a dummy variable for Hispanics were significant at the .05 level. The strongest variable was involvement (.15), followed closely by education (.13), and perceived knowledge (.12). Occupation seemed to be related, but fell just outside the bounds of significance.

The findings on the first three variables help confirm our expectation that attitudes toward technology were conditioned by whether one was a user or not. Involvement, education, and perceived knowledge help determine one's status in the techno-economic system and, in turn, this conditions one's evaluation of science and technology. Noteworthy is that income plays no significant independent role in determining attitudes. Education and a willingness to adapt to using new technologies are much stronger determinants.

Confirmation of our expectation is further supported by the results on race. Even when possible ramifying conditions are controlled—income, occupation, education—Blacks retain significant negative attitudes toward science and technology. As with gender, culturally conditioned differences remain among Blacks but not among Hispanics. The results for Hispanics—slight and insignificant slope—appear to indicate that Hispanics are more thoroughly integrated into the techno-economic system. The overall results suggest that Blacks have been grouped among the "nonusers." Losers in the process of technological change are those whose lives have been only marginally touched in any beneficial way by the changes in society.

**Predicting Evaluation**

A last regression equation attempted to explain the overall evaluation. For this calculation, we restricted the sample to only those who cared to give a definite evaluation about whether things had gotten better or worse. About 190 respondents said both or did not respond and were excluded from the sample. Of the explanatory variables, using both demographics and technological indices, only four were statistically significant: attitudes toward technology, education, gender, and income. Both level of involvement and perceived knowledge dropped out of this model as independent determinants of overall evaluation.

Given the results of the previous equations, it appears that positive overall evaluations of social change are a product of two distinct paths. First, there is the education/attitude path. Higher education and more positive evaluation of science and technology—interrelated but distinct sources of variation—produce a higher overall evaluation. Respondents along this path are more likely to think the changes over the last 20 years have made life better. A second path is through income, again certainly related to education, but separable as a distinct source of variation affecting overall evaluation. Respondents with higher incomes are likely to agree that things have gotten better in the past 20 years. Both of these paths appear to identify winners, though we can argue that the notion of "winning" has several facets. On the one hand, winners are those who are in the upper income brackets despite any involvement with modern science and technology; they may have benefited from changes without any direct involvement with instruments of change. On the other hand, winners seem also to be defined by adaptability; they are in a position to take advantage of the opportunities presented by science and technology, either because of education or through an affective dimension acquired for idiosyncratic reasons. In either case, positive evaluations of the changes over the last 20 years are a product of those paths and we can speculate that positive evaluations of the changes induced into society over the next 20 years, as Texas more thoroughly becomes an information society, will continue to be a product of similar forces.

One final note is that gender differences is a significant determinant of evaluation, although its contribution to overall explanation is relatively small. Coefficients show that males have a slightly more positive evaluation of changes than do females.

# *Appendix:*
# *Questions on*
# *Science and Technology*

ST1. Scientific and technical development is accompanied by bigger and bigger risks for society that are difficult to overcome. Do you

— strongly agree
— agree
— disagree
— strongly disagree
— or are you not sure
— refused/NA

ST2. Science and technology have produced more and better jobs for people. Do you (same as ST1)

ST3. Increased use of computers has been a great benefit to society. Do you (same as ST1)

ST4. I find it difficult to talk about science because I don't know enough about it. Do you (same as ST1)

ST5. Over the last 25 years, that is since about 1960, do you consider that the life of people in the United States has, in general, changed?

— a great deal
— some
— a little
— hardly at all
— don't know
— refused/NA

ST5A. In your opinion, have people's lives changed more for the better, or more for the worse?

— better
— worse
— some of both
— don't know
— refused/NA

ST5B. In what way is it worse (better)?

ST5C. Considering the changes that have come about in the last 25 years, how important a part do you think those connected with scientific discoveries have been playing?

— very important
— somewhat important

— not very important
— not important at all
— don't know
— refused/NA

ST6. Do you use a computer?

— in your work: yes, no, don't know
— at home: yes, no, don't know

# PART V

# Media, Information Technology, and Change

# 11

# Texas According to the
# New York Times

FREDERICK WILLIAMS
DENISE FYNMORE

*How is attempted economic and social change covered by the press, particularly the prestigious national press? Like other areas of the country, Texas has occasionally received coverage in the* New York Times *of its attempt to encourage the development of an information age economy, particularly in microelectronics. The present chapter illustrates how uses of modern computer data base records of newspaper coverage can be efficiently accessed to study the profile of coverage of a particular topic in a region of the country. In this research, data base files of the* New York Times *were searched for the years 1980 through 1986 to study coverage of social and economic change in Texas. Frederick Williams is director of the Center for Research on Communication Technology and Society at the University of Texas at Austin. Denise Fynmore, at that time, served as administrative assistant in that organization.*

## *"Let Them Rot in the Sun!"*

This epithet was popularly reported as the Easterner's attitude about Texas when the price of oil crashed in the mid-1980s. It was likely a response in kind to the Texas bumper sticker of a few years earlier in the era of high oil prices, namely: "Freeze a Yankee!"

Epithets aside, there has been a continuing interest within Texas about how the state is viewed by "outsiders." In an era of prosperity and with the attempt to encourage a high-tech economy, did the rest of the country or world know what was happening in Texas? Is Texas a favorable place to locate your business? Should you invest in Texas companies? Should you immigrate? In all, what is the image of Texas as it attempts to enter into the information age?

The attempt to gain an objective assessment of national press coverage of Texas was the main motive of the present study, although there was a special interest to see if the attempts at promoting the economic growth of the state were gaining national attention (and investors). Further, as with the above epithet, many who have learned of this study were also anxious to know if the outside press were promoting a negative or stereotyped view of the state, a practice called "Texas Bashing" in journalistic circles.

For several reasons, the *New York Times* was chosen as the object of our study of Texas coverage. As a highly respected newspaper, the *Times* should be reasonably objective about Texas. It supports a state bureau office in Houston. Its readership expects distinctively national perspectives on news events, ones presumably free from local or regional biases. Finally, files of this publication are easily researched using electronic data base search and retrieval techniques.

This is a report, then, on how the *New York Times* covered Texas during the years 1980 through 1986. The research method could be applied to any city, state, or country that wished to examine its progress through the analysis of press coverage.

## Overview of the Survey and Results

### Scope of the Survey

Electronic files of the "city edition" of the *New York Times* were examined via the National Newspaper Index accessed using the Dialog Information Service for the years 1980 to 1986. Based partly on this examination and partly on categories of a priori interest, eight categories of articles were chosen for analysis. These included:

- high tech (computers, telecommunication, microelectronics, some biotechnology)
- oil (the petroleum business)

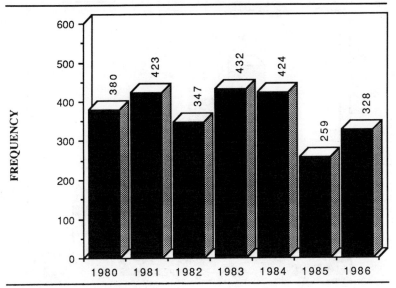

Figure 11.1    Article Frequency

- other business (specific businesses other than high tech and petroleum, banking in many instances)
- politics
- education
- crime
- sports
- recreation, travel, and celebrations

Key words were chosen to define each topic to be searched in the Index's *NYT* files. Each search resulted in a subfile of article citations from which selected information could be gathered and that provided a frequency count of articles in the category. Column inches for each article were noted in the citations and these together with the frequencies and average length of articles were calculated on a yearly basis.

## What Is in the
*Times* About Texas?

The Index contained 2593 articles on Texas for 1980 through 1986. Figure 11.1 shows how these are divided across those years.

We were much more interested in the topics of these articles, however. Figure 11.2 presents an analysis of topical coverage, in this

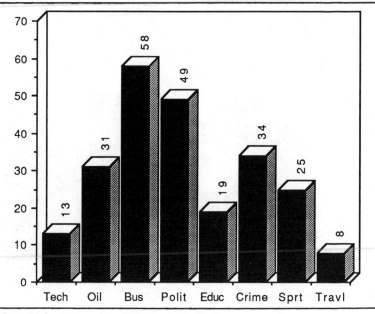

Figure 11.2    Average Annual Frequency by Topic

case, averaged annually. Notice that "business" (excluding technology and oil) accounts for the greatest average annual frequency (58). If technology and oil are added to this, the total average is 102, which is far greater than any other topic covered. All types of business account for a grand total across 1980 through 1986 of 719 articles, with average annual column inches of 1270, and an average article length of 10.6 inches. This is a mix of a few long articles and many brief (1 to 3-column-inch) ones. Also, these are an underestimate of business coverage because many further business-related articles (e.g., government) were not included in the classifications because they did not represent specific businesses. Clearly, the business of Texas is the most important topic covered by the *Times*.

For a state that was attempting to encourage high-tech industrial growth while facing declining oil profits, it is noteworthy that only 13 articles annually on specific businesses from 1980 through 1986 were about high-tech industries compared with 31 for petroleum businesses, and other businesses (mostly banking), 58. The category of politics and government also receives major attention in the *Times*, averaging 49 stories and 723 column inches per year. Next are crime and sports

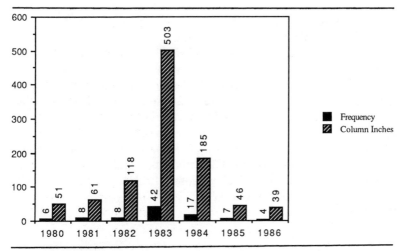

Figure 11.3    High Tech

categories, averaging 34 and 25 stories per year, respectively, and 326 and 367 total column inches per year. Education is next in amount of coverage, averaging 19 articles and 268 column inches per year. Finally are articles on travel, recreation, and celebrations, accounting for an average of 8.3 articles per year and 185 column inches per year.

## Coverage of "High Tech"

"High-tech" industries (microelectronics, computers, telecommunications, but also including biotechnology) were of special interest to us as reflecting an economic future for Texas. Stories on this topic were differentiated from those on other types of businesses. Figure 11.3 shows that, with the exception of 1983, the coverage is not of high frequency or length.

The most frequent high-tech coverage in the *New York Times* tracks the largest microelectronics employer in Texas—Texas Instruments. The greatest frequency of articles as well as accumulated column inches is for the year 1983, where Texas Instruments is either the main topic or among the topics of 42 articles. The year 1983 was not particularly good for Texas Instruments, as they sought to sue Compaq Computer Corporation for design infringements, defects were found in the TI 99-4A home computer, losses were predicted in quarterly earnings, the home computer market was failing, Texas Instruments laid off workers, and chief executive officer William Turner retired. The eventual big news to Texas of that year—the coming of the Microelectronics and Computer Technology Corporation ("MCC") to Austin—was relegated to a single 10-column-inch story on May 18. There was no other substantial coverage in 1983 of the MCC plan for development in Texas.

In addition to MCC, there were some notable omissions from the stories over the seven-year period. One, for example, is the paucity of coverage of the Texas operations of Southwestern Bell, by far their largest operating area. So, too, is there a relative absence of Trammel Crow's notable "Infomart," the Dallas-based permanent computer and telecommunications trade displays housed in a replica of London's Crystal Palace. Files for the *New York Times* yield only Andrew Pollack's "Supermarkets for Computers" (December 2, 1982), 20 column inches.

### Is There a "Texas Stereotype"?

Despite whether Texans complain about distortions or exaggerations of their lives and culture as imposed by Easterners (and New Yorkers, in particular), an analysis of coverage in the *New York Times* does not offer much evidence of the "Texas stereotype." The bizarre does show up in the news from time to time—for example, witchcraft, an especially grisly murder, odd cowboys, a child-mayor, or eccentric millionaires. Some characters or events would not have half the color if they did not occur in Texas—for example, old-style politicians, football rallies out of control, chili cook-offs, textbook controversies, or "no-pass, no play" becoming a heated political issue.

Yet, for the most part, the coverage of Texas by the *Times*, especially when assembled and analyzed in large "sweeps" by computer, seems straightforward. When the coverage by the *Times* of current economic problems in Texas is subjectively compared with in-state publications, there seems to be much less of a rehashing of the past, or seeing the crises through interpretations of people who are part of the problem. If there is a bias by the *New York Times* in its coverage of Texas, it may be that its reporters see the future of this state in a bit more comprehensive view than those who regularly rub elbows in Austin with lobbyists and the PR crowd.

**Research Implications**

Clearly, a newspaper data base search, coupled with texts of selected articles, is an efficient method for studying press coverage of social or economic change. This same method could be easily applied to any city, state, region, or country (we have recently done a study of Saudi Arabia). Also, it could be used to assess comparative coverage as, for example, a comparison of coverage by a sample of major Texas dailies as compared with national press. In retrospect, most of the reaction to the present study has been mild surprise that Texas is treated so evenly by the *Times*.

# 12

# Relations of Occupations to
# Uses of Information Technologies

## STEPHEN D. REESE

*Presumably, as an information society evolves, its citizens become more professionally and personally involved with information technologies. Although there are frequent studies of individuals' uses of technologies—for example, how many households have personal computers—there has been relatively little in-depth analysis of such data. In the present research, Stephen Reese analyzes the relationships between uses of various information technologies, and demographic, particularly occupational, characteristics of the user. From such analyses, he is able to develop a tentative model by which we might examine the relation of information technology use to professional involvement in the information society. Reese is on the faculty of the Journalism Department in the UT College of Communication. His past research has often involved survey data, particularly relationships between demographic characteristics and media use.*

## Background

### Jobs in the Information Society

Many of the most important questions regarding our postindustrial "information society" revolve around the changing nature of work. Whose jobs will be eliminated? Whose will be enhanced? What training and skills will be needed to advance? Questions of larger social impact are equally compelling. Will occupational and social mobility be greater

215

or less? Will an eroding industrial middle class leave gaps between a growing information elite and an expanding service-based underclass? The present study focuses on work, in particular, information work. It examines how workers use and relate to the key tools of the information work force—communications technologies.

Occupations locate workers in the social structure. Some persons have more advantageous locations in the system hierarchy than others by virtue of their jobs. Some workers have a better chance than others to take advantage of information society trends to advance or consolidate their positions. These locations, in turn, color the views and affect the behavior of those who are in them. This study is not concerned so much with what information workers do, but rather how what they do spills over into other areas of their lives. Specifically, having an information job should help predict not only how or if workers use technology on the job, but also what use they make of technologies at home and how they regard larger issues of science and technology in general.

### The Shifting Work Force

The production and use of information, and the technologies that facilitate that work, are said to occupy a central role in the "knowledge industries" that are supplanting an industrial economy centered on the production of objects. These new industries are based on handling information and symbols (Porat, 1978). As Daniel Bell (1976) says, a postindustrial society is based on services. What counts is not raw muscle power, or energy, but information.

In Marc Porat's (1977) analysis, "knowledge producers" (e.g., scientists, engineers, doctors, and lawyers) originate and market knowledge to others, often through the "knowledge distributors," who include educators, professional communication workers, and librarians. "Market specialists" (e.g., salesmen, administrators, and planners) represent the planning and control apparatus of the economy. As such, they monitor and create information within market systems and shuttle it about via information processors (e.g., clerks, bookkeepers, secretaries, tellers, or bank tellers). Based on this information-use criterion, the present study reconceptualizes a traditional set of occupational categories: professional, administrative/managerial, clerical/service, and blue collar.

Professionals roughly encompass both the knowledge producers and the distributors, given their largely creative informational orientation involving advanced education, mastery of a body of knowledge, and a largely informational output. Managers and administrators operate within systems, monitoring the environment, relaying and acting on information passed on from above and below, similar to Porat's "market specialists." The clerical/service category most resembles the information processor category, although it contains technically noninformational service workers. A previous study, however, suggests that the service workers would constitute 47% of this category and be demographically similar to the clerical/information processors (Reese et al., 1986). Finally, the blue-collar category refers to the traditional industrial occupations.

Although three of the four (excluding blue-collar) categories could be considered information workers in a broad sense, professional and administrative/managerial workers occupy a more advantageous occupational location than clerical/service workers. They have a more creative role in message production and greater control. In a different context, the political scientist Harold Lasswell (1948/1971, p. 90) has made a similar distinction. Referring to communication in social formations, he suggests that message handlers may be contrasted with those who affect the content of what is said. "Symbol specialists" are separated into the "manipulators" (controllers) and the "handlers." The first group typically modifies content, while the second does not. Therefore, that group of information workers that modifies content will be termed "knowledge workers," including both professionals and managers.

## Use and Adoption of New Technologies

Workers clearly differ in their need for communication technologies on the job. Given the nature of information work, though, we would expect workers also to differ in their adoption of home communication technologies. For example, information workers would have a potentially greater need for home computers than noninformation workers. This blending of workplace and home for the information worker is a growing phenomenon, making it important to examine the use of both work and home technologies.

Williams (1982, p. 136) notes that communications technologies allow many information workers to bring their work home rather than transport themselves to their jobs. Conceptually, too, it is more difficult to identify where information workers produce their commodity. If they are valued based on what they know, it makes little difference where they acquire the information they hold, whether home or office. In addition to adopting technologies that are purely functional to their work, information workers should be more likely to adopt other technologies as well. The fact that many information workers have direct experience with various telecommunication and information technologies through their jobs makes it more likely that related technologies would be adopted and used outside of the workplace.

Several studies of new communication technology adoption support this notion. For example, Rogers's (1983) concept of "technology clusters" suggests that adoption of one device triggers adoption of other related innovations. Familiarity with one technology increases one's understanding of and receptivity toward others. Even knowing how automatic bank teller machines operate predicts more positive attitudes toward new media technology (Carey, 1981). Other related studies have found that experience with personal computers is associated with positive attitudes toward other new media (Ledingham, 1983; Stover-Tillinghast and Visvanathan, 1983).

**Attitudes Toward**
**Science and Technology**

In addition to affecting technology use and adoption, the present study hypothesizes that, given the strategic advantage of the knowledge workers, they will hold more favorable attitudes toward science and technology. Several studies have examined public attitudes toward science, technology, and computers (e.g., Lee, 1971; LaPorte and Metlay, 1975; Taviss, 1972), finding a generally positive though mixed regard for technologies. These studies, however, predated the large-scale introduction of information technologies for both home and office use. A more recent study (Reese, 1987) examined attitudes toward these technologies related to both social and individual issues. High socio-economic status predicted more optimistic views regarding the social impact of the new technologies. Youth was associated with optimism toward both the social impact and the personal control the new technologies would bring.

Other research supports the more general conclusion that those in a position to take advantage of new technologies evaluate it more favorably (Pelto and Pertti, 1973; Winner, 1977; Chapter 10 in this volume). Based on these findings, an individual's occupation should color attitudes toward science and technology, beyond the effect expected from socioeconomic status alone. Those workers who stand to benefit most from technology should be most favorable toward it.

**Research Questions**

Given the conceptual distinctions, this study compares these workers in their use of technologies on the job, specifically computers. How do they differ in the extent to which they use computers and the applications to which they are put? An equally important question is how workers differ in adoption of home communication technologies. Adoption of three technologies (cable TV, videocassette recorders, and home computers) is compared. Finally, workers are compared on their attitudes toward science and technology, to determine how relative strategic occupational position affects these views.

*Research Method*

The data were gathered in late July and early August of 1986 as part of the Texas Poll conducted by the Texas A&M Public Policy Resource Laboratory.

Respondents' occupations were field-coded into four categories: professional, administrative/managerial, clerical/service, or blue collar. Three Likert-type items measured respondents' attitudes toward the risks of and provision of jobs by science and technology, and the social benefit of computers. These were combined into a summed index (0, 1, 2, or 3) representing the number of positive responses (disagreeing that science and technology carry risks, agreeing that they produce jobs, and that computers benefit society). A factor analysis indicated that they shared the same underlying dimension. Another Likert-type item evaluated how much respondents felt they knew about science.

Respondents were asked whether they had cable TV, pay channels "like HBO," a satellite dish, videocassette recorder, or home computer (yes, no). In addition, they were asked if they used a computer at work and if they used one at home. If yes, they were asked the primary uses to which they put the computer.

TABLE 12.1

Occupational Differences in Computer Use and Uses[a]

(in percentages)

| | Professional | Administrative/ Managerial | Clerical/ Service | Blue Collar |
|---|---|---|---|---|
| Use computer at work | 58 | 58 | 53 | 19 |
| Use computer at home | 29 | 30 | 16 | 12 |
| Primary uses of computer at work[b] | | | | |
| 1. Accounting | 6 | 11 | 9 | 4 |
| 2. Information retrieval | 8 | 8 | 9 | 3 |
| 3. Data entry | 4 | 4 | 9 | 1 |
| 4. Word processing | 5 | 2 | 5 | 1 |
| 5. Programming | 5 | 3 | 3 | 3 |
| 6. General office | 2 | 5 | 5 | 1 |
| 7. Analysis | 3 | 1 | 0 | 2 |
| 10. Other | 5 | 2 | 4 | 1 |
| | (n = 170) | (N = 125) | (n = 200) | (n = 140) |

a. Excluding those keeping house (14%), retired (16%), and unemployed (6%) in the total sample (N = 986).
b. Ranked in order by most frequently cited application across occupational categories.

## *Results*

### Computer Use

Table 12.1 shows differences in computer use and applications. These results emphasize just how pervasive computers have become in the workplace. A majority of information workers use a computer at work, figures that don't differ that much across the three information work categories: professional (58%), managerial (58%), and clerical (53%). Even 19% of blue-collar workers reported using one. When comparing home computer use, however, the knowledge workers (professional and managerial) were almost twice as likely as clerical workers to be users. Given the conceptual basis of their product, knowledge workers are more likely than others to put computers to uses in ways that transcend the workplace. A variety of computer work applications were also reported (although the number of respondents reporting each are too small to detect any significant subcategory differences). It appears, however, that business applications predominated, matching the growth

TABLE 12.2

Occupational Differences in Adoption of Home Communication
Technologies and Attitudes Toward Science and Technology
(in percentages)

| | Professional | Administrative/ Managerial | Clerical/ Service | Blue Collar |
|---|---|---|---|---|
| Percentage having | | | | |
| Cable TV | 60 | 62 | 60 | 49 |
| Pay TV channels | 70 | 60 | 66 | 73 |
| Satellite TV dish | 4 | 10 | 8 | 6 |
| Videocassette recorder | 57 | 68 | 42 | 49 |
| Home computer | 31 | 33 | 20 | 14 |
| Percentage agreeing[a] | | | | |
| Science and technology carry risks[b] | 41 | 44 | 55 | 45 |
| Science and technology produce jobs[c] | 89 | 85 | 73 | 69 |
| Computers benefit society[d] | 86 | 88 | 80 | 74 |
| R doesn't know enough about science[e] | 34 | 45 | 56 | 51 |
| | (n = 170) | (n = 125) | (n = 200) | (n = 140) |

a. Percentage responding either "agree" or "strongly agree."
b. "Scientific and technical development is accompanied by bigger and bigger risks for society that are difficult to overcome."
c. "Science and technology have produced more and better jobs for people."
d. "Increased use of computers has been a great benefit to society."
e. "I find it difficult to talk about science because I don't know enough about it."

in those equipment and software developments. No single application appeared to predominate in any occupational category.

**Other Technology Use**

Table 12.2 compares technology adoption and attitudes. Workers did not differ significantly in adoption of cable (and, of those, the number having pay channels). Knowledge workers were more apt to have the more costly VCRs and home computers than clerical and blue-collar workers. They also differed in attitudes toward and perceived knowledge about science and technology. Clerical workers were most likely to think that technology carries substantial risks, while for the other three items, they were joined by the blue-collar workers in expressing more negative responses than the knowledge workers.

TABLE 12.3

Multiple Regression Analysis of New Technology Adoption
Using Demographic, Occupational, and Attitudinal Predictors

| | Technology Adoption[a] | | |
|---|---|---|---|
| | Cable | VCR | Computer |
| Step 1 | | | |
| Education (d3) | .05 | .04 | .12** |
| Black | .02 | .00 | .02 |
| Hispanic | .07* | −.01 | .01 |
| Gender[b] | .01 | −.05 | −.02 |
| Age | −.09** | −.25** | −.15** |
| Family income | .12** | .28** | .15** |
| Step 2 | | | |
| Clerical | .04 | −.06 | .01 |
| Managerial | .04 | .08** | .07 |
| Professional | .04 | −.01 | .04 |
| Blue collar[c] | −.01 | .01 | −.06 |
| Step 3 | | | |
| Use computer at work[d] | −.02 | .01 | .09** |
| Step 4 | | | |
| Positive regard for science[e] | .02 | .04 | .09** |
| Feeling informed about science[f] | .05 | .00 | .06 |
| Total $R^2$ | .04 | .20 | .12 |

NOTE: Figures are standardized beta coefficients for variables entered hierarchically and reported at the step entered.
a. Dummy coded with adopting the technology = 1, else 0.
b. Three dummy coded variables: 1 if Black, Hispanic, and female, else 0.
c. Dummy coded occupational variables: 1 if R's occupation fell in each category, else 0.
d. "Do you use a computer in your work?" 1 if "yes," else 0.
e. Summed positive responses (0, 1, 2, or 3) to three science attitude items: disagreeing that science and technology carry risks; agreeing that they produce jobs, and that computers benefit society.
f. Disagreeing that R doesn't know enough about science.
*p < .05; **p < .01; N = 1000.

These differences, however, could easily be confounded with differences in socioeconomic status. If occupation is a useful analytical concept, it should predict differences beyond those attributable to other demographic differences. The regression analyses in Table 12.3 were performed to determine how occupational and attitudinal factors were related to technology adoption. Although entertainment and work-oriented technologies have been frequently lumped together in other studies, comparing their different predictors is revealing.

In each case, cable TV, VCR, and computer adoption was associated (although weakly) with youth and wealth. Those, however, were the only common predictors. As expected, computer adoption was more predictable from occupational factors, that is, being a managerial worker and using a computer at work. In addition, education and positive regard for science and technology are also positively associated with computer adoption, strengthening the conceptual relationship between computers and information age mobility.

The implicit model of this study has been to view occupations as a social location. As such, workers may be viewed as occupying more or less advantageous locations in an information society social system. These locations may partly be viewed as a function of demographic factors, on which workers in one occupation differ from those in another. But workers in different occupations should also differ in their attitudes toward uses of technology. Viewed this way, a different analysis procedure would seem appropriate, one that could analyze all these factors simultaneously. In this way, we may determine the unique contribution of occupational influences in conjunction with other factors.

### Discriminate Analysis of Occupational Groups

Table 12.4 presents the results of a discriminant analysis, presented spatially in Figure 12.1. Treating the occupational categories as four groups, discriminant analysis constructs a dimension that maximally separates the groups. Thus the contribution of any given variable to the discriminating dimension can be evaluated holding all others constant. (If there were only two groups, discriminant analysis would be equivalent to multiple regression with a dummy dependent variable.) The demographic, science and technology attitudes, and technology use variables were used as predictors, and a stepwise procedure of discriminant analysis employed to eliminate those variables without satisfactory discriminating power. The procedure locates the variable that best discriminates between the groups, finds the next best discriminator given the first, and so on.

Multiple discriminant function analysis based on the remaining variables yielded three significant discriminating functions (Wilks's lambda = .51, .78, and .96, $p < .01$). Table 12.4 reports standardized canonical coefficients, which may be interpreted like beta weights in

TABLE 12.4
Discriminant Analysis of Occupational Groups
with Demographic, Attitudinal, and Technology
Adoption Predictors

| | Function 1 | | Function 21 | | Function 3 | |
|---|---|---|---|---|---|---|
| Education | .82 | (.92) | −.13 | (−.26) | −.43 | (−.27) |
| Family income | .02 | (.53) | −.13 | (−.25) | .15 | (−.27) |
| Black | −.11 | (−.22) | .01 | (.05) | .09 | (.04) |
| Regard for science | .14 | (.39) | −.19 | (−.30) | .03 | (.06) |
| Gender | .28 | (.12) | .79 | (.83) | .03 | (−.05) |
| Hispanic | .16 | (−.07) | .26 | (.30) | .00 | (−.02) |
| Use computer at work | .15 | (.44) | .37 | (.17) | .37 | (.33) |
| Age | .15 | (−.09) | −.13 | (−.10) | .32 | (.16) |
| Satellite TV dish | .04 | (.00) | .13 | (.05) | .40 | (.40) |
| VCR | −.01 | (.21) | −.21 | (−.26) | .62 | (.58) |
| Home computer | .08 | (.27) | .05 | (−.06) | .28 | (.34) |
| Eigenvalue | .52 | | .24 | | .04 | |
| Canonical correlation | .59 | | .44 | | .19 | |
| Degrees of freedom | 33 | | 20 | | 9 | |
| Wilks's lambda | .51 | | .78 | | .96 | |
| Significance | p = .000 | | p = .000 | | p = .01 | |

NOTE: A stepwise procedure was used to identify the significant discriminating variables in the order of their contribution: education, income, age, gender, Hispanic, Black, regard for science, computer at work, and the technology items. Variables are ordered above based on their function loadings. Standardized canonical coefficients and structure coefficients (in parentheses) are reported.

multiple regression. The structure coefficients reported are analogous to loadings in factor analysis and represent the correlation of a variable with the underlying function. Pehadzur (1982) notes that these loadings are useful in naming a function, as their square indicates the squared variance between the measure and the function, and suggests that values of .30 and above be treated as meaningful. Based on these coefficients and loadings, the three functions were likened to social location axes and termed "learned," "born," and "acquired."

As can be seen, Function 1 is primarily a function of education and, to a lesser extent, income, race, and regard for science and technology. High values of Function 1 are associated with being well educated, well-off, non-Black, and holding positive views toward science. High values of Function 2, on the other hand, are associated with being female and Hispanic, as well as with holding a negative view of science and technology. Function 3 accounts for the least variance, but does

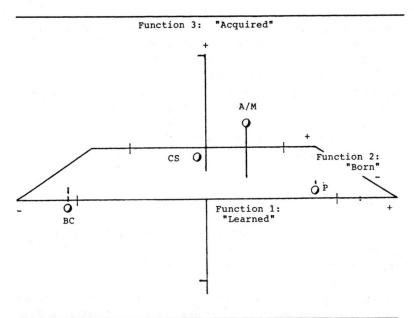

**Figure 12.1** Spatial Analysis of Occupational Group Centroids Plotted Along Three Discriminant Analysis Functions, or "Social Location" Axes

NOTE: Hatch marks on Functions 1 and 3 represent one standard deviation. Function 2 is two standard deviations from front to back. Locations are approximate. Centroid values on Functions 1, 2, and 3: P—professionals (.89, −.31, −.18); AM—administrative/managerial (.31, −.17, .38); CS—clerical/service (−.16, .70, −.04); and BC—blue collar (−1.13, −.48, −.07).

significantly separate the groups with a dimension primarily characterized by adoption of technology, including using computers at work, and owning satellite dishes, VCRs, and home computers (thus the term "acquired").

Figure 12.1 shows the relationships among the groups more vividly. The key discrimination among information and blue-collar workers is, of course, education, a qualification greatly affecting mobility in the work force. This is coupled with a favorable view of science and technology, which separates the professional at one end from the blue-collar workers at the other. Function 2 reflects the predominance of females in the clerical and service occupations. Gender is the variable that loads most strongly. Interestingly, although clerical workers use computers in their jobs, as Table 12.1 showed, this does not translate into a favorable view toward science and technology in general. The attitudes variable loads negatively on Function 2, indicating that clerical workers are more negative than the rest.

Function 3 is an "acquired"-technology dimension. The managers are distinguished from other occupations by their greater tendency both to use computers at work, as well as to acquire satellite TV, VCRs, and computers at home. Thus, taken as a whole, these dimensions suggest that the strategic position of the knowledge producers is reflected, not only in their socioeconomic status, but also their use, adoption, and attitudes toward technology.

### Discussion

This study shows that one's occupation clearly relates to the use of communication technologies and how they are regarded. Not surprisingly, information workers use computers much more at their jobs than blue-collar workers. Beyond that, however, the higher-level information workers, termed "knowledge workers" in this study (professional and administrator/managers), are more likely to use computers at home as well, in addition to other technologies. They also tend to have a more positive regard for science and technology than other workers. Combining these findings with demographic differences helps conceptualize occupations in terms of strategic location, which here is viewed as a function, not only of socioeconomic advantage, but also optimism toward science and technology and acquisition of communication technologies.

This focus on relative position derives from the belief that many of the most important questions to be asked about the information society are "distributive" in nature. The distinctions in occupational location should remind us that not all information workers will occupy the elite levels of an information age (as indeed they didn't in the industrial age). Rather, as many critical scholars have charged (Mosco, 1982; Schiller, 1981), information age trends may have a bifurcating effect on the work force, enabling some to consolidate their position while creating a large underclass of low-paid service workers. Although these workers may be considered part of the information work force, they will not occupy as advantageous a position as the knowledge producers, but could represent the "drones" of the knowledge industries. This study suggests such occupational processes but cannot address them directly, given that it only presents a cross section of the work force. Research is needed to monitor these suggested trends and evaluate whether information age tendencies facilitate or constrain social and occupational mobility.

This initial analysis does show that occupation is a useful analytical concept, in that it accounts for meaningful differences in information-related characteristics: uses of and regard for technology. This study consolidated occupations in very general categories for analysis. Future research, however, should more explicitly identify what people do at their information jobs, and how technology is used. That is, what are the essential features of information work that cause those workers to think and behave differently than others? We know from economic analyses discussed earlier that the information work sector is growing, but we also need to find out more about the workers who fill those jobs. Who are they, what they do, and what they think? By beginning to understand how workers differ as a function of their work, we can anticipate the tools, attitudes, and resources that will be required for future information society mobility.

# 13

# Predicting Media Uses

## PAMELA J. SHOEMAKER

*For nearly a half century, media researchers have posed various relations between the use of mass media and the processes of social and political change. The two seem to go hand in hand, although the relationships are complex. In any study of how the agendas are set for the type of information society change, it will be of likely benefit to understand how people are using mass media. In the present research, Pamela Shoemaker examines relationships between demographic characteristics of citizens and their uses of media in Texas and is able to compare these figures over a period of time. As is found in so many studies of mass media, the more educated individual tends toward use of print in a variety of information sources as compared to the less educated counterpart who tends more toward electronic media or none at all. Pamela Shoemaker is with the Department of Journalism at the University of Texas at Austin and is Director of the University's Survey Research Office.*

## Focus of the Research

A 1985 survey of Texas adults (Shoemaker, Reese, & Danielson, 1985) found that they spend on the average more than seven hours each day with television, newspapers, radio, and magazines—almost the same amount of time as is spent working or sleeping. The purpose of this research was to study further Texans' sources for news and public affairs information and to look at differences in media use patterns among subgroups of the population.

Using data collected by both the Texas Poll at Texas A&M University and the Department of Journalism at the University of Texas at Austin, the chapter will first look at the sources of information on which Texans rely for news about government and public affairs. Second, we will look at the amount of attention that Texans pay to news about political and government on the local, state, national, and international levels. Third, we will estimate the amount of time that Texans spend with television, newspapers, magazines, and radio. Fourth, we will discuss the use of and demand for Spanish-language mass media in Texas.

## Survey Data

Data used in these analyses came from two sources: the first was a bilingual telephone survey of Texas adults conducted during spring 1984 by the University of Texas at Austin, Department of Journalism. The study was funded by the Gannett Foundation. A total of 1218 half-hour telephone interviews were completed, 308 of which were with respondents who reported that they were at least partially of Hispanic ethnic origin. The second drew from quarterly telephone surveys of 1000 Texas adults that have been conducted since late 1983 by the Texas A&M University Public Policy Laboratory. The "Texas Poll" questionnaires included questions about media use in the spring, summer, and winter 1984 polls; in the summer 1985 poll; and in the summer 1986 poll. The summer 1986 sample (N = 1000) was stratified by ethnicity, with Hispanics being oversampled.

In addition to demographic questions, most items inquired about which media were relied upon for different types of news, including special affairs, newspaper, magazine, radio and television exposure, and use of Spanish-language media. Copies of the questionnaires may be obtained from the author.

## Results

### Where Texans Get News of
### Government and Public Affairs

A majority of Texans rely on television for news about government and public affairs. Table 13.1 shows that education is the best single

TABLE 13.1

Discriminant Analyses of Three Media Reliance Variables
by Demographic Variables (education, income, age, gender,
ethnicity, and years lived in Texas)

| Reliance on Television, Newspapers, Radio, Magazines, or Other People for | Demographic Variable | Partial $R^2$ | F |
|---|---|---|---|
| Local news* | Education | .04 | 6.37[c] |
| | Ethnicity—Anglo dummy variable | .01 | 2.47[a] |
| | Income | .01 | 1.57 |
| | Age | .01 | 1.50 |
| | Ethnicity—Hispanic dummy variable | .00 | .64 |
| | Years lived in Texas | .00 | .51 |
| National news* | Education | .02 | 16.01[c] |
| | Ethnicity—Anglo dummy variable | .01 | 5.12[a] |
| | Age | .00 | 1.05 |
| | Income | .00 | .84 |
| | Years lived in Texas | .00 | .49 |
| | Ethnicity—Hispanic dummy variable | .00 | .36 |
| General news** | Education | .03 | 6.88[c] |
| | Gender—male dummy variable | .02 | 3.41[b] |
| | Ethnicity—Anglo dummy variable | .01 | 3.16[b] |
| | Income | .01 | 2.01 |
| | Age | .00 | .99 |
| | Ethnicity—Hispanic dummy variable | .00 | .67 |
| | Years lived in Texas | .00 | .43 |

a. $p < .05$.
b. $p < .01$.
c. $p < .001$.
*Texas Poll (Summer 1986); N = 856.
**Texas Poll (Winter 1984); N = 868.

discriminator of media reliance (on television, newspapers, magazines, radio, or other people) for news of government and public affairs, with ethnicity (the dummy variable for Anglos) also being a statistically significant discriminator. Anglos are slightly more likely to depend on newspapers for political information than are Hispanics and Blacks.

Figures 13.1 to 13.3 show the three media reliance measures broken down by education and reveal that a majority of Texans, regardless of their educational level, rely on television for news about government and public affairs. This television reliance is especially pronounced when looking at national news, with nearly three-fourths of all Texans

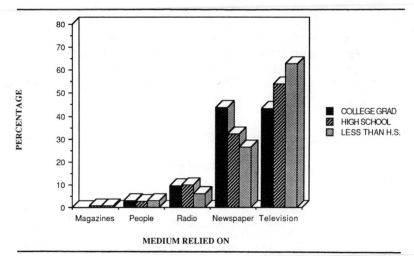

**Figure 13.1    Texans' Media Reliance for Local News, by Education**
SOURCE:    Texas Poll (summer 1986).

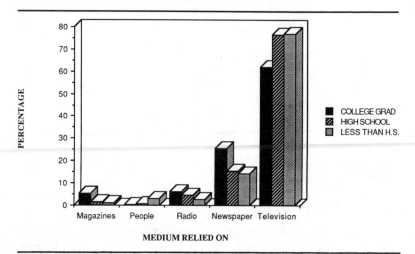

**Figure 13.2    Texans' Media Reliance for National News, by Education**
SOURCE:    Texas Poll (summer 1986).

saying that they get most of their information about national politics from television, compared with just over half who say they get most of their information about local politics from television.

Although education discriminates between those who depend on

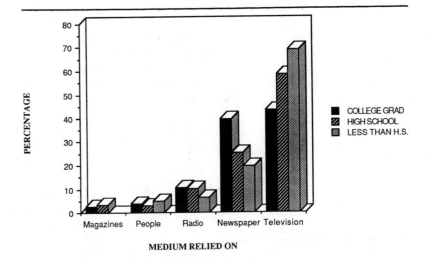

**Figure 13.3**   Texans' Media Reliance for News About Government and Politics, by Education (local/national not specified)
SOURCE:        Texas Poll (winter 1984).

newspapers and television for national news (Figure 13.2), the biggest effect of education on media reliance is in local news (Figure 13.1), with college education acting to suppress reliance on television. Those with a college education are equally likely to say that they rely on television as on a newspaper for local news.

Comparing the Figure 13.1 and 13.2 results with Figure 13.3 provides an interesting comparison of operational definitions, with Figure 13.3 not breaking out local and national news, but asking instead about media reliance for general information about government and politics. The results fall somewhere in between the local and national results, suggesting that specifying the type of news is important in future studies.

**Texans' Attention to
Public Affairs News**

As Table 13.2 shows, education is the most important predictor of attention to public affairs news on the state, national, and international levels, whereas income and age are the best predictors of attention to local news. People of high education and income, as well as older people, are the most likely to pay attention to governmental and

TABLE 13.2

Stepwise Regression Analyses of Demographic Variables
(education, income, age, ethnicity, gender)
on Texans' Attention to Public Affairs News on the
Local, State, National, and International Levels
(N = 1020)

| Attention to | Independent Variables Entering Equation | Standard Beta | Total $R^2$ |
|---|---|---|---|
| Local government and politics* | Income | .10[b] | .01[b] |
| | Age | .10[b] | .02[c] |
| | Education | .08[a] | .02[c] |
| State government and politics* | Education | .17[c] | .03[c] |
| | Gender—male dummy variable | .11[c] | .04[c] |
| | Age | .09[b] | .05[c] |
| National government and politics* | Education | .29[c] | .09[c] |
| | Gender—male dummy variable | .14[c] | .11[c] |
| | Age | .10[c] | .11[c] |
| | Income | .10[a] | .12[c] |
| International affairs* | Education | .29[c] | .08[c] |
| | Gender—male dummy variable | .20[c] | .12[c] |
| | Age | .07[b] | .12[c] |

a. $p < .05$.
b. $p < .01$.
c. $p < .001$.
*UT—Austin (1984).

political news. Table 13.2 also shows that men are somewhat more likely to pay attention to state, national, and international news, although there is no gender difference for attention to local government.

**Texans' Media Exposure**

Table 13.3 shows that Texans are frequent consumers of television and radio newscasts. Texans listen to radio newscasts on an average of nearly five days a week and watch one or more television news programs three or four days a week. The only differences in broadcast exposure among Hispanics, Anglos, and Blacks is in the overall amount of time spent watching television, frequency of viewing national evening TV news, and frequency of viewing late evening local news. Separate regression analyses were performed to assess the relationship between ethnicity (dummy coded) and these broadcast variables after simultan-

TABLE 13.3
General Broadcast Media Use Among Texas Adults,
Means (and standard deviations)

| Broadcast Media Variable | Hispanics N = 306 | Anglos N = 729 | Blacks N = 111 | Statistical Significance |
|---|---|---|---|---|
| Hours per day spent | 2.68 | 2.43 | 2.32 | F = 1.22 |
| listening to radio | (2.63) | (2.55) | (2.67) | n.s. |
| Days per week listen to | 4.58 | 4.66 | 4.39 | F = .50 |
| radio news | (2.79) | (2.75) | (2.88) | n.s. |
| Hours per day watch television[b] | 2.93 | 2.71 | 3.28 | F = 5.16 |
| | (2.02) | (1.81) | (2.17) | p < .01 |
| Days per week watch national | 1.36 | 1.44 | 1.68 | F = 1.09 |
| morning news | (1.96) | (2.04) | (2.10) | n.s. |
| Days per week watch national | 2.17 | 2.98 | 3.02 | F = 11.84 |
| evening news[a] | (2.29) | (2.59) | (2.54) | p < .001 |
| Days per week watch early | 3.28 | 3.49 | 3.84 | F = 1.87 |
| evening local news | (2.66) | (2.72) | (2.86) | n.s. |
| Days per week watch late | 3.29 | 3.58 | 3.97 | F = 3.00 |
| evening local news[b] | (2.71) | (2.67) | (2.50) | p < .05 |

a. In a separate regression analysis, the relationship between ethnicity (dummy coded) and the dependent variable held up after simultaneous controls for age, gender, income, and education. R-square for ethnicity was significant beyond the .05 level. All analyses are from the UT–Austin, 1984, data set.
b. In a separate regression analysis, the relationship between ethnicity (dummy coded) and the dependent variable was not statistically significant after simultaneous controls for gender, age, income, and education. All analyses are from the UT–Austin, 1984, data set.

eous controls for demographic variables. Only the relationship between ethnicity and watching the national evening TV news held up after controls.

Table 13.4 shows the results of a stepwise regression analysis, using the television exposure measures as dependent variables and entering demographic variables into each equation according to their importance in explaining variance in television exposure. The results show that education and income are negatively related to the overall amount of time spent watching television, with those having the least education and making the least money watching the most. In addition, women watch more television than men.

The best predictor of exposure to television news was age, with older Texans watching more morning national news shows and more early evening local news than younger ones. This may be more a function of

TABLE 13.4

Stepwise Regression Analyses of Demographic Variables
(education, income, age, ethnicity, gender)
on Texans' Television Exposure (N = 784)

| Television Exposure Variable | Independent Variables Entering Equation | Standard Beta | Total $R^2$ |
|---|---|---|---|
| Hours spent per day watching television* | Education | $-.25^c$ | $.06^c$ |
| | Income | $-.16^c$ | $.08^c$ |
| | Gender—male dummy variable | $-.11^c$ | $.09^c$ |
| Days per week watch national morning news* | Age | $.13^c$ | $.02^c$ |
| Days per week watch national evening news* | — | | |
| Days per week watch early evening local news* | Age | $.36^c$ | $.13^c$ |
| | Ethnicity—Anglo dummy variable | $-.07^a$ | $.14^c$ |
| Days per week watch late evening local news* | — | | |

a. $p < .05$.
b. $p < .01$.
c. $p < .001$.
*UT—Austin (1984).

job schedules than interest, because age did not explain variance in watching other television news programs.

Age is also important in predicting radio exposure (Table 13.5), but age is negatively associated with overall radio listening and listening to radio news. In addition, men are more likely to listen to radio newscasts than women.

Print media exposure is covered in Tables 13.6 to 13.8. A discriminant analysis of whether the respondents read daily newspapers thoroughly shows that age, education, ethnicity (Anglo dummy variable), and income are the best discriminators. College graduates are more likely to say that they read a newspaper thoroughly than are those with less education. Texans read newspapers an average of four days a week and spend just under 30 minutes with them. Most Texans read a newspaper nearly every day, especially college graduates. Ethnicity is related to the frequency of print exposure (even after controls for demographics), but

TABLE 13.5

Stepwise Regression Analyses of Demographic Variables
(education, income, age, ethnicity, gender)
on Texans' Radio Exposure (N = 784)

| Radio Exposure | Independent Variables Entering Equation | Standard Beta | Total $R^2$ |
|---|---|---|---|
| Hours per day listen to radio* | Age | $-.21^c$ | $.05^c$ |
| Days per week listen to radio newscasts* | Gender—male dummy variable | $.15^c$ | $.02^c$ |
| | Age | $-.08^a$ | .03 |

a. $p < .05$.
b. $p < .01$.
c. $p < .001$.
*UT—Austin (1984).

TABLE 13.6

Discriminant Analysis of Whether a Newspaper Is Read
Thoroughly by Demographic Variables (education,
income, age, gender, ethnicity, and years lived in Texas)

| Newspaper Reading | Demographic Variables | Partial $R^2$ | F |
|---|---|---|---|
| Does the respondent read a daily newspaper thoroughly?* | Age | .02 | $18.73^c$ |
| | Education | .01 | $11.57^c$ |
| | Ethnicity—Anglo dummy variable | .01 | $7.39^b$ |
| | Income | .01 | $4.39^a$ |
| | Gender—male dummy variable | .00 | 2.95 |
| | Ethnicity—Hispanic dummy variable | .00 | .35 |
| | Years lived in Texas | .00 | .21 |

a. $p < .05$.
b. $p < .01$.
c. $p < .001$.
*Texas Poll (Winter 1984); N = 868.

not to time spent with newspapers and magazines on days when they are read (Table 13.7). Anglos are the heaviest readers, both in frequency of newspaper use and in the number of magazines read.

The best predictors of print media exposure are age, education, and income (Table 13.8). Older Texans who have the most education and income are the most frequent readers of newspapers and magazines.

TABLE 13.7
General Print Media Use Among Texas Adults,
Means (and standard deviations)

| Print Media Variable | Hispanics | Anglos | Blacks | Statistical Significance |
|---|---|---|---|---|
| Number of magazines subscribed to or read regularly[a] | .76 (.77) | 1.24 (.94) | .96 (.88) | F = 33.13 p < .001 |
| N = | 308 | 738 | 117 | |
| Time spent in a day reading magazines (0 = none, 1 = 1-29 minutes, 2 = 30-59, 3 = 60-89, 4 = 90-119, 5 = 120+) | 1.68 (1.16) | 1.72 (1.13) | 1.43 (1.21) | F = 2.66 n.s. |
| N = | 206 | 653 | 97 | |
| Days per week that a daily newspaper is read[a] | 3.43 (2.94) | 4.33 (2.86) | 3.72 (2.89) | F = 11.31 p < .001 |
| N = | 308 | 738 | 116 | |
| Time spent in a day reading daily newspapers, (0 = none, 1 = 1-29 minutes, 2 = 30-59, 3 = 60-89, 4 = 90-119, 5 = 120+) | 1.62 (.89) | 1.72 (.95) | 1.65 (1.07) | F = 1.12 n.s. |
| N = | 244 | 671 | 105 | |

a. In a separate regression analysis, the relationship between ethnicity (dummy coded) and the dependent variable held up after simultaneous controls for age, gender, income, and education. R-square for ethnicity was significant beyond the .05 level. All analyses are from the UT–Austin, 1984, data set.

## Spanish-Language Media Use

Although Hispanics are more likely than Anglos and Blacks to use Spanish-language media, many Hispanics do not use Spanish-language media at all (Table 13.9). Radio is used more by Hispanics than any other Spanish-language medium, with television second. More than half of Hispanics said that they listen to and watch Spanish-language broadcast media at least part of the time when they use broadcast media,

TABLE 13.8

Stepwise Regression Analyses of Demographic Variables
(education, income, age, ethnicity, gender)
on Texans' Use of Magazines and Newspapers
(N = 784)

| Print Exposure | Independent Variables Enter Equation | Standard Beta | Total $R^2$ |
|---|---|---|---|
| Days per week read | Income | $.18^c$ | $.03^c$ |
| a daily newspaper* | Age | $.18^c$ | $.06^c$ |
| | Education | $.11^b$ | $.07^c$ |
| | Gender—male dummy variable | $.08^a$ | $.08^c$ |
| Time per day spent | Age | $.10^b$ | $.01^b$ |
| reading a news- | Income | $.10^b$ | $.02^c$ |
| paper* | | | |
| Number of magazines | Income | $.28^c$ | $.08^c$ |
| subscribed to or | Education | $.17^c$ | $.10^c$ |
| read regularly* | Age | $.11^c$ | $.11^c$ |
| Time per day spent | Education | $.11^c$ | $.01^c$ |
| reading magazines* | Age | $.12^c$ | $.03^c$ |
| | Income | $.08^a$ | $.03^c$ |

a. $p < .05$.
b. $p < .01$.
c. $p < .001$.
*UT—Austin (1984).

but less than one-fourth of the print media consumed is published in Spanish. In fact, more than half of Hispanics say that having a Spanish-language daily newspaper to read is not at all important to them (Table 13.10).

Table 13.11 shows that education, income, and age are powerful predictors of Spanish-language media use among Hispanics. It is the older, less-well-educated, and lower-income Hispanic who wants Spanish-language mass media. Young Hispanics are virtually identical to young Anglos in their mass media usage.

## Conclusions

We have investigated the extent to which Texans use the mass media, including their sources for information about government and public affairs, their attention to news about government, their media exposure, and the demand for Spanish-language mass media. We have also tried to

TABLE 13.9
Spanish-Language Use Among Texans,
by Ethnicity (in percentages)

| Spanish-Language Media Variable | Hispanics N = 306 | Anglos N = 735 | Blacks N = 116 | $x^2$ Statistical Significance |
|---|---|---|---|---|
| Overall, how much of television watched is in Spanish?[a] | | | | |
| None | 41.2 | 92.8 | 90.6 | 386.97 |
| Less than half | 34.0 | 6.8 | 8.5 | p < .001 |
| About half | 13.7 | .1 | .9 | |
| More than half | 5.2 | .3 | .0 | |
| All | 5.9 | .0 | .0 | |
| How much of television news watched is in Spanish?[a] | | | | |
| None | 61.2 | 96.2 | 92.3 | 258.33 |
| Less than half | 17.9 | 3.5 | 7.7 | p < .001 |
| About half | 8.1 | .1 | .0 | |
| More than half | 4.6 | .1 | .0 | |
| All | 8.1 | .0 | .0 | |
| How many of the newspapers and magazines read are in Spanish?[a] | | | | |
| None | 77.1 | 98.6 | 98.3 | 164.61 |
| Less than half | 9.8 | 1.2 | 1.7 | p < .001 |
| About half | 5.6 | .1 | .0 | |
| More than half | 2.3 | .0 | .0 | |
| All | 5.2 | .0 | .0 | |
| How much of the radio listened to is in Spanish?[a] | | | | |
| None | 37.5 | 94.1 | 93.1 | 475.64 |
| Less than half | 23.1 | 5.3 | 6.0 | p < .001 |
| About half | 13.0 | .4 | .9 | |
| More than half | 2.3 | .1 | .0 | |
| All | 24.1 | .0 | .0 | |

a. In a separate regression analysis, the relationship between ethnicity (dummy coded) and the dependent variable held up after simultaneous controls for age, gender, income, and education. R-square for ethnicity was significant beyond the .05 level. All analyses are from the UT—Austin, 1984, data set.

## TABLE 13.10
### Attitudes Toward Spanish-Language Newspapers
### Among Texans, by Ethnicity
### (in percentages)

| | Hispanics N = 305 | Anglos N = 736 | Blacks N = 115 | $\chi^2$ Statistical Significance |
|---|---|---|---|---|
| How important is it for you to have a daily newspaper to read in Spanish?[a] | | | | |
| Not at all | 51.8 | 95.9 | 91.3 | 340.33 |
| A little | 13.4 | 3.0 | 6.1 | p < .001 |
| Somewhat | 14.1 | .8 | 1.7 | |
| Very | 20.7 | .3 | .9 | |

a. In a separate regression analysis, the relationship between ethnicity (dummy coded) and the dependent variable held up after simultaneous controls for age, gender, income, and education. R-square for ethnicity was significant beyond the .05 level. All analyses are from the UT—Austin, 1984, data set.

## TABLE 13.11
### Stepwise Regression Analyses of Demographic Variables
### (education, income, age, ethnicity, gender)
### on Texans' Hispanics' Use of Spanish-Language Mass Media
### (N = 263)

| Spanish-Language Media Variable | Independent Variables Entering Equation | Standard Beta | Total $R^2$ |
|---|---|---|---|
| Overall television use* | Education | −.38[c] | .14[c] |
| | Age | .24[c] | .19[c] |
| | Income | −.18[b] | .22[c] |
| Television news use* | Age | .42[c] | .18[c] |
| | Income | −.23[c] | .23[c] |
| Radio use* | Education | −.44[c] | .19[c] |
| | Income | −.21[c] | .23[c] |
| Print media use* | Income | −.22[c] | .05[c] |
| | Age | .17[b] | .08[c] |

a. p < .05.
b. p < .01.
c. p < .001.
*UT—Austin (1984).

differentiate among the mass media use patterns of various subgroups of the population.

Education turns out to be a powerful predictor of many types of media use, with more highly educated Texans using more media, particularly the newspaper, and paying more attention to news about government and public affairs. Hispanics of higher education are less likely to want and to use Spanish-language media, relying instead on English-language news sources.

Age was positively associated with watching morning and evening television newscasts and with reading magazines and newspapers, but negatively associated with radio listening.

Ethnicity seldom entered the stepwise regression analyses that we conducted to assess the most important predictors of media use, showing that most differences in media use between ethnic groups are a function of socioeconomic status. Some ethnicity-related media differences persist, however, even after controls for socioeconomic status. With about 21% of Texans being at least partially of Hispanic descent, the impact of the Hispanic (particularly Mexican) culture and language has strongly influenced the Texas life-style. Today there are 10 Spanish-language publications in Texas reaching more than 500,000 people, as well as many radio stations that program primarily or exclusively in Spanish. Spanish-language television programming is available to most people either through broadcast or cable/satellite channels.

We have shown that, while Texans are heavy media consumers, those media are primarily English-language, even among Hispanics. The demand for Spanish-language mass media tends to be concentrated in the older part of the Hispanic population, with older Hispanics being far more likely to read or wish to read Spanish-language newspapers than young Hispanic adults.

# 14

# Computers in Texas Schools

## Key Issues for
## Education in the Information Age

NOLAN ESTES
VICTORIA WILLIAMS

*The computer seems a natural for training youngsters as citizens for the information age. Yet despite the intense interest in the use of small or personal computers in the schools beginning in the early 1980s, we find in Texas, as in most of the United States, that computers are gravitating more toward a topic of instruction rather than a technology used to improve or to make more efficient instruction in the basic subjects. In this chapter, Nolan Estes, who served for many years as Superintendent of the Dallas Public School System, and Victoria Williams, author of several computer books, take the position that we must redirect efforts at the use of computers in our schools. Given the mandates in Texas schools for education for a technological era, computers must be brought much more back into the mainstream of the instructional process. Nolan Estes is now Professor of Education at the University of Texas at Austin. Victoria Williams is Assistant Superintendent of the Lake Travis Independent School District.*

## The Mandate for
## "Computer Literacy"

Although the personal computer revolution has not changed our schools in the manner predicted by many enthusiasts in the late 1970s, computers and so-called computer literacy have gained a place in Texas schools. This is an important facet of growth in a state that wishes to be competitive in the information age. Currently, in Texas schools, Computer Literacy must be taken for one semester by all seventh- or eighth-grade students. At the high school level, any student wishing to receive an advanced diploma or an advanced diploma with honors must take one year of computing. That one year may be drawn from the following courses:

Computer Mathematics I or II,
Business Data Processing and Introduction to Computer Programming,
Vocational Data Processing and Vocational Computer Programming,
Business or Vocational Word Processing, and
Computer Science I or II.

Although Texas is well on the way to implementing these requirements, we feel that there is a larger challenge for uses of computers to prepare our children for the information age.

## Education for the Information Age

Now that all of the attention is subsiding, surely it is not as exciting a time for personal computer enthusiasts as the early 1980s; sometimes it is not even comfortable either. But does this mean that the computer revolution in our schools is over? Or did it ever happen? Educational computing, as in business and the home, or the industry itself, is undergoing a proverbial "shake-out." The use of computers in education has not really declined. Mostly, it is the "hype" that has subsided—the demise of overextended (in promises as well as finances) manufacturers of hardware and software, the futurist authors (returned to legitimate science fiction!), and the quickie magazines featuring stories of second-graders studying calculus on their TI-99As (also gone).

It staggers the imagination to envision some of the educational implications intrinsic to our transition from an industrial society to an information one. The astronomical increase in the need information handling will not only significantly increase the demands on education but will force us to stretch our limited resources still further to meet them. We must train a new work force as we move from being industrial to information oriented. Moreover, by the year 2000, the alignment of world powers is expected to depend on nations that have mastered and made the most effective use of the new technology. Thus the need to produce a computer-literate younger generation is the current challenge for educators not only in Texas but in United States if not most countries of the world.

As of summer 1986, according to the Texas Poll, one in every five Texas households had a computer. One of every three Texans, both men and women in the work force, worked with computers. Although Texans are generally positive about technology, even with income and education held constant, women tend to feel less comfortable with their knowledge of science and technology, indicating a need to focus educational effort on this segment of our school population.

As Texas educators, our mandate for growth has two implications. First, we must train people in the way computers and related technologies can make them more effective both professionally and personally. But, second, we are also challenged to increase our own productivity as professionals in the educational process.

That we are challenged to increase our own professional productivity was stressed as early as the 1970s by Ted Bell, U.S. Secretary of Education, who aptly said that unless we integrate the microcomputer technology into our school operations, this new technology may become a competitor rather than a helper. Tom Pyzant, Superintendent of Schools in Oklahoma City, echoed this sentiment in an AASA convention paper, saying, "Unless those of us who are responsible for providing leadership in education have the longer view than in the 90's, we in public education are going to be doomed to an unending struggle. That longer view can only be a vision of the future." In his comments to the 1986 World Conference on Computers in Education, Henry Becker of the Center for Social Organization of School at Johns Hopkins University reflects this ambivalence when he remarks that

> the large part of me that loves computers is overjoyed at the tremendous increase in computer-related activity in U.S. schools in the past two years. But the responsible part of me that is concerned with the efficiency and cost-effectiveness of providing instruction to millions of young people in the establishments we call schools is somewhat skeptical about the meaning and consequences of this activity.

We cannot forecast with accuracy what tomorrow will bring, but we can, as leaders, help shape the future by the decisions we make today! And this means getting comfortable with technology.

## Computers as an
## Educational Technology

What makes computer technology different from other instructional technologies—films, slides, tapes, television—that each had so much promise but that seemed to fall by the wayside as the classroom has seemed largely unchanged? The answers to this question are fourfold.

First, pressure for using computer technology continues to come from outside the profession, including parents, board members, and citizens. Most of the microcomputer efforts seen thus far in our schools have come despite our own profession. We've taken software that, for the most part, has been developed by hardware manufacturers. Never before has such technological pressure from outside education been so strong an influential force for change.

Second, the cost and versatility of small computer technology has put previously financially unattainable equipment into a now-affordable range. A piece of equipment costing a million dollars in the 1960s costs only a few thousand dollars today and will probably cost only hundreds of dollars in the 1990s. Software costing thousands in the 1960s and hundreds today will be available to the consumer for tens of dollars in 1990.

Third, this technology, unlike previous innovations, increasingly interacts with other information-handling technologies. Records with paper printers, videodiscs, compact discs, videotape, the telephone network, and a host of other communication devices will allow the learner to look, listen, and talk and in return receive responses from a friendly computer.

Fourth, and perhaps the most important motivation for educators, is the ability of the computer to improve the individual instructional process. Students are able to interact one-on-one with a piece of equipment, and unlike other technologies, students can perceive valuable learning experiences pegged to their achievement and interest levels. Research has long shown that, at best, a teacher with 25 to 30 students can spend but two to four minutes a day one-on-one with individuals. A friendly computer can do this all day long, with greater patience and without bias.

Simply put, computer technology personalizes learning; it frames learning within individualized situations, and combines immediate feedback with infinite patience. In addition, the animated screen display, as in video games, attracts and captures the attention of the student.

## Are Teachers Obsolete?

No—quite the contrary. Just as the print media of 500 years ago did not replace the oratorical requirements or importance of the teacher, computer-based forms of educational technology will not render the teacher obsolete. We cannot deny that the new technology will change or alter the way we do business in the classroom. The emphasis in the next decade, however, will be focused more on learning how to learn than on the acquisition of information.

Teachers will be helping students to learn how to classify and reclassify information, to change categories, to move from category to category, to switch from concrete to abstract information, and to look at problems from different viewpoints. In essence, teachers will focus on how to teach students to teach themselves.

Concerning cost-effectiveness, time is on the side of technology. The per-pupil cost of education in the United States has been steadily rising at 10% per year compounded over the past 10 years. The cost of computer technology, on the other hand, has been dropping at the rate of 25% per year in the last 20 years.

## The Status of Texas

Educational reform measures have put Texas ahead of many states in the use of instructional technology. According to Geoffrey Fletcher of the Division of Instructional Technology of the Texas Education Agency, there is, at minimum, a laboratory with 10 computers in each of the 1012 middle or junior high schools and each of the 1305 high schools in the state. This is due to a middle school computer literacy course requirement and a high school requirement for students desiring an advanced high school transcript to take a computing course. It is estimated that there is a minimum of five computers in 75% of the state's 3486 elementary schools. Beginning in 1988, all elementary schools will phase in computing applications through the basic curriculum.

*The State Board of Education Rules for Curriculum* also permits the alternative delivery of instruction by technology. To foster the use of instructional technology, the state board of Education has established computer-based instruction demonstration sites in Texas. In addition, two legislative bills were passed in 1985 to assist schools in hardware and software acquisition. House Bill 1303 allows the purchase of computers and related equipment from a state bid list, saving money and eliminating the need for districts to go out for bid individually. House Bill 1304 established a software advisory committee to create an approved list of software to be used in Texas schools. The bill provided for statewide software purchasing and licensing agreements and the development of a state long-range technology plan. Some state funding is also available for research and development through the 20 regional education service centers. In addition, the Texas Learning Technology Group has been coordinated through the Texas Association of School Boards as a consortium of school districts interested in the development of instructional technology systems. The first project of the group is an interactive videodisc delivery system for physical science.

The state has developed an electronic networking system that offers services in electronic mail and electronic conferencing and supports an electronic bulletin board containing education policy, announcements, and a variety of other school information.

There are a number of telecommunications systems in use throughout the state for the delivery of instruction and teacher in-service training. The Educational Service Center Region IV INTERACT System provides an alternative delivery system of offering courses for credit. INTERACT provides four channels of one-way video and two-way audio capability using a microwave transmitter for video and audio out and telephone lines for talk back. The Educational Service Center Region 20 TI-IN Satellite Network also makes possible the offering of courses that otherwise would be difficult for districts to provide. TI-IN uses a two-channel satellite video/audio transmission system. The system offers a variety of credit courses and teacher in-service programs. Education Service Centers have receive sites that allow the commissioner of education and other education agency staff to address large numbers of educators with minimal travel. In the Dallas area, the Regional Instructional Television Consortium supports broadcast rights for four channels of video. The microwave signal is received and rebroadcast by many of the local cable television companies, extending the range of the service in the Dallas region. A Guidance Information System provides counselors on-line access to career and college data bases to aid students in vocational decisions.

Texas has also adopted legislation, policies, and official guidelines related to technology in teacher education, staff development, and graduation requirements. Current certification requires new teachers to earn three university semester hours of computer literacy. A university-based teaching certification program exists leading to computer information systems certification. A system of "Advanced Academic Training" is provided for all curriculum areas and delivery systems. Technology training can take place within the framework. The system is linked to a statewide career ladder with merit pay to motivate educators.

The Texas Education Agency currently is implementing a Public Education Information Management System to increase accountability, coordinate information management practices, reduce paperwork, and streamline the process of data collection and analysis.

Overall, technology has penetrated most aspects of education in Texas. A path has been made for the growth of the use of computer technology to increase educational productivity in a state where test scores have been low compared to national levels of student achievement. Although the promise and potential of technology are present, the uniqueness of computers as an educational technology will be significant in determining the progress of the state.

# 15

# *Advertising as an Index of Change*

GARY B. WILCOX
JUDITH KAPLAN

*If the use of media is considered as a change agent in populations, the use of advertising might be considered an even more specific definition of types of information related to change. After all, advertising is directed at specific behaviors and buying habits and even trends of changes. In this chapter, researchers Gary Wilcox and Judith Kaplan offer a preliminary examination of advertising as an index of change. They find not only, as expected, that fluctuations in the advertising business are a barometer of the economy, but also that there are differences in the types of media that shoppers use for buying information. Gary Wilcox is on the faculty of the Department of Advertising at the University of Texas, where Judith Kaplan is a graduate student.*

## The Texas Advertising Business

Advertising in Texas has continued to grow and expand from the late 1970s until recently. The industry enjoyed greater expenditures in all the major media. In general, the industry grew consistently in terms of both the number of agencies and the number of clients increasing. This industry growth brought many advertising agencies larger national accounts, such as American Airlines and Compaq Computers, as well as new and better talent.

Unfortunately, in the early part of 1986, the advertising business in Texas entered a frustrating period. The economic problems in Texas have resulted in a soft advertising industry and, as a result, many in the advertising industry have been forced to cut back the size of their staffs.

> [The] ... story is becoming more typical in the Southwest as billings and account losses force small and mid-size shops to cut back or fold. The loss of jobs has affected a broad range of people in advertising, from recent college graduates to managers with 20 years of experience. Some are leaving for hotter markets while others are changing careers or taking odd jobs to make ends meet. Many are depressed and frustrated [Vinson, 1986, p. 6].

*Adweek* (Southwest Edition) found that, in 1986, 16 of the 50 largest Southwest advertising agencies reported decreased billings from 1985, while only 9 agencies reported decreases from 1984 to 1985. Both large and small agencies reported 1986 billings below their 1985 levels (Reeves, 1987). Large agencies, who usually have several national advertisers as clients, saw a decrease in ad expenditures in Texas because they felt that the economic downturn had been responsible for decreased spending power. Because Texas could not provide the kind of growth national businesses needed, many were forced to reduce regional marketing programs. In addition to lost national revenues, smaller agencies, who primarily have local and regional business, also saw clients cutting or eliminating budgets.

According to *The Standard Directory of Advertising Agencies*, agency growth slowed considerably from 1985 to 1986 (1985/1986). Although most of the larger agencies continued to report increases, they were much smaller than in previous years. Houston has been the hardest hit of the Texas cities as many agencies laid off staff members. A number of agencies have even been forced to sell their Houston offices as the clients reduced or eliminated their advertising budgets. Those agencies that handled energy-related accounts, especially second-tier agencies, have lost much of their business.

The top three industries in Texas prior to the drop in the price of oil were energy, real estate, and banking. All three of these industries are in trouble in 1987 and no longer have the advertising expenditures they once did. Furthermore, dependent industries such as home builders, developers, retailers, and financial institutions have likewise been forced to cut budgets in an effort to survive.

TABLE 15.1
Shopping Information from Media: 1986

| Medium | Percentage | N |
|--------|-----------|---|
| Newspapers | 68.8 | 589 |
| Radio | 4.2 | 40 |
| Television | 11.2 | 107 |
| Magazines | 6.2 | 59 |
| Mail | 21.2 | 202 |

## Where Texans Get Their Shopping Information

### Background

The present study involved analysis of statewide survey data on where Texans get their shopping information. The study also allowed comparisons between surveys taken in 1984 and 1986, a period of contrasting prosperity in the state. The key item that was a part of a larger quarterly survey taken by the Texas Poll was the question: "Where do you get most of your shopping information—from newspapers, radio, television (magazines; used only in 1986), or advertisements you get in the mail?"

Each study involved analysis of responses from a base sample of 1000 Texans selected randomly for the poll.

### Findings for 1986

We present first in Table 15.1 the results from the 1986 survey, which clearly show that the newspaper is the preferred source of shopping information. Usable responses were gained from 977 Texas residents. When asked where they get most of their shopping information, over two-thirds of the sample responded "newspapers." As can be seen in Table 15.1, direct mail ran a distant second (21.2%) followed by television (11.2%), magazines (6.2%), and radio (4.2%). (Results here or in the tables may sometimes sum to over 100% because a few respondents gave several answers although they were not encouraged to do to.)

Significant differences in media use for shopping information were noted for the demographic variables—sex, age, and ethnic origin. Table

TABLE 15.2
Media Usage for Shopping Information
by Sex: 1986

| Medium | Male % | N | Female % | N |
|---|---|---|---|---|
| Newspapers | 63 | (299) | 60 | (357) |
| Radio | 6 | (26) | 3 | (14) |
| Television | 10 | (47) | 10 | (60) |
| Magazines | 4 | (19) | 7 | (40) |
| Mail | 17 | (80) | 21 | (122) |

Chi-square = 12.693; $p < .05$.

TABLE 15.3
Media Usage for Shopping Information
by Age Group: 1986

| Medium | 18-29 % | N | 30-44 % | N | 45-61 % | N | 62+ % | N |
|---|---|---|---|---|---|---|---|---|
| Newspapers | 56 | (141) | 64 | (245) | 68 | (146) | 57 | (112) |
| Radio | 5 | (18) | 3 | (12) | 3 | (7) | 4 | (8) |
| Television | 12 | (29) | 8 | (32) | 6 | (13) | 16 | (32) |
| Magazines | 7 | (18) | 6 | (22) | 3 | (7) | 6 | (12) |
| Mail | 20 | (49) | 19 | (71) | 20 | (42) | 17 | (34) |
| Total | 100 | (250) | 100 | (382) | 100 | (215) | 100 | (198) |

Chi-square = 21.679; $p < .05$.

15.2 reveals varying media use for shopping information between males and females. Females were more likely to obtain shopping information from mail and magazines than males; males reported a greater reliance on newspapers and radio for shopping information than females.

Examination of media use for shopping information by age groups in Table 15.3 revealed further patterns. First, the age categories 18-29/62+ and 30-44/45-61 reported similar usage patterns. The 30-44 and 45-61 age groups exhibited a greater reliance on newspapers as a source for shopping information than the other age groups. The 18-29 and 62+ age groups reported a much higher use of shopping information obtained from television than the other two age groups. Radio, magazine, and mail use among the four groups was fairly similar.

TABLE 15.4
Media Usage for Shopping Information
by Ethnic Origin:  1986

| Medium | Anglo | | Black | | Hispanic | |
|---|---|---|---|---|---|---|
| | % | N | % | N | % | N |
| Newspapers | 62 | (468) | 48 | (55) | 69 | (99) |
| Radio | 4 | (29) | 3 | (4) | 4 | (6) |
| Television | 10 | (73) | 15 | (18) | 7 | (10) |
| Magazines | 5 | (40) | 12 | (14) | 3 | (4) |
| Mail | 19 | (144) | 22 | (26) | 17 | (24) |
| Total | 100 | (753) | 100 | (117) | 100 | (143) |

Chi-square = 21.653; $p < .01$.

Table 15.4 indicates that the respondents' ethnic origin also significantly affected their media choice habits. In this sample, Anglo and
Hispanic respondents had very similar media choice preferences while
Black respondents were significantly less likely to rely on newspapers for
shopping information. Blacks reported much more frequent reliance on
television and magazines for shopping information than either Anglo or
Hispanic respondents. In all the demographic comparisons, however,
the order of media use for shopping information remained fairly
consistent.

### Comparisons with 1984

A comparison of 1986 with 1984 survey results showed a significant
increase in the respondents' uses of newspapers as a source of shopping
information from 1984 to 1986. In the earlier study, newspapers were
reported as the most frequent source of shopping information by 62% of
the respondents, followed by mail (29%), television (23%), and radio
(13%). Magazines were not included in the 1984 survey. Use of radio,
television, and mail as a source for shopping information dropped
significantly from 1984 to 1986.

### Conclusions

For shopping information, the overwhelming media choice of
Texans is the newspaper. Although newspapers were the dominant

medium in 1984 as well, there was a significant increase in the reported use for 1986 while television, radio, and mail exhibited a significant decrease in use for shopping information. Media usage for shopping information was also found to be related to several demographic variables with significantly different usage patterns noted by sex, age, and ethnic group.

The use of newspaper as the major source for shopping information is consistent with previous research by Larkin and others (1977). The sharp decrease in the use of radio and television between 1984 and 1986 could be attributed to two explanations. First, the change in the economic climate in Texas may be playing a role in changing media usage patterns. As the energy-related industries cut their work forces, the out-of-work residents may have left the state in search of employment elsewhere. The loss of energy-related employees and the influx of new technological firm employees may have resulted in changing demographics, such as income and education levels, thus producing different media usage habits.

Second, the slowdown in the economy may also signal the manner in which consumers seek information prior to product purchase. With less disposable income available, the consumer may be spending more time evaluating different product alternatives and offerings. In doing so, their use of newspaper as a source increased, causing a decline in the reporting of other media. As noted in previous research, print media, specifically newspapers, are more likely to carry shopping information.

Despite all the attention given to the electronic media in the so-called information age, the newspaper may remain the most important advertising vehicle, especially for daily shopping information and for the more educated population.

# PART VI

# Epilogue

# 16

# Prominent Citizens
# Look Back on Change

PATRICIA WITHERSPOON

*The study of social and economic change in the information age is in no way restricted only to economic data, public attitudes, or technology transfer. Another important source of information is to see change through the eyes of prominent citizens, particularly those who have experienced great change in their own lives. In this concluding chapter, which our research group felt was aptly an "epilogue" to our studies, Patricia Witherspoon interviews ten Texans who are successful and well known but who also represent different aspects of Texas life. From these discussions, the researcher was able to draw certain themes that are uniquely Texan. Witherspoon asks one of the broad questions of any society, or Texas, in the information age: Are there certain qualities of the population or the culture that are likely to remain distinctive? Her interviewees think so and the present chapter describes the results. Patricia Witherspoon is Associate Dean of the University of Texas College of Communication. Dr. Witherspoon is currently conducting a major project involving the study of organizational communication in the Ford, Carter, and Reagan presidencies.*

## Personal Views of Change

The study of change in a society is a study of its people, whose efforts create and continue the economic, educational, political, and cultural institutions that unite them with a collective identity. Although a society's changes can be analyzed by studying the demographics and opinions of its masses, they also can be viewed through the eyes of a few individuals who have served that society as agents or examples of change.

Such views are particularly interesting in a society undergoing rapid change, as in the case of Texas. Cotton, cattle, and oil have symbolized the state's economy in the last 150 years. Now, as the state faces economic problems prompted by the decline of the oil industry, be it temporary or permanent, and as the Muse of "high tech" acts as a beacon of economic hope, several important questions are emerging. If a "New Texas" is evolving, what, if anything, remains the same among its people—among their values, life-styles, and elements of their culture? This study looks at change through the observations and life experiences of 10 distinguished citizens (see Table 16.1), 10 changemakers from various regions of the state who have commented on the future of Texas and reminisced about its past. Remembrances of places and people are of critical importance to this study, because how one remembers the past affects how one views the future.

The participants in this study place great importance on the relationship between Texas' past and future. Amid myriad changes that have affected them, they possess a confidence in the state's future based on a pride in its history. As a result, several of the comments recurring throughout conversations with these individuals reflect images of the state's past: Texans value "rugged individualism" yet also possess a concomitant sense of community, necessary in the development of any frontier; they respect "the land" as well as qualities identified historically with Texans such as bravery, friendliness, and independence.

Not surprisingly, these 10 individuals who represent the fulfillment of the American dream view the future of Texas positively, noting that most of the significant changes seen in their lifetimes have been positive changes. Pondering the future, they accept, sometimes even applaud, the coming of new technologies to Texas as aids to strengthen, but not replace, the economies that built the state. Moreover, they expect future generations of the state's citizens to appreciate its history and retain values that are a part of that history.

Memories evoked during the 10 interviews create a vivid scrapbook: white houses surrounded by green Bermuda grass and pecan trees; swimming in the Guadalupe River; a Sunday outing in a rented gig; traveling in old cars along dirt roads on vacations to Colorado; evening band concerts; fireworks shot off in the country on summer nights; church bazaars; the State Fair; and huge meals at birthday celebrations where the men were served first and the women and children second. Remembrances include listening to cowboy stories about the trails to

TABLE 16.1

The Ten Texans

*Jane Weinert Blumberg* (Seguin)—Chairman of the Board, Seguin State Bank and Trust Company; Member, University of Texas System Board of Regents (1977-1983) and Texas Lutheran College Board of Regents (1965-present); Member, Democratic National Committee (1972-1980).

*Janey S. Briscoe* (Uvalde)—First Lady of Texas (1972-1978); Member, University of Texas System Board of Regents (1981-1987); Founder, First Lady's Volunteer Program.

*Clotilde P. Garcia* (Corpus Christi)—Physician and surgeon; former school teacher and principal; Inductee, Texas Women's Hall of Fame (1984); Regent of Del Mar College (1960-1982).

*Barbara Jordan* (Houston)—Holder, Lyndon B. Johnson Centennial Chair in National Policy, University of Texas at Austin (1982-present); Member, U.S. House of Representatives (1972-1978); Member, Texas Senate (1966-1972); Inductee, Texas Women's Hall of Fame (1984).

*Mary Faulk Koock* (Austin)—Businesswoman; Vice President for Marketing and Public Relations, Republic Bank South Austin (1972-1983); author of books on American and Texas cuisine; food columnist.

*Tom Lea* (El Paso)—Painter and writer: mural artworks displayed in public buildings in El Paso, Dallas, Washington, D.C.; easel works exhibited in several Texas museums and the Pentagon; World War II war correspondent for *Life* magazine.

*Wales Madden, Jr.* (Amarillo)—Attorney; Member, Board of Directors, Mesa Petroleum Company and First National Bank of Amarillo; Member, UT Board of Regents (1959-1965); Trustee, Trinity University (1967-present); Chairman, the University of Texas Centennial Commission.

*\*W.D. Noel, Jr.* (Odessa)—Independent oilman and investor; Chairman of the Board, The Rexene Corporation and El Paso Products Company; Cofounder and director, Texas Commerce Bank, Odessa, and director of banks in San Angelo and Houston.

*A.W. Riter, Jr.* (Tyler)—Chairman of the Board and Chief Executive Officer, Interfirst Bank, Tyler; Member, Board of Directors, TCA Cable TV, Inc.; President, Texas Bankers Association (1984-1985); State Vice President (Texas), American Bankers Association (1986-present).

*Charles C. Sprague* (Dallas)—President Emeritus, University of Texas Health Science Center at Dallas; Member of Executive Council, Association of American Medical Colleges (1984-1986); Chairman, Board of Directors, Association of Academic Health Centers (1985-1986); First President of the UT Health Science Center, Dallas (1972-1986).

*Now deceased; the author gratefully acknowledges his contributions to this study.

**Kansas; marching with mother in the Women's Christian Temperance Union parade; welcoming the new minister to town with a fried chicken**

dinner; celebrating holidays in south Texas with both Mexican and American customs; and going to school only after the cotton picking season was over. There are also memories of seeing the Ku Klux Klan burn a white cross on land now owned by Willie Nelson; smelling poverty in the dilapidated cars of Oklahomans migrating west; and listening to a stand-up radio in the middle of the night as the King of England announced his abdication.

These memories helped identify one major similarity among the interviewees. These Texans are products of close-knit families that valued religion and/or civic responsibility, and this element of their pasts apparently affected their personal and professional development as well as their view of Texas. As Barbara Jordan emphasized, "Strong family support, good religious background, sense of self . . . were values, principles articulated to me, driven into me, demonstrated to me, which served me well."

The opinions and life stories of these individuals from different backgrounds, different occupations, and different parts of Texas form a "patchwork quilt" of reflections and experiences. Several themes emerged, however, as the interview data were analyzed, and they are common threads in the "patchwork quilt"—significant comments about Texas, its people, and its future. These themes are the major focus of this study.

## Themes of Change

*Texans are imbued with a frontier spirit, and a belief that all things are possible through hard work.*

Tom Lea reveals much about the frontier of Texas through his paintings and writings, and his work reflects his love for "the image of the people that came to a tough land." His mural in El Paso's courthouse is a 54-foot long characterization of the types of people who built Texas, with an epigraph that says, in part, "Now the old giants are gone. We little men live where heroes once walked the inviolate earth." According to Lea, one example of a frontier "giant" in Texas was Richard King, founder of the King Ranch. King came to Texas, saw the potential in the land around him, and involved his children in its development.

According to the participants in this study, the frontier spirit possessed by "heroes" of the past still exists in present-day Texans. It is a drive to build and create, to cast one's lot in the state's future. W. D. Noel of Odessa, for instance, helped build that city in west Texas beginning in the 1930s. Having worked his way through the University of Texas, via summer employment in oil fields, he came to Odessa and four years later began his own oil company. As he emphasizes, one had the opportunity to build and participate in the development of a community. Opportunities were abundant because there was so much to be done. The frontier demanded sacrifices, but it rewarded individuals willing to work hard and perform well.

Almost every participant in this study mentioned the "can-do" attitude of Texans. Janey Briscoe suggests that Texans do not like to admit there is some task they cannot do, some problem they cannot solve. Barbara Jordan emphasizes that "no task is too large, too impossible or too improbable for a Texan." One can reap the rewards of labor if one believes in, and practices, a work ethic. Several of the stories told during the research are testaments to that belief.

Mary Faulk Koock recalls the life of her father, the son of migrant farmers, who as a young man helped educate himself by reading in a wagon at night. He later became a member of the first law class at the University of Texas. Wales Madden describes his early desire to take part-time and summer jobs, not because he had to, but because the work ethic was a value learned from his father. Clotilde Garcia was the product of a work ethic through which six of seven children in her family became medical doctors. Living in a time and culture when educating daughters was an unpopular expenditure, but encouraged by parents who were former teachers, she remembers a 70-mile, daily, round-trip bus ride to the south Texas junior college where her education began.

After 150 years of growth and development, Texas is still regarded by the 10 interviewees as a frontier because it faces a set of new challenges. Now it must compete in a world economy and cultivate its people as a resource as well as other natural resources above and below the ground. It is still regarded as a land of opportunity, a place with continuing potential for economic, educational, and cultural growth.

*Texas has been a land of opportunity that has enabled native sons and daughters to remain in the state and cultivate its resources.*

Because of a lack of natural resources to sustain economic growth, or the existence of major and continuing economic problems, natives of some states in this country have had to leave their homelands. Wales

Madden remembers at the age of five or six seeing dilapidated cars of migrant families travel west from Oklahoma across the panhandle of Texas, recalling he could "smell the poverty" in those cars. He saw the children his age "who were obviously in worse circumstances than I and I worried about that and I worried about their parents and the way they looked and the way they had so little." To the individuals interviewed for this study, Texas historically has been a land of opportunity, fulfilling the economic needs of its natives as well as those who have come from other places to share its resources. Charles Sprague did leave Texas for a time to take a prestigious position in a medical school outside the state. There he was assured by those who hired him that they were committed to the growth and development of the medical complex he would direct. Over time he discovered their lack of dynamism in seizing opportunities to realize the potential in the health institution. Several years later, a group of Texas businessmen attempted to recruit him back to Dallas as Dean of the Southwestern Medical School. They said they were committed to creating the best medical school possible and were willing to commit the necessary resources, which they ultimately did. Sprague came home to Dallas because the opportunities he sought were in Texas. According to him, these businessmen were visionaries, risk-takers, and their attitude was indicative of those who built an environment to provide opportunities for the state's citizens. Barbara Jordan considered leaving the state during the 1960s, but not for economic reasons. As she recalls the night in 1964 when she lost her second race for a seat in the Texas legislature: "I drove around by myself for a long time thinking I could go back to Boston where I had gone to law school and maybe try to make my political mark there because people in Boston may think I have something to offer." Shortly thereafter, a Supreme Court case on reapportionment caused the creation of new state senatorial districts, and Jordan realized that she previously had carried the area in one of these new districts. In 1966 she ran for the state senate in that district. "I ran that race and I won that race and I never moved out of Texas." In her words, "It was a long time coming," but Texas finally was changing into a land of opportunity for all its citizens.

Not surprisingly, the recent decline in the state's economy is one of the most significant changes that has affected Texas, according to the individuals interviewed in this study. Whether the state can remain a land of opportunity for its citizens is a question they face as inhabitants of a society undergoing rapid change. Nevertheless, several interviewees perceive that many of the Texans who leave their state eventually return to visit and/or live. In their opinions, the unique history, culture, and geography of Texas develops an allegiance toward and an affection for the state among its citizens and finally draws them "home."

*Texans have a respect for and an identification with "the land."*

All of the 10 individuals interviewed in this study have an appreciation of "the land" in Texas, even those who were born, raised, and still live in urban areas. To them, "the land" is a manifestation of physical beauty as well as the source of the food, fiber, and energy economies that built the state.

Almost every interviewee recalls a favorite image or "mental picture" of Texas. Such images include the Palo Duro Canyon at sunset; the east Texas pine forests; the rocky, barren hills surrounding the Rio Grande; the sandy beaches of the Gulf Coast; the rolling hills of the black farm country in north central Texas, and a line of oil wells silhouetted against the horizon. Perhaps the most picturesque example was volunteered by Jane Blumberg, who indicates that her idea of earthly paradise would be to stand "in a field of bluebonnets at dawn in a gauze dress, facing a Gulf breeze."

A concern about the future of these "images" was articulated by some of these Texans, concern emanating from a loyalty to the industries that helped build their lives as well as a respect for land as a natural resource. Speaking of the urban sprawl Texas has experienced, Janey Briscoe and Mary Faulk Koock express the hope that some areas of Texas will be protected in perpetuity from commercial development and its environmental effects.

This identification with, and indeed respect for, the land is an acknowledgment of its role in the development of Texas. It is valued as the source of the agricultural and petroleum industries that built the state's economy. Additionally, Tom Lea emphasizes, Texans view their ancestors as victors over the land as well as its cultivators, as people who fought a war of independence to win the land, settle it, and then develop it as an economic resource. Their land was a prize, if also a burden.

Modern-day ranchers and farmers may view their acres similarly. Janey Briscoe, for instance, suggests that one cannot survive in agriculture without coping with the physical and emotional demands involved with working the land. Indeed, she describes "her country," south Texas, as "hard, hard country" that "almost demands you be a giant in your own time."

The "land" of Texas is important to its citizens as a source of "spiritual" as well as economic sustenance. Speaking of the generations who settled and continue to live in the Hill Country of central Texas, Barbara Jordan observes that "the soil feeds their souls." And, although Texas is now an urban state with far more of its people living in cities than on farms, there was a sentiment among the interviewees that after decades and perhaps centuries of change in Texas, the importance of "the land" will remain. Several of them might agree with the campaign motto used by Jane Blumberg's grandfather earlier in this century when he ran for a seat in the Texas legislature: "Civilization begins and ends with the plow."

*Texans possess identifiable qualities or characteristics. They are brave, tenacious, friendly, good-humored, and independent.*

Many common qualities were identified in several interviews as some of the characteristics that Texans possess. The ones named describe pioneers, risk-takers, visionaries, and entrepreneurs. To the interviewees, bravery and tenacity are qualities in individuals who value a heritage that includes Stephen F. Austin's colonists, William B. Travis's fated volunteers at the Alamo, and Sam Houston's victors at San Jacinto.

According to Wales Madden, the Texans who volunteered to serve in this country's wars have been different from other Americans because they identified closely with the nations struggling for freedom. "Having grown up in an environment where people fought to get their freedom, their approach to life was different from those who were handed it." Tom Lea agrees, emphasizing that because Texas fought for its independence and "stood alone as a republic for awhile," "being isolated and being alone [from the rest of the United States] made us remember it more." At the same time, he suggests, Texans who fought in World War II became better citizens of the world as they became more aware of the lives led by peoples in foreign lands. In his opinion, these Texans became "considerably less provincial" in their view of other cultures and nations.

*Courageous* and *independent* were two of the other adjectives the interviewees used to describe Texans, not only because of the state's past, but because of the future it faces. According to A. W. Riter and W. D. Noel, Texans are "free thinkers" and would rather solve their own problems than ask someone to help them. Similarly, Charles Sprague views Texans as "big thinkers" because "there is something attractive to people in Texas about bigness."

Several of the interviewees describe Texans as courteous, compassionate, good-humored, and friendly. According to Jane Blumberg, one characterization of a Texan is someone skiing down a snowy slope in Colorado while greeting the skiers he passes. Moreover, she comments, Texans practice the art of inclusion as new citizens migrate into the state. Nonnatives appear to be welcomed quickly as "Texans." Such "hospitality," W. D. Noel suggests, generally is observed because Texans evaluate people by the personal qualities they possess and by what they contribute to their occupations and their environments. In general, they are not evaluated by their wealth or lineage.

A discussion of a Texan's identifiable characteristics would not be complete without mentioning a commonly held belief that Texans brag incessantly about their state. Of those individuals who mentioned this trait, all feel that the perception of a Texan's inclination to pat him- or herself on the back is exaggerated. According to Clotilde Garcia, Texans are a prouder people than citizens of other states because of their Spanish heritage as well as other aspects of their history. In Mexico, she emphasizes, people identify with their state (e.g., Nuevo Leon, Chihuahua), not their nation. The uniqueness of this heritage includes an influential history, language, and culture. Increasingly, the direct descendants of this heritage, the Mexican American population, are becoming an important economic, political, and sociocultural force within Texas.

Jane Blumberg's definition of Texas and its citizens summarizes the thoughts expressed by most of the interviewees: Texas is a large section of land inhabited by people who came early or came late and who have been influenced by this place and by each other . . . who, whatever the diversities, share qualities of courage, tenacity, and a love of place.

*Texas is synonymous with diversity, but Texans have a sense of community that has helped build the state and will continue its development.*

The geography of Texas is synonymous with diversity. As Jane Blumberg muses, the east Texas pine woods bear so little resemblance to west Texas that if one went to sleep in St. Augustine and woke up in Marfa, he or she would be somewhat disoriented. And yet, she maintains, despite this diversity, there is an identification with being

"Texan" among the state's citizens regardless of the regions in which they reside or how and when they arrived.

Concomitantly, although one may think of rugged individualism as a pioneer trait, a sense of community is needed to unite individuals in building a society. Texans recall the volunteers at the Alamo and the colonists led by Stephen F. Austin as examples of such individuals. Responding to this heritage, according to Barbara Jordan, Texans have a sense of community and unity unlike that pervading other regions of the country.

Jordan witnessed an example of this "sense of family" during her years in Congress. Every Wednesday at noon, the Texas delegation lunched together. She observed that other state delegations did not seem to share the cohesiveness that united the Texans. Regardless of political party or ideology, she recalls, "We were just friends and we liked each other and we looked out for each other and we were unified wherever we could be unified. That to me is true Texan."

Another example of community is that described by Clotilde Garcia, whose parents settled in Mercedes, Texas, early in this century. Most of the Mexican American population of that town came from Mexico during its revolution. Many were lawyers, teachers, and members of other professions. This community of individuals valued education, and according to Garcia, Mercedes has produced more Mexican American doctors, lawyers, and teachers than any other community in the Rio Grande Valley of Texas.

This "sense of community" built the regions of Texas, and several towns and cities now have realized the benefits of cooperation among their communities and the attendant implications for the state's future. The Dallas-Fort Worth airport is an example of cooperation between communities. Similarly, the Austin-San Antonio Corridor is being developed through the cooperative effort of two cities for mutual benefit. The coming to Texas of the Microelectronics and Computer Technology Corp. (MCC) also was the result of such efforts. When Mayor Henry Cisneros of San Antonio learned that his city no longer was under consideration as a site for the consortium, he worked to bring that organization to Austin.

Other examples of entrepreneurial cooperation include a task force appointed by the mayor of Dallas several years ago. According to Charles Sprague, business leaders from the private sector and heads of research institutions were chosen to develop ways to continue the in-migration and development of high-technology and new technology firms. Additionally, a consortium of leaders, including A. W. Riter, from communities in east Texas are working to attract new firms and industries for long-range economic progress. The "sense of community" so important to the creation of Texas is now crucial to its development.

*The coming of the "information age" to Texas has been a boon to the state because it has resulted in a more informed citizenry.*

According to Jane Blumberg, the knowledge base in American society has expanded faster in the last 100 years than "dough in a warm oven." Almost all the interviewees acknowledge that, in Texas, "the information age" has created a more informed populace.

Several of the interviewees express concern about past images of Texans that picture them as ignorant, uncultured, and unsophisticated. Although they agree that the quality of education in the state has improved in recent decades, due in large part to "the information age," they stress the need for continuing improvement in the elementary and secondary school system and continued financial support for Texas' research universities. They also recognize the educational and socio-cultural impact of "the information age" on future generations, who will need to evaluate and/or assimilate more information than previous generations.

Several individuals remember daily newspaper reading as a valued family activity, where parents would read to children and discuss the day's events. They acknowledge, however, that electronic media, especially television, have been important sources of information for children about the world outside Texas, and have created a more cosmopolitan understanding of the world among the state's adults. They also marvel at the global society that the instant transmission of information has created; a society, according to Tom Lea, in which Texans are "forewarned about what kind of mischief and what kind of achievement is going on around us."

While approving of the positive effects of "the information age," a few individuals are concerned about the amount of information to which Texans are exposed. As Barbara Jordan suggests, in the future, Texas will need people who can determine how vast amounts of data can be applied to human uses without being overwhelmed by that data. Consequently, she emphasizes, Texas will need teachers during the next decades who will both nurture and educate the state's children to prepare them for effective and enlightened decision making. Future citizens will need to understand the difference between having information and finding solutions to problems. As Jane Blumberg warns, "Information and knowledge are not wisdom. The telephone book is full of facts but it doesn't contain a single idea."

*The emergence of new technologies will strengthen, not replace, the economies that built Texas.*

Most of the 10 Texans interviewed have an appreciation of, if not a loyalty to, the cattle, cotton, and oil industries that built Texas. All these individuals indicate that new technologies will have positive effects on the economy of Texas, but they differ on the degree to which the economy will be affected by them.

Several of the interviewees are confident that the development of new technologies in Texas will have a dramatic and positive impact on the state's economy. Barbara Jordan espouses the belief that industries based on the development of new technologies, such as computers and new forms of telecommunications, may serve as the state's economic base. A. W. Riter suggests that high-technology industries may replace the great wealth created previously by high oil prices, because "the oil and gas industry . . . will never be what it once was." Consequently, he emphasizes, Texas must give these industries a high priority when allocating the state's resources for economic development.

Drs. Garcia and Sprague praise the effects of new technologies on the field of medicine, particularly in diagnosing as well as treating medical problems, and Dr. Sprague forecasts that "ten years from now every doctor will have a computer." These individuals, as well as Mary Faulk Koock and A. W. Riter, also predict several potential effects of a strong high-technology economy, including the cultural homogenization of the state, the creation of more socioeconomic differences between rural and urban Texas than even now exist, increased educational and cultural development within the state's communities, and the enrichment of the intellectual community of Texas owing to the in-migration of outstanding scientists and professionals from a variety of technology-related fields. From his vantage point in Amarillo, Wales Madden expects the opportunities new technologies may provide to improve communication among the distant points on Texas' map.

Although each of the interviewees expresses a respect for the contributions new technologies, and related industries, may make to the Texas economy, a few individuals emphasize that their main purpose should be to undergird and strengthen existing industries, such as agriculture and the petrochemical industry. W. D. Noel believes that Texas has a more broad-based economy than many people realize, but other facets of the economy have been overshadowed by the oil industry and that industry will "continue to be important for a long time." Smokestack industry will remain a part of the Texas economy, he suggests, but will become much more sophisticated with new technologies including perhaps robots.

Several of the interviewees express confidence that the cattle industry will continue to be an important part of the Texas economy, underscoring Janey Briscoe's comment that "it is difficult to see high technology prefabricating steaks." These individuals believe, however, that agriculture as an industry can be improved through the application of new technologies. Mrs. Briscoe compares high technology to "a strong right arm for existing industries," saying it may be a new beacon of light for others to follow, but for people like her, whose lives have been intertwined with the development and success of the agricultural industry, "there will be a place for us." Moreover, she cautions, the success of new technology industries will depend on the success of businesses that support those technologies. Consequently, as several of these individuals suggest, high tech will help the Texas economy, but it will not and should not be its sole support and it cannot single-handedly save Texas from economic disaster.

*Future generations of Texans should appreciate the state's history and retain the values upon which that history is based.*

Each of the interviewees has a kinship with the future of Texas. Clotilde Garcia has delivered over 7000 babies during her career. Most of the individuals have children and/or grandchildren. All have devoted much of their lives to working for or with children through public service or private volunteer work. Consequently, the future of Texas, as well as its past, is important to these Texans. Each has definite opinions on the values he or she wants future generations to retain as heirs to the state's heritage.

The "values" listed by the 10 interviewees include integrity, honesty, courage, a sense of responsibility, and other values rooted in Judeo-Christian beliefs. Several emphasize the importance of the work ethic for future generations, even though new technologies may provide them an easier life than previous generations experienced. According to W.

D. Noel, growing up in a frontier takes character, discipline, and purpose—a dedication to creation. And, A. W. Riter remarks, because Texas is facing new challenges as a result of dramatic social and economic changes, its future will be a new frontier. Charles Sprague suggests that new generations of Texans must have a sense of self-worth, self-esteem, and self-confidence that comes from purpose, not ego. Additionally, Barbara Jordan expresses hope that future Texans will have a social conscience that will "open more quickly to the new mosaic," that is, the composite cultural picture of races, religions, and ethnicities that will be Texas. Moreover, Clotilde Garcia emphasizes, future Texans should appreciate the contributions made by Mexican American colonists and by each group of individuals who have settled in the state. Jordan also hopes for a generation that will not be content until Texas is among the top 10 states in the nation in providing educational and human services to its people.

Every person interviewed for this study believes strongly that future generations of Texans should appreciate the state's history. Several individuals mention the Alamo as an example of this history not only because the battle within it was a significant event in the state's war for independence, but because it continues to be a symbol of the Texas "spirit." It is a continuing link with the past in a society that has survived 150 years of tumultuous change.

*The most significant changes in Texas have been positive changes, and have major implications for the state's economic and educational future.*

The major changes in Texas that the 10 interviewees have witnessed are identified as the following:

- the state's evolution from an agricultural to an industrial economy and the concomitant shift in the population from rural to urban areas;
- changes in the state's demographic characteristics caused by in-migration from other states and an increase in the minority population, particularly the Hispanic population;
- The development of metropolitan areas in Texas and a related increase in the cultural offerings within these and other communities in the state (as W. D. Noel comments, prior to 1930, Texas did not have a true metropolitan area);
- the improvement of education in the state, particularly at the postsecondary level, owing to an investment of the state's resources in higher education;

- a change in attitude toward minorities in Texas and the advancement of minorities in the socioeconomic and political structures in the state;
- the "recent" decline in the oil and gas economy;
- the introduction of high- and new technology businesses as an important component of the state's economy; and
- the development of a two-party system, instead of one party with conflicting political philosophies.

In assessing the effects of these changes, the participants in this study acknowledge the major differences between their lives and those of their parents or others of the previous generation. The latter individuals faced more economic difficulties as adults in a state still developing its economy. Economic survival was a major goal in their lives. The development of cheap energy, according to W. D. Noel, spared their children from "back-breaking labor" and "eliminated the necessity for all of the children to stay home [from school] and help make a living for the family." Additionally, over time, education became more accessible, especially at the postsecondary level. In general, the quality of life of the 10 interviewees has been better than that of their parents because the means for cultivating the state's resources improved, as did the ability of its people to use them.

Unfortunately, some of the technological changes that have made the lives of Texans easier have combined to change forever certain elements of a treasured past. As Jane Blumberg observes, the quality of life in small communities is not as good as it once was—television and air conditioning have taken neighbors off the front porch and put them behind closed doors and windows, thereby affecting a sense of "neighborhood" that permeated such communities for many years.

The changes that have been listed have resulted in a variety of positive effects on the state, including a better educated populace, a higher standard of living, and an increased tolerance of different religions, races, and ethnicities. Several participants in this study acknowledge problems Texans face, however, such as drug abuse and the breakup of nuclear families, which citizens in other states also are facing. Such problems, they suggest, stem from the changing mores and increased stress found in rapidly changing, technologically developing mass societies.

Of greatest concern to most of the interviewees is the recent decline of the oil and gas economy in Texas that built cities, universities, and individual fortunes as well as a variety of economic and sociocultural structures within the state. As Wales Madden emphasizes, never again will Texas have "the complacency of knowing that you have a huge natural resource . . . upon which you can depend for employment of the people and production of revenue." In Texas, as in all societies, change will require adaptation for survival, as well as growth.

### A Unifying Theme

Texans are now fighting for economic, not political, independence. They face challenges in a frontier that is more civilized, but also more complex, than the one their ancestors encountered during the last century.

In reviewing all the themes described in this study, and the data obtained from 10 interviews, one unifying theme emerged: the importance that these distinguished Texans place in the relationship between past and future. They share an optimism about the future of Texas based on a pride in its past. To some Texans, such confidence may be unrealistic and out of touch with the severe economic problems the state and many of its citizens are facing. Jane Blumberg read a quotation by Marcus Aurelius toward the end of her interview, however, that aptly reflects the sentiments shared by the 10 participants in this study:

> Never let the future disturb you. You will meet it if you have to with the same weapons of reason which today arm you against the present.

### Appendix A:
### Author's Note

All the individuals interviewed for this study are native Texans between the ages of 50 and 80, and have spent much, if not all, of their lives in the region of Texas they represent in this study. Several are over the age of 65. While a few of these Texans have lived briefly in other parts of this country, all have visited other states and/or nations.

There are many distinguished citizens in Texas, and the purpose of this project was to talk with 10 such individuals, knowing they do not represent a random sample of the population. Interviewees were chosen subjectively, using a variety of criteria. Some of these individuals have been publicly recognized for outstanding contributions to their fields, such as law, medicine, and banking. Others have been recognized statewide, and nationally, for their contributions to education, public service, and the arts. A few are also the sons and daughters of changemakers who made their contributions to Texas earlier in this century.

These individuals were interviewed between June and December 1986. Each interview generally lasted from one to two hours and took place in each individual's home or office. Eleven questions made up the "core" of each interview, although additional questions were used as needed to probe initial responses to these questions. A listing of the questions is found in Appendix B.

Because the purpose of this study was to ascertain observations and opinions about change in Texas, the questions used in the interviews were designed to elicit perceptions of change from different "angles." That is, an effort was made at the beginning of each interview to discuss each individual's past, then elicit his or her opinions on changes in the state observed during adulthood. Finally, the author sought to obtain comments about the future of Texas as the home of succeeding generations. Specifically, 11 questions were designed to provide information on the following topics:

— remembrances about growing up in Texas
— values learned as a child
— geographical and/or sociocultural images of Texas developed and communicated during one's lifetime
— the most significant changes observed in Texas (both pleasing and disturbing)
— perceived generational differences among Texans as related to quality of life
— effects of "the information age" on the state's citizens
— effects of new technologies on Texas, including its economy and culture
— preferred values and images of the state for future generations of Texans to retain

## Appendix B:
## Ten Texans Talk About Change

1. What do you remember about growing up in Texas? What are your fondest memories about being a child in this state?

2. What "lessons of life" or values were you taught as a child?

3. What images of Texas have you carried with you during your life? What about Texas do you like to describe to people in other states and/or countries?

4. What are the most significant changes you've seen occur in Texas since you were a child?

5. Which changes please you? Why?

6. Which changes disturb you? Why?

7. How is your life as an adult in Texas different from that of your mother's and father's?

8. How do you anticipate the lives of adults in Texas 20 years from now will be different from your adult life in Texas?

9. What are your thoughts about the "information age" as it is affecting Texas?

10. What effects will new technologies (computers, telecommunication systems) have on the state, for example, on its economy, its culture?

11. What values/images of Texas would you like succeeding generations of Texans to retain?

# *Appendix*

## *Summaries of Additional Studies[1]*

### Texas Agriculture in the Information Age

Heather E. Hudson
Martin Burch
The University of Texas at Austin

Agriculture in the United States is undergoing major pressures from the changing American global economies. The farmer's world is influenced not only by drought and freezing weather but by interest rates and international markets. An abundant harvest of high-quality crops is no longer a guarantee of profitability. Successful farming today requires innovation, ingenuity, and a keen awareness of changing markets. In this changing environment, information has become a strategic tool for planning, management, and marketing of agricultural products.

Although new industries and services are diversifying the economic base, agriculture will continue to be a mainstay of the Texas economy. Agriculture itself is in transition, however, as farmers and ranchers turn to new means of obtaining and using information to improve productivity and profitability. The introduction of computers and specialized software coupled with improved telecommunications services are changing the way farmers manage and market their crops.

This paper provides an overview of current activity in the uses of computers on Texas farms, plus several additional examples of other information technologies.

### Perspectives on the Economy of Texas

M. Ray Perryman
Leigh Humphrey
Baylor University

This paper described relevant phases of a project at Baylor University Forecasting Service designed to integrate economic modeling initiatives into a unified framework. The major aspects of the study include

(1) significant expansion of the existing Texas Econometric Model;

(2) development of a complete subregional empirical system capable of generating detailed economic projections of output, income, sales, employment, wages, productivity, and other variables on a regional area, metropolitan area, and county basis;

(3) integration of the system described above with an industry-occupation matrix to permit complete labor market profiles on a disaggregated sectoral basis; and

(4) linkage with an input-output matrix system to permit detailed economic impact assessments to be conducted.

The project has implications as a part of the information complex of Texas, as it offers a mathematically consistent basis for providing projections for several million variables of relevance to the state economic environment. Consequently, it provides a unique information asset that offers important applications for economic development and diversification efforts throughout the state. As related to the topic of Texas in the information age, the project will permit the assessment of the impact of specific information and communication industries in a wide variety of contexts. The report offers descriptions of the basic methods involved in the project, as well as illustrations within the context of selected information and communications industries.

## *Higher Education and the New American Economy*

**Bryan D. Jones**
**Arnold Vedlitz**
**with**
**Michael Beardsley**
**Texas A&M University**

A major issue in the information age is the extent to which state governments can encourage the development of a technology-based economy. The present paper focuses on the policy instrument for achieving this end, namely, state funding for higher education. Major findings include the following:

(1) The quality of the higher education system, measured by federal R&D garnered by universities in the state, is strongly related to economic development, as measured by professional and managerial jobs, by scientists and engineers per capita, and by per capita income.

(2) State expenditures for higher education are related, albeit more modestly, to the quality of the higher education system.

(3) Generalized support for higher education is more directly related to university quality than are state-level R&D appropriations.

(4) A comparison of Texas and California indicates that California has supported its institutions of higher education at a higher level and more consistently over the years than has Texas. As a consequence, California universities are of higher quality. The state has a higher proportion of professionals and managers in its work force, and more scientists and

engineers; its citizens enjoy a higher level of income on average. If policymakers in Texas wish to encourage the development of the second, forward-looking type of economic structure, they ought to

- make a substantial, continuing, dependable, and long-term commitment to building excellence in higher education;
- distinguish universities and colleges according to their mission in funding allocations (education experts distinguish the following classes of universities: major research, research, intermediate, small, comprehensive college, general BA college, two-year academic, and two-year occupational)—findings here suggest the importance of the research mission of universities in the economic development process;
- relax constraints on universities in the development of new programs and projects—institutions in Texas currently lack the full flexibility to meet changing economic conditions;
- fund both basic and applied research—both can lead to major practical applications, and the former will have more of an impact on the research infrastructure than the latter;
- put more research funds under the control of university presidents to help build the research infrastructure; and
- encourage a more proactive role for government and the state's universities in the economic development process—government can be the handmaiden of business in moving toward a brighter economic future, but old negative ideas about government must be put aside for it to do so.

## NOTE

1. Information on these reports may be obtained by writing to the Center for Research on Communication Technology & Society, College of Communication, University of Texas at Austin, Austin, TX 78712.

# References

Bavelas, A. 1968. "Communication Patterns in Task Oriented Groups." Pp. 503-511 in *Group Dynamics*, edited by D. Cartwright and A. Zander. New York: Harper & Row.

Bell, D. 1976. *The Coming of Post-Industrial Society*. New York: Basic Books.

———1981. "The Social Framework of the Information Society." In *The Microelectronics Revolution*, edited by Tom Forester. Cambridge: MIT Press.

Beniger, J. 1986. *The Control Revolution*. Cambridge, MA: Harvard University Press.

Bennis, W. G. and P. E. Slater. 1968. *The Temporary Society*. New York: Harper & Row.

Bingham, R. and J. Blair, eds. 1984. *Urban Economic Development*. Beverly Hills, CA: Sage.

Bourne, L., ed. 1982. *Internal Structure of the City*. New York: Oxford University Press.

Bureau of Economic Analysis. 1985. Austin: Texas Department of Commerce.

Carey, J. 1981. "Selling Videotex to Archie Bunker." In *Telecommunications and Productivity*, edited by M. Moss. Reading, MA: Addison-Wesley.

Devereux, E. A., T. Ferguson, W. Fisher, S. Magee, S. McDonald, E. Sharpe, Jr., R. Smilor, J. Smith, S. Szygenda, F. Williams, H. Woodson, and M. Wilson. 1987. *Economic Growth and Investment in Higher Education*. Austin: University of Texas, Bureau of Business Research.

*Directory of Texas Manufacturers*. 1986. Austin: University of Texas, Graduate School of Business, Bureau of Business Research.

Dizard, W. 1982. *The Coming Information Age*. New York: Annenberg/Longman.

Drucker, P. 1969. *The Age of Discontinuity*. New York: Harper & Row.

Duncan, J. W. 1986. *Business Starts in 1986*. New York: Dun & Bradstreet.

Dunkelberg, W. C. 1985. *Financing Small Business*. Washington, DC: National Federation of Independent Business.

Dunn, Edgar S. 1980. *The Development of the U.S. Urban System*. Baltimore: Johns Hopkins University Press.

Dyer, J., D. Hill, A. Vedlitz, and S. White. 1985. "The Partisan Transformation of Texas." Paper presented at the American Political Science Association's Annual Meeting, New Orleans, August 29-September 1.

Dyer, J., F. Williams, and D. Haynes. 1986. "Texans' Attitudes Toward Science and Technology." Report from the New Texas Project. Austin: University of Texas, Center for Research on Communication Technology and Society.

"The Economic Review and Forecast." 1985. Supplement to *Austin Magazine*, Austin Chamber of Commerce (October).

"The Economic Review and Forecast." 1986. Supplement to *Austin Magazine*, Austin Chamber of Commerce (October).

Elazar, Daniel. 1984. *Federalism: A View From the States.* New York: Thomas Crowell.

Ellul, J. 1964. *The Technological Society.* New York: Knopf.

Etzioni, A. and C. Nunn. 1974. "The Public Appreciation of Science in Contemporary America." *Daedalus* 103:191-205.

Federal Communications Commission. 1983. *Statistics of the Communication Industry.* Washington, DC: Government Printing Office.

General Appropriation Bill. 1986-1987. Texas State Legislature, 1985, for 1986-1987 Fiscal Year.

Gruben, W. C. and K. R. Phillips. 1986. "Understanding the Texas Unemployment Rate." Pp. 17-30 in *Economic Review.* Dallas: Federal Reserve Bank of Dallas (November).

Hanneman, G. 1986. "Applying the Idea: Telecommunications and Economic Development." *NATOA News* (March/April):1 ff.

Inglehardt, R. 1977. *The Silent Revolution: Changing Values and Styles Among Western Publics.* Princeton, NJ: Princeton University Press.

Ladendorf, K. 1983. "The Anticipation Ends: MCC Moves in, But Is Still Feeling Some Growing Pains." *Austin American-Statesman* (September 12).

LaPorte, T. and D. Metlay. 1975. "Technology Observed: Attitudes of a Wary Public." *Science* 188(April):53-59, 121-127.

Larkin, E. F. and G. L. Grotta. 1977. "The Newspaper as a Source of Consumer Information for Young Adults." *Journal of Advertising* (Fall):5-10.

Larsen, J. K. et al. 1987. "Industry-University Technology Transfer in Microelectronics." Tempe: Cognos Associates and Arizona State University, Program in Information Management, School of Public Affairs.

Lasswell, H. 1971/1984. "The Structure and Function of Mass Communication in Society." In *The Process and Effects of Mass Communication,* edited by Wilbur Schramm and Donald Roberts. Urbana: University of Illinois Press.

Ledingham, J. 1983. "The Information Society: Fact or Charming Mythology." Paper presented at the International Communications Association, Dallas, Texas.

Lee, R. 1971. "Social Attitudes and the Computer Revolution." *Public Opinion Quarterly* 34:53-59.

Legislative Budget Board. 1984-1985. Fiscal Size Up, Texas State Services, Biennium, 61.

Leinberger, C. and C. Lockwood. 1986. "How Business Is Reshaping America." *Atlantic* (October):43-52.

Machlup, F. 1962. *The Production and Distribution of Knowledge in the United States.* Princeton, NJ: Princeton University Press.

Marcuse, H. 1964. *One Dimensional Man.* Boston: Beacon.

Marshall, E. 1979. "Public Attitudes to Technological Progress." *Science* 205:281-285.

Martin, J. 1978. *The Wired Society.* Englewood Cliffs, NJ: Prentice-Hall.

Masuda, Y. 1982. *The Information Society.* Bethesda, MD: World Future Society.

Minneapolis Telecommunications Task Force. 1985. *Telecommunications and Economic Development in Minneapolis.* Minneapolis, MN: Author.

Mosco, V. 1982. *Pushbutton Fantasies.* Norwood, NJ: Ablex.

Moss, M. 1985. "Telecommunications and the Future of Cities." Paper presented at the Landtronics Anglo/American Conference, London, June 19-21.

National Commission on Excellence in Education. 1983. *A Nation at Risk: The Imperative for Educational Reform.* Washington, DC: Government Printing Office.

National Science Foundation (NSF). 1981. *Research and Development in Industry.* Washington, DC: Author.

National Science Foundation (NSF). 1983. *Research and Development in Industry*. Washington, DC: Author.

National Science Foundation (NSF). 1984. *Federal Funds For Research and Development*. Vol. 30-33. Washington, DC: Author.

Ouchi, W. 1984. *The M-Form Society: How American Teamwork Can Recapture the Competitive Edge*. Menlo Park, CA: Addison-Wesley.

Panel on Policies and Prospects for Metropolitan and Nonmetropolitan America. 1980. *Urban America in the Eighties*. Washington, DC: Government Printing Office.

Pehadzur, E. 1982. *Multiple Regression in Behavioral Research*. New York: Holt, Rinehart & Winston.

Pelto, D. and J. Pertti. 1973. *The Snowmobile Revolution: Technology and Social Change in the Arctic*. Menlo Park, CA: Cummings.

Pelton, J. 1981. *Global Talk*. Brighton, Sussex, England: Harvester Press.

Pion, M., B. George, and M. W. Lipsey. 1981. "Public Attitudes Toward Science and Technology: What Have the Surveys Told Us?" *Public Opinion Quarterly*, pp. 303-316.

Porat, M. 1977. *The Information Economy: Definition and Measurement*. Special Publication 77-12, U.S. Department of Commerce, Office of Telecommunications. Washington, DC: Government Printing Office.

———1978. "Global Implications of the Information Society." *Journal of Communication* 28(1):70-80.

Rabier, A. J. and R. Inglehardt. 1977. *Euro-Barometer 7: Science and Technology in the European Community*. Ann Arbor, MI: Inter-University Consortium for Political and Social Research.

———1978. *Euro-Barometer 10A: Scientific Priorities in the European Community*. Ann Arbor, MI: Inter-University Consortium for Political and Social Research.

Reese, S. 1987. "Information Work and Workers: Technology Attitudes, Adoption and Media Use." Prepared for presentation to the Human Communications Technology Special Interest Group, International Communications Association Conference, Montreal.

———, P. Shoemaker, and W. Danielson. 1986. "Social Correlates of Public Attitudes Towards the New Communication Technologies." *Journalism Quarterly* 63:675-682.

Reeves, M. 1987. "1986 Tough on SW Shops." *Adweek* (Southwest Edition; March 16), p. 1.

Rogers, E. 1983. *Diffusion of Innovations*. New York: Free Press.

———and J. K. Larsen. 1984. *Silicon Valley Fever: Growth of High Technology Culture*. New York: Basic Books.

Schiller, H. 1981. *Who Knows: Information in the Age of the Fortune 500*. Norwood, NJ: Ablex.

Schmandt, J. and R. Wilson, eds. 1987. *Promoting High Technology Industry: Initiatives in Policies for State Governments*. Boulder, CO: Westview Press.

Shoemaker, P. J., S. D. Reese, and W. A. Danielson. 1985. *Media in Ethnic Context: Language and Communication in Texas*. Austin: University of Texas, Department of Journalism.

Smilor, R. W., G. Kozmetsky, and D. V. Gibson, eds. 1988. *Creating the Technopolis: Linking Technology Communication and Economic Development*. Cambridge, MA: Ballinger.

Snyder, D. P. 1984. "The Strategic Context of Management in America, 1985 to 1995." Bethesda, MD: Snyder Family Enterprise (November).

*The Standard Directory of Advertising Agencies: The Red Book*. October, 1985-January, 1986. New York: American Association of Advertising Agencies.

Stover-Tillinghast, D. and N. Visvanathan. 1983. "The Electronic Newspaper: Building a Profile of Potential Users." Paper presented to the Association for Education in Journalism and Mass Communication, Corvallis, Oregon.

Taviss, I. 1972. "A Survey of Popular Attitudes Toward Technology." *Technology and Culture* 13:606-621.

TENRAC. 1980. *Annual Report* (December).

TENRAC. 1983. *Texas Energy Development Fund*. (September).

Texas College and University Systems, Coordinating Board. 1984. *Public Senior Institutions and Agencies of Higher Education in Texas: Research Funds Report for the Fiscal Year Ended August 31, 1984*. Austin, TX: Author.

Texas Department of Health. 1986. *Population Data System*. Austin, TX: Author.

Texas Science and Technology Council. June 1984-June 1985. *Annual Report*. Austin, TX: Author.

U.S. Bureau of the Census. 1980. *1980 Census: General Population Characteristics*. Washington, DC: Government Printing Office.

U.S. Bureau of the Census. 1973 through 1983. *County Business Patterns*. Washington, DC: Government Printing Office.

Vinson, M. 1986. "Jobless Ad Pros Find Work Scarce." *Adweek* (Southwest Edition; September 8):6.

Wigand, R. T. 1987. "Taming the Desert: High Technology Development in the Phoenix Area." In *Technopolis: Technology and Economic Development in the Modern City State*, edited by R. W. Smilor, G. Kozmetsky, and D. V. Gibson. Boston: Ballinger.

Williams, F. 1982. *The Communications Revolution*. New York: New American Library.

Willis, M. D. 1987. *Employment Trends: Texas and the United States from 1970-1985*. Austin: University of Texas, Bureau of Business Research.

Winner, L. 1977. *Autonomous Technology*. Cambridge: MIT Press.

Yankelovich, D. 1982. "Changing Attitudes to Science and the Quality of Life: Edited Excerpts from a Seminar." *Science, Technology, and Human Values* 7:23-29.

# Index

advertising: business changes, 251-256; in Texas, 251-253
Austin, MCC site selection, 99-106
Austin-San Antonio corridor, 67-90

business growth, 44, 52

cable TV use, 220-221
change: newspaper coverage, 207-213; personal views, 259, 261, 272-274; themes, 262-272
computer literacy, 243-244
computers: attitudes toward, 195-197; use in Texas schools, 243-249

diversification trends, 57-58

economic development, 19-25
economy, attitudes toward, 187-188
education, 28-29, 31, 53, 209-210
employment trends, 55, 57
entrepreneurship, 60

foreign investment, 61-62

Governor's Science and Technology Council, 159-171
graphics, change, 52-53
growth spin-off analyses, 76-82

high tech: news coverage, 207-213; growth, 58-60

information: economy, 15-18; sector, 36-38; sector growth, 35-54; society, 13-32; society, negative views, 27-28; society

study, 13-29; subsectors, 39-41; technologies, use of, 19-23, 215-227

job growth, 41, 44

M-form society, 115-116, 159-160, 170
MCC (Microelectronics and Computer Technology Corp.): effects on state, 109, 112; general, 14, 75, 84, 159, 161-164, 166, 171, 268; origin, 93-99; recruitment, 91-116; site selection, 99-106
media exposure, 234-238
media uses, prediction of, 239-242
Mexico, 62-63

news sources, 230-233

pay TV use, 220-221
political parties, change, 179-184
postindustrialism, 15-18

quality of life, 83-85

R&D: general, 29-30, 69-70, 148-149, 155-156; spending in Texas, 148-153
religion and morals, change, 185, 187
research funding, 148-153
rural economy, 23

schools, computer use, 243-249
Science and Technology Council, 159-171
science and technology: attitudes, 191-204, 218-219; background, 142-147; directions, 154-155; future, 153-157; policy, 141-157; questions, 203-204; state role, 141-142